W9-CLQ-304

Roadmap to the InterNIC InfoGuide

One of the services offered by the Internet Network Information Center (InterNIC, introduced in Chapter 1) is the InfoGuide, a collection of useful information about the Internet and its resources. You can reach the InfoGuide via ftp (`ftp is.internic.net`), gopher (`gopher is.internic.net 70`), or W3 (use the URL `http://www.internic.net/`). When you get connected, you'll find the following directories:

Beginners, Start Here (`beginners`):   Information for new Internet users. Glossaries, overviews, brief introductions to Internet tools, and lists of books about the Internet.

About the InfoGuide (`about-infoguide`):   Information about the InfoGuide itself, how to use it, submit files, and offer suggestions.

About InterNIC Information Systems (`about-internic`):   All about InterNIC Information Systems.

About the Internet (`about-internet`):   Information about the Internet: statistics, history, and Internet organizations.

Getting Connected to the Internet (`getting-connected`):   The latest information on Internet access providers all over the world.

Using the Internet(`using-internet`):   A one-stop encyclopedia of Internet applications from E-mail to W3.

Internet Resources (`resources`):   A subject-oriented collection of select documents and pointers to other subject-oriented resources.

Advanced Users (`advanced`):   Tips for systems administrators, network programmers, and others with an interest in the technical side of the Net.

Frequently Asked Questions at InterNIC IS (`faq`):   The InterNIC's most requested documents.

Scout Report (`scout-report`):   What's new on the Internet as reported by the InterNIC Infoscout.

For every kind of computer user, there is a SYBEX book.

All computer users learn in their own way. Some need straightforward and methodical explanations. Others are just too busy for this approach. But no matter what camp you fall into, SYBEX has a book that can help you get the most out of your computer and computer software while learning at your own pace.

Beginners generally want to start at the beginning. The **ABC's** series, with its step-by-step lessons in plain language, helps you build basic skills quickly. For a more personal approach, there's the **Murphy's Laws** and **Guided Tour** series. Or you might try our **Quick & Easy** series, the friendly, full-color guide, with **Quick & Easy References**, the companion pocket references to the **Quick & Easy** series. If you learn best by doing rather than reading, find out about the **Hands-On Live!** series, our new interactive multimedia training software. For hardware novices, there's the **Your First** series.

The **Mastering and Understanding** series will tell you everything you need to know about a subject. They're perfect for intermediate and advanced computer users, yet they don't make the mistake of leaving beginners behind. Add one of our **Instant References** and you'll have more than enough help when you have a question about your computer software. You may even want to check into our **Secrets & Solutions** series.

SYBEX even offers special titles on subjects that don't neatly fit a category—like our **Pushbutton Guides**, our books about the Internet, our books about the latest computer games, and a wide range of books for Macintosh computers and software.

SYBEX books are written by authors who are expert in their subjects. In fact, many make their living as professionals, consultants or teachers in the field of computer software. And their manuscripts are thoroughly reviewed by our technical and editorial staff for accuracy and ease-of-use.

So when you want answers about computers or any popular software package, just help yourself to SYBEX.

For a complete catalog of our publications, please write:

SYBEX Inc.
2021 Challenger Drive
Alameda, CA 94501
Tel: (510) 523-8233/(800) 227-2346 Telex: 336311
Fax: (510) 523-2373

SYBEX is committed to using natural resources wisely to preserve and improve our environment. As a leader in the computer book publishing industry, we are aware that over 40% of America's solid waste is paper. This is why we have been printing the text of books like this one on recycled paper since 1982.

This year our use of recycled paper will result in the saving of more than 15,300 trees. We will lower air pollution effluents by 54,000 pounds, save 6,300,000 gallons of water, and reduce landfill by 2,700 cubic yards.

In choosing a SYBEX book you are not only making a choice for the best in skills and information, you are also choosing to enhance the quality of life for all of us.

The Internet Roadmap

The
Internet
Roadmap

Second Edition

Bennett Falk

SYBEX®

San Francisco • Paris • Düsseldorf • Soest

Developmental Editor: David Peal
Editor: James A. Compton
Technical Editor: Samuel Faulkner
Book Designer: Helen Bruno
Chapter Art and Screen Graphics: Helen Bruno, Ingrid Owen
Technical Art: Cuong Le
Page Layout and Typesetting: Len Gilbert
Proofreader/Production Coordinator: Kristin Amlie
Indexer: Ted Laux
Cover Designer: Ingalls + Associates
Cover Illustrator/Photographer: Robert Kopecky

Screen reproductions produced with Collage Plus.
Collage Plus is a trademark of Inner Media Inc.

SYBEX is a registered trademark of SYBEX Inc.

TRADEMARKS: SYBEX has attempted throughout this book to distinguish proprietary trademarks from descriptive terms by following the capitalization style used by the manufacturer.

Every effort has been made to supply complete and accurate information. However, SYBEX assumes no responsibility for its use, nor for any infringement of the intellectual property rights of third parties which would result from such use.

First edition copyright ©1994 SYBEX Inc.

Copyright ©1994 SYBEX Inc., 2021 Challenger Drive, Alameda, CA 94501. World rights reserved. No part of this publication may be stored in a retrieval system, transmitted, or reproduced in any way, including but not limited to photocopy, photograph, magnetic or other record, without the prior agreement and written permission of the publisher.

Library of Congress Card Number: 94-68433
ISBN: 0-7821-1586-1
ISBN: 0-7821-1586-1S

Manufactured in the United States of America
10 9 8 7 6 5 4 3

Acknowledgments

Many people deserve thanks for their help in bringing this project to completion. My colleagues at Sybase (particularly in Technical Support) have been a constant source of encouragement and puzzling questions. The members of the East Bay FOG provided an opportunity to test some of the ideas in this book on a new audience. Jim Compton and David Peal helped shape the ideas into a book. Sarah, Chloe, and Selina are muses in their own right. Mary Eisenhart provided friendship, the nudge that started all this, and a monthly opportunity to think and write creatively.

Thanks above all to Margaret Moreland.

at a Glance

Table of Contents

Part Three The Internet Community's Applications

Appendices
— — — — —

Introduction

This book introduces the basics of working with the Internet, primarily for people who will connect to the Internet by phone. You'll learn what the Internet is and how to use it from your computer. Along the way, some key information resources will be introduced as starting points for exploring the Internet. You'll soon find that the Internet doesn't stand still, but the topics covered here will give you everything you need to get started with the Internet as it is now and to grow with it as new applications and resources are introduced.

What You Need to Know before You Start

About all that's needed for you to get something out of this book is some degree of comfort with using some sort of computer. Exactly what sort of computer you're comfortable with doesn't really matter: you'll find something familiar on virtually every computer you work with on the Internet.

What does "some degree of comfort" mean? Basically, there are three skills that will be helpful to anyone reading this book. First, you should know in general what files, disks, and directories (or folders) are, and you should know how to do things with files, disks, and directories—how to move a file from one disk to another, how to move around in a hierarchy of directories, how to take a file from one directory and put it into another, and the like. (If you're taking advantage of the Windows implementations now available for many of the Internet tools introduced in this book, the Windows File Manager provides a fairly painless way of handling these tasks.) A second helpful skill is being able to tell the difference between the application programs that you use to do the work you're interested in and the operating system that runs on your computer. This boils down to being aware of what commands to issue when. (Typing the operating system command "dir" when you're running a word processor is unlikely to produce a directory listing.) Finally, it is helpful if you've had some experience using your computer to talk to a modem.

There are a few things you *don't* have to know before reading this book. Knowledge of the UNIX operating system is not required. Computers running UNIX *are* common on the Internet and among Internet access providers. Knowing UNIX is a good thing; but it is definitely not a prerequisite for doing things on the Internet. (See also Appendix D, "Just Enough UNIX," for general information about using UNIX.)

Knowing how networks work isn't required either. You can become quite proficient at using network resources without understanding the technical details of what's going on.

How to Read This Book

This book has three parts and five short appendices. In Part I, we'll discuss what the Internet really is, concentrating on three things: the physical network (the cabling that holds the Internet together), the protocols (the tools that get messages from one place to another), and network applications (the programs that put you in touch with the network).

We'll also step through using a simple Internet program named `finger`. Chapter 2 discusses the mechanics of getting connected to the Internet by phone from your own home computer. Read the chapters in Part I if you're interested in how the Internet works. Any user can work smarter and faster by understanding the framework of the Internet.

Part II discusses `ftp`, `telnet`, and electronic mail. These are the Internet's most basic tools: they are more or less universally available, and they are building blocks for many Internet services. Read the chapters in Part II if you are trying to locate or retrieve a specific file, or trying to communicate with a specific person or group of people. Just about every Internet user needs to know something about `ftp`, `telnet`, and e-mail.

Part III presents Internet tools developed by the Internet user community. User-developed applications (like `gopher` and the World Wide Web) provide a simpler interface for Internet resources. The most visible contributions from the Internet community are in the USENET News, an immense bulletin board that serves as a forum in which literally thousands of topics are discussed. Read Part III if you want quick access to these popular data sources. You'll learn to use global search tools that truly put the world at your fingertips.

The appendices contain practical information about a number of topics.

The Internet Roadmap is as close to random-access as a book can be. Like any roadmap, it has more than one starting point and more than one destination. Chapter 1 will give you some helpful background for everything else, but you can read the rest of the Roadmap in the order that is most helpful for you. If you want to send e-mail to a friend, start with Chapter 5. If you're eager to start doing things right away, begin with gopher in Chapter 6—it's the easiest tool to jump-start Internet exploration. Wherever you start, enjoy the trip.

Typographical Notes

A book and a computer are different media, and what is clear on your screen may occasionally be confusing in print. To bridge that gap, this book uses a few simple typographical conventions:

1. Internet addresses and the commands used in various Internet programs appear in a monospace typeface.

2. In dialogs between a user and a program on the Internet, the user's input appears in **boldface** type, and any explanatory notes appear in *italic* type:

```
telnet> open well.sf.ca.us  Open a connection to well.sf.ca.us
```

3. If a line of program output on the screen won't fit on a single line in this book, the character ➡ tells you that we broke the line; the program didn't:

```
# Geographic Name Server, Copyright 1992 Regents of the
➡University of Michigan.
# Version 8/19/92. Use "help" or "?" for assistance, "info"
➡for hints.
```

Stay in Touch

And finally, don't forget to write:

```
roadmap@sybex.com
```

## PART ONE

Introducing

the

Internet

- The two chapters in Part 1 provide a general orientation to what the Internet is and how it works. Chapter 1 discusses the three things that make the Internet work: the *cabling* that holds the Internet together, the *network protocols* that allow different types of computers to communicate on the Internet, and the *client/server architecture* that you'll encounter in programs that use the Internet. Along the way, you'll also be introduced to the `finger` program and some of the information resources it can be used to reach. Chapter 2 discusses how to connect to the Internet by phone. Internet access providers offer two different kinds of services: conventional dialup access and protocol dialup access. An overview describes what these services are and what you'll need to get up and running with either type of service.

CHAPTER **1**

What Is
the Internet?

"It was a trick question!" the Vice President for Research and Development grumbled as he walked into the board room. He had been bested again in the Internet Hunt. "Everybody knows the melting point of Tungsten! I just forgot that its symbol in the periodic table is W."

- The people seated at the conference table shifted uneasily in their chairs. The VP dropped a pile of printouts on the table and smiled: "Fortunately, our new tomato is being very well-received in the marketplace. These are this morning's reports from the retailers in our marketing test."

- In Davis, the owner of a produce store composed a piece of electronic mail for the biotechnology company's director of marketing in Chicago. The new tomatoes were selling like hotcakes, but they were also causing problems with his regular suppliers who resented competing with a biotech firm in the produce market. He was about to send the message when a brilliant idea occurred to him. He would copy the message to all the tomato suppliers with e-mail access. With luck, the marketing director and the suppliers could work this out between themselves.

- Minutes later the director of marketing received this message and frowned at her screen. The new tomato would fail if the growers rejected it outright. Were they really resentful or were they bluffing? Curious about their competitive position, she logged in to a database in Fresno to check the price and availability of imported tomatoes. Could she risk playing hardball with tomato growers?

- Somewhere in central California a tomato grower was seated at a personal computer connected to the same database in Fresno. He searched through biotechnology bulletins, trying to figure out if the tomato would help or hurt his business. He also wondered what it would be like to have a few new tomato seeds for his private garden. Finding nothing new, he checked his e-mail. There were messages from a store owner in Davis and another from someone he didn't know in Chicago. He read the Chicago mail and smiled: he would have some seeds within a week.

- All these people are using the Internet, a global network of computer networks that is both a medium for communication and reference resource on virtually any subject.

A View of the Internet from 30,000 Feet

The Internet is the world's largest computer network, a distinction it has earned by virtue of being a "network of networks." The Internet is an outgrowth of a network (ARPANET) established roughly a quarter-century ago to meet the needs of researchers working in the defense industry in the United States and a few of their colleagues in other countries. The ARPANET grew slowly, from a handful of computers in 1971 to more than 1000 in 1984. Working with the ARPANET, researchers came to regard high-speed computer networks as an indispensable tool for academic research in all fields, and in 1986 the US National Science Foundation established NSFNET to provide network connections to more research institutions and improve international network cooperation. In 1987, the Internet served more than 10,000 computers. By 1989 the network had grown to more than 100,000. In 1990, the ARPANET ceased to exist, but the Internet continued to grow: 1 million computers in 1992, 2 million in 1993. The Internet has now spilled out of the academic world to offer both information access and a fast, inexpensive means of communication to the general public. It will be the next public utility. It is the reality behind the "Information Superhighway" buzzword.

Yes, But What Can I Do With It?

If you're like most new Internet users, the first thing you probably want to know is what the Internet will enable you to do. There's a basic chicken-and-egg problem here: it's difficult to explain what you can do on the Internet without first explaining some things about how the Internet works and how you get connected to it. On the other hand, if you don't know what you can do with the Internet, why should you bother to get connected to it in the first place? Most of this book will explain in detail how to do things on the Internet. This chapter and the next one will explain some basic Internet concepts and how to go about getting an Internet connection.

To use the Internet, you have to be working with a computer that is connected to it. This could be a PC, a Macintosh, or a multi-user system (UNIX-based, for example). This book assumes that you've connected to the Internet via a phone line, but (as you'll see in Chapter 2) even dialup connections come in several flavors. Depending on the computer and how it's connected to the Internet, you might have to log in before you can execute commands. (Chapter 2 shows how to make a dial-up get connection to the Internet. See Appendix C for information about logging in.)

A Simple Internet Command: Finger

Once you've logged in, you can execute commands that use your computer's Internet connection. Of all the commands that access the Internet, the easiest to use is the network application named finger. Finger was originally developed to display information about a computer's users. The finger command is part of the suite of utilities that have grown up around the Internet network software. You'll find versions of finger for all sorts of different operating systems (DOS, Windows, UNIX, and so on). The examples here show the UNIX version because UNIX-based computers are common among Internet access providers. To execute it, just type the word finger followed by the login name of the user you want information about. Figure 1.1 shows an example.

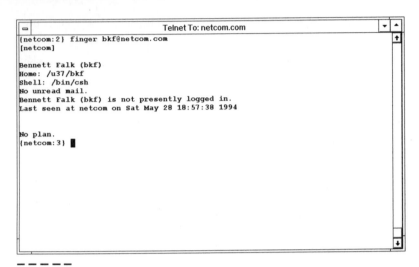

```
⊟                    Telnet To: netcom.com                    ▼ ▲
{netcom:2} finger bkf@netcom.com                              ↟
[netcom]

Bennett Falk (bkf)
Home: /u37/bkf
Shell: /bin/csh
No unread mail.
Bennett Falk (bkf) is not presently logged in.
Last seen at netcom on Sat May 28 18:57:38 1994


No plan.
{netcom:3} ▮


                                                              ↡
```

Figure 1.1   A sample finger session.

The interesting thing about finger is that, if you're connected to the Internet, it can tell you about users on other computers. To get this information, you need to know both a user's login name and the name of the machine on which the user has an account. If you know these things, however, the finger command can tell you some things about that user: their name, home directory, the time of their last login, and whether they have any unread electronic mail. Finger also displays the contents of a file named .plan if there is such a file in the user's home directory. (The "No Plan" message in the example indicates that there is no .plan file for the user bkf.) You can put anything you like in your .plan file, and as you'll see shortly, many Internet users use their .plan files creatively. If you have a user name on the computer you use, try executing the finger command using that name. If finger prints a message similar to the output above, you're ready to proceed. Your command may return a message like

finger: Command not found.

This means that the `finger` command is not available to you. That's a serious obstacle, but it's hardly the end of the world. See the accompanying sidebar for hints on coping with this.

WHEN FINGER IS FICKLE – – – – – – – – – – – –

There are three unusual conditions you might encounter when you try to execute the `finger` command.

Finger can't find the user: If you provide the name of a nonexistent user, `finger` will respond this way:

```
finger etaoin          "etaoin" is a mistyped user name.
Login name: etaoin     In real life: ???
```

Finger can't find the computer: If `finger` can't interpret the computer name you've given it, it will respond in this way:

```
finger bennett@shrdlu.com
unknown host: shrdlu.com
```

This can be caused by mistyping the computer name when entering the command. If so, execute the command with the correct name. If you've typed the name correctly and still receive the "unknown host" message, your computer's connection to the Internet may be faulty (or the computer may not be attached to the Internet at all). Ask the system administrator for help.

Your computer can't find `finger`: Finally, you may get this response:

```
finger aurora@xi.uleth.ca
finger:  Command not found.
```

This means that your computer can't find the `finger` command to execute it. The `finger` command is widespread, but not ubiquitous. There is a way to work around this using the `telnet` command. The name you supply to `finger` has the format `user@computer.name`. If your computer can't find the `finger` command, try `telnet` with the computer name and the number 79. If `telnet` connects successfully, type the user name and press Return, as in this example:

```
telnet xi.uleth.ca 79
Trying...
Connected to xi.uleth.ca.
Escape character is '^]'.
aurora
Login name: aurora     In real life: Aurora Finger
Directory: /userfiles/others/oler/solar/aurora Shell: /bin/true
Never logged in.
Plan:
=============================================
S.T.D. HOURLY AURORAL ACTIVITY STATUS REPORT
=============================================
---<Output Truncated>---
```

It is possible that you will get a "Command not found" message in response to your `telnet` command as well. If this happens, you should confirm with the computer's administrator that it really is connected to the Internet.

A Finger on the Internet's Pulse

If you were able to execute the `finger` command using your own user name, you're ready to do a simple test of your computer's Internet access. The command you'll use is

```
finger spyder@dmc.iris.washington.edu
```

Be sure to spell everything correctly and to place punctuation marks just as shown. This command will `finger` a user named spyder at a computer named `dms.iris.washington.edu`. When you execute this command, it will return, in addition to the expected user information, a summary of recent earthquake activity similar to that shown in Figure 1.2. The .plan file for spyder contains information about seismic events. To display this file, your `finger` command makes a connection over the Internet to a computer at the University of Washington.

Congratulations, you're using the Internet.

The Earthquake Information Service maintained by the University of Washington is one of many information resources accessible via the `finger` command. Here are a few of the other services that can

---

A CLOSER LOOK AT THE finger COMMAND – – – – – – – –

Now that you're familiar with domain names, we can make a little more sense of the `finger` commands listed for NASA and weather information in our opening exercise. Remember that a `finger` command looks like this:

```
finger user@computer
```

To `finger` a user elsewhere on the Internet, the computer name (everything to the right of the "@") should be in domain name format. When you `finger solar@xi.uleth.ca`, for example, you're querying a computer named `xi` at the University of Lethbridge (`uleth`) in Canada (`ca`). Notice that some of the names have more fields than others. The tropical storm forecasting service is located on the host named `typhoon` in a local domain named `atmos` at Colorado State University (`colostate`), which is in the top-level `edu` domain.

9

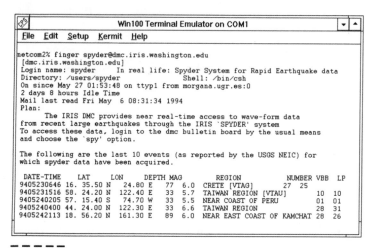

```
                          Win100 Terminal Emulator on COM1          ▼  ▲
 File   Edit   Setup   Kermit   Help

 netcom2% finger spyder@dmc.iris.washington.edu
 [dmc.iris.washington.edu]
 Login name: spyder      In real life: Spyder System for Rapid Earthquake data
 Directory: /users/spyder            Shell: /bin/csh
 On since May 27 01:53:48 on ttyp1 from morgana.ugr.es:0
 2 days 8 hours Idle Time
 Mail last read Fri May  6 08:31:34 1994
 Plan:
      The IRIS DMC provides near real-time access to wave-form data
 from recent large earthquakes through the IRIS `SPYDER' system
 To access these data, login to the dmc bulletin board by the usual means
 and choose the `spy' option.

 The following are the last 10 events (as reported by the USGS NEIC) for
 which spyder data have been acquired.

  DATE-TIME    LAT    LON   DEPTH MAG        REGION        NUMBER VBB  LP
 9405230646 16. 35.50 N  24.80 E   77  6.0  CRETE [VTAG]      27   25
 9405231516 58. 24.20 N 122.40 E   33  5.7  TAIWAN REGION [VTAU]   10   10
 9405240205 57. 15.40 S  74.70 W   33  5.5  NEAR COAST OF PERU    01   01
 9405240400 44. 24.00 N 122.30 E   33  6.6  TAIWAN REGION        28   31
 9405242113 18. 56.20 N 161.30 E   89  6.0  NEAR EAST COAST OF KAMCHAT 28   26
```

- - - - -

Figure 1.2 This finger command produces a summary of recent earthquake activity.

be reached with `finger`:

Earthquake information	`finger spyder@dmc.iris.washington.edu`
	`finger quake@geophys.washington.edu`
News from NASA	`finger nasanews@space.mit.edu`
Solar activity	`finger aurora@xi.uleth.ca`
	`finger solar@xi.uleth.ca`
	`finger daily@xi.uleth.ca`
Tropical storm statistics	`finger` ➥`forecast@typhoon.atmos.colostate.edu`

A Closer View of the Internet

Some people compare the Internet to a highway system. To others the networks and connections that make up the Internet seem more like a cloud. Describing what you *do* on the Internet is no easier. To say that the Internet provides information access and communication does not begin to describe the breadth of what it offers.

In spite of the Internet's size and diversity, however, there are three basic things that make the Internet work, and these components fill the same roles regardless of how big the network gets or what it is used for. Understanding the Internet's essential parts will make the Internet easier to use and give you an advantage in adapting to new developments and responding to problems.

The Internet's most basic component is a physical network. The Internet behaves as though all the computers in all the participating networks were joined by a giant cable. In fact, all the computers on the Internet *are* joined by connectors—not by one cable, but by thousands. All these connectors are coordinated to work like a single cable linking all the computers on the Internet. Many features of the Internet can be attributed directly to this physical network, the cabling that holds it all together.

The cabling, however, it is just a starting point. The physical network can transmit gibberish as easily as it carries real information. What makes the traffic over the Internet's many cables meaningful is the language in which the information is broadcast. The Internet has a language of its own; in fact it has several. These languages are *protocols*. Protocols are the languages through which the computers on the Internet communicate. They divvy up the physical network into discreet locations and enable one location to send messages to another.

Finally, neither the cable nor the network protocols are things that human beings directly interact with. Most of what you will see when you use the network are software tools or applications. But network applications are different from single-user applications on stand-alone computers. The distinguishing feature of a network application is its structure or architecture, and it is not possible to do justice to the Internet without talking about network applications.

The Tao of Cable

Considered as a piece of cable, the Internet is like a very long string to which millions of tin cans are attached. (The Tin Can Network is shown in Figure 1.3.) More than two million computers participate in the Internet, and they are all held together by cabling—very much as string holds a tin can network together. The Internet's physical network functions like an immense, single circuit—a giant party line that carries everyone's data.

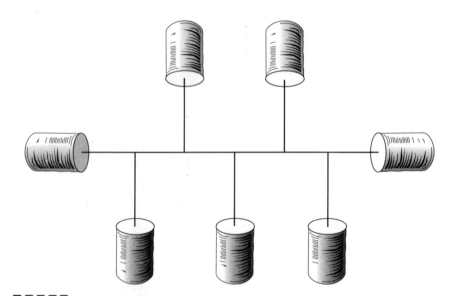

Figure 1.3   The tin can network.

More than any other component, the cabling defines the network. The cable determines what it means to have an Internet connection (if you aren't connected to the physical network somehow, you aren't "on" the Internet). The cable also affects the network's performance (how long it takes to retrieve something from another computer on the network). The cost of an Internet connection is influenced by the cost of establishing and maintaining the physical network, and ownership of the physical network has traditionally established who has the right to make policies about what the network can and can't be used for.

It's All Connected

People get access to Internet by using computers that are connected to the physical network. Computers connected to the Internet are said to *host* the network, and the phrase *network host* refers to a computer connected to the Internet's physical network. This host may be part of your local area network (LAN), or it may be maintained by a commercial access provider such as America Online or Netcom. Throughout this book, *hosts* and *computers* will be used interchangeably.

The network cables themselves don't really care what sorts of computers are connected to them. On the Internet, you will encounter computers of all sorts (supercomputers, massively parallel computers, mainframes, supermicros, and personal computers), but none of them will seem any faster than the cable that gives you access to them.

Attaching a computer to the Internet is usually a matter of connecting it to a local network that is, in turn, connected to the Internet. There are privately owned local networks in businesses and on campuses everywhere. If the local network where you work is connected to the Internet, you have Internet access through the computer you use on that network. When you subscribe to an Internet access provider, chances are you're subscribing to a local network, and not to a single computer that happens to be connected to the Internet. Local networks are commonly held together by cabling that can provide excellent service over short distances (less than a mile). A common physical medium for local networks is Ethernet.

TIP –

If you use a workstation on an Ethernet-based LAN, the Ethernet connection is either a small, metal "T" with a cable running through it attached to the back of the computer or a small plastic box with a few lights blinking red, green, or amber attached to the computer by a modular cable. If you work at a computer that is attached to a LAN, be extremely careful around the physical connector. Ethernet transceivers can easily find their way underfoot to be stepped on or tripped over. Detaching an Ethernet connection improperly can interrupt network service across the entire LAN. In general, it's a good idea to leave maintenance of the physical LAN connection to your network administrators.

Somewhere on any local network connected to the Internet is a *router*. The router is the local network's point of connection with the Internet. This can get complicated: the local network may use one kind of cabling to connect its computers with each other and get its Internet connection over an entirely different kind of cable. A router is a computer that bridges the gap between whatever medium is used for the LAN and the long-distance line that provides access to the Internet at large, Figure 1.4 illustrates this. The router insulates the LAN and the Internet from each other: it protects the LAN from having to process a large volume of network traffic going to other sites,

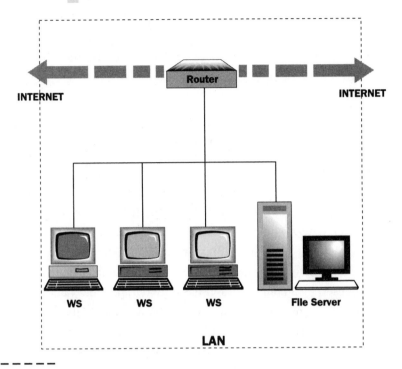

Figure 1.4 A local network connected to the Internet.

and it protects the Internet from the interruptions of service (crashes) that are the lot of local networks everywhere.

The long distance (or wide area) portions of the Internet's physical network are essentially dedicated telephone lines, and the Internet cannot currently be extended to places that don't have a telephone line network adequate for data transmission. Parts of eastern Europe, Africa, and Asia (or any place where the telephone system is not highly developed) have fewer and slower Internet connections than, for example, the United States, France, and Japan.

The long distance lines that carry Internet traffic differ from the lines for voice phones in two important ways. They tend to be point-to-point lines (which means that the circuit is always open between the two points the line connects), and they have a greater capacity for carrying data.

The Speed of Ones and Zeros

Not so long ago, the fastest way to move a lot of information from one place to another sixty miles away was to load a station wagon with magnetic tape and drive for an hour. When data moves from place to place, its speed is determined largely by the medium that carries it.

The capacity of any line is measured in bits of data transmitted per second. (Bit is short for "binary digit." It is the smallest unit of information used by a computer, and has only two possible values: 0 and 1. Typically, computers use eight bits to represent a single character.) Ethernet-based local networks currently transmit data at speeds up to 10 million bits per second (or 10 Mbps) over distances up to one kilometer. This rate translates to roughly 1.2 million characters, nearly six hundred screenfuls of information, per second.

Building a global network one kilometer at a time would be tedious and expensive. Telephone lines provide good long distance coverage and a choice of transmission speeds. Voice-grade phone lines like the one your modem uses can transmit data at speeds up to 28,800 bits per second, or 28.8 kbps (kilobits per second). This works out to a little less than two screenfuls (25 lines by 80 characters per line) of data each second—much slower than Ethernet.

Beyond voice grade lines, there are "leased" lines: dedicated phone lines between two points. Leased lines are capable of carrying data at rates between 56 and 64 kbps. The lines connecting the first four sites on the Internet's precursor, ARPANET, more than twenty years ago carried data at

56 kbps (about 3.5 screens of information per second).

The demand for higher-capacity lines has produced the service grades that are commonly used in wide area networking in North America. T1 lines, widely used as major data arteries, have a capacity of 1.5 million bits per second (Mbps) or 94 screens of data per second. T3 grade lines transmit data at thirty times that rate (45 Mbps or just over 2800 screenfuls per second). T3 lines were first introduced to the Internet in 1991 and are currently used throughout the Internet's North American backbone. A map of the T3 backbone is shown in Figure 1.5.

Paying for the Internet

Cabling is not free. And while it is usually clear who pays for and owns a local network, it is not always clear who should bear the cost of installing and maintaining the connections between networks that

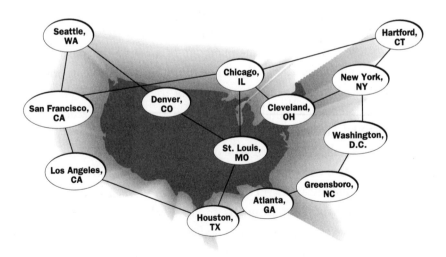

Figure 1.5   North American T3 backbone.

make the Internet a reality. The cost of connecting a local network to the Internet is usually paid by whoever owns the local network. That owner negotiates a connection with a site already connected to the Internet and pays for the dedicated line that connects the local network to the Internet site. Commercial Internet access providers usually pass their costs back to their subscribers through monthly charges or hourly usage fees.

The T3 backbone mentioned above is a critical piece of the network in North America, and its maintenance has not been left to chance. Since 1986, the National Science Foundation has funded this part of the Internet through its NSFNET project.

Acceptable Use

No one owns the Internet as a whole, and it is remarkably free of network-wide regulation. Certainly all the parts of the Internet (individual networks, some local and some quite large) are owned by someone, and the owners of local networks set policies for the appropriate use of the resources they make available to the larger community.

Because public funds maintain one of the Internet's most substantial components, the T3 backbone of the physical network, there are some basic ground rules for the use of the backbone. The NSF has formulated an Acceptable Use Policy that applies to traffic using the NSFNET facilities on the network.

This policy gives us a view of the network as a tool for education and academic research. It advocates the use of the Internet for things like communications between researchers, collecting information about and applying for grants and research contracts, and administering of research programs and academic professional societies (ominously referred to as "disciplinary societies").

Some kinds of commercial activity (advertising, consulting for pay, general use by "for-profit" institutions) are declared to be unacceptable. Most of the vignettes at the beginning of this chapter describe common uses of the Internet that are, strictly speaking, unacceptable under the NSFNET policy.

However, the Internet is rapidly changing. The commercial sector is the fastest growing portion of the Internet user community, and many of the large regional networks that make up the Internet have acceptable-use policies that are far less restrictive of commercial activities than the NSFNET policy. Gradually, an infrastructure to support commercial use of the Internet is being built alongside the structure that protects the interests of the academic community. The Commercial Internet Exchange (CIX) is a consortium of businesses attempting to define the ground rules for the role of business in a public network.

Quite apart from acceptable-use policies, there is a general consensus among Internet users about the proper use of the Internet. The network is a cooperative venture, and you should not do anything that would place at risk the network, its users, or the agencies that contribute resources to the Internet.

TIP –

Check with your Internet access provider for its use policy. You should also ask the access provider about NSFNET backbone access and your obligation to abide by the NSF Acceptable Use Policy.

The Dance of Protocols

Of course, no one thinks it's particularly difficult to use a piece of cable, no matter how large: you simply pull the string tight and shout into the tin can attached to it. You don't usually have to read a manual to learn how to use a piece of cable.

Communicating through a medium as complex as the Internet, however, raises some issues that never occur to two people trying to talk into tin cans joined by a piece of string. Imagine for a moment the effect of a million talkers on the tin can network with a single string carrying everyone's speech to all the attached cans. The jumble of noise coming over the network would make it virtually impossible for anyone to find a partner in dialogue.

A monitor attached directly to a part of the Internet's physical network would show something similar to the cacophony of voice traffic over string. You would see a jumble of messages going to and from nearby sites, possibly interspersed with messages (irrelevant to any local site) on their way from one distant place to another.

Unlike users of our tin can network, however, partners in dialogue over the Internet routinely do find each other. Messages travel long distances and arrive at their destinations intact. The component of the network that makes this possible is a collection of *protocols* that handle different aspects of delivering messages from one place to another. Network protocols are special-purpose languages that computers use to communicate with each other. Some protocols choreograph the movement of messages, some check the integrity of what was sent, and some "massage" data from one format into another.

The use of protocols is not unique to computer networks. For example, the familiar act of addressing an envelope to be put in the mail is a kind of protocol. The address and return address on an envelope are messages to the post office describing where the letter is to go under various circumstances. These messages must appear in their expected places on the envelope and must use a format the postal service understands if the envelope is to be deliverable.

20

Protocols on the Internet

Protocols do their work behind the scenes. The task of translating messages into and out of protocols is handled silently by network hosts, and human users are spared the drudgery of addressing by hand the individual packets that cross the network. Every message transmitted over the Internet passes through at least three levels of protocol: a *network protocol* to oversee getting messages from place to place, a *transport protocol* to manage the integrity of what is transmitted, and an *application protocol* that turns the network transmission into something a human being can recognize as the answer to a request that was dispatched through a network application. These protocols are nested or layered very much like the boxes in Figure 1.6.

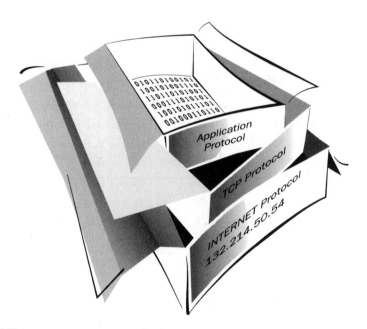

Figure 1.6 The layering of protocols.

The protocol used by the Internet for getting messages from one machine to another is called the Internet Protocol (IP). The Internet Protocol is a *network protocol*, and its job is to manage the logistics of getting a message from the sending machine to the receiving machine.

Messages delivered by the Internet protocol are called *packets*, and they are quite small, fifteen hundred or fewer bytes. Since this is much smaller than many of the messages and files that are transmitted over the Internet, it is common for a transmission to require multiple packets.

Collecting related packets, putting them in the proper order, and verifying that none are garbled are all tasks outside the scope of the Internet Protocol itself. The Internet has two *transport* protocols that deal with the integrity of network transmissions (particularly those that span multiple packets): the Transmission Control Protocol (TCP) and the User Datagram Protocol.

Finally, there are *application* protocols, which take care of formatting requests formulated by users and the data that returns in response to those requests. There are about as many application protocols as there are applications on the Internet. Mail, `telnet`, `ftp`, `archie`, `gopher`, WAIS, and World Wide Web—you'll learn about using these applications later in this book—each has its own protocol.

The Internet Protocol and the Transmission Control Protocol are paired so frequently that it is common to speak of TCP/IP networks. For years, TCP/IP has been the protocol of choice among manufacturers of multiuser computers, and there are several TCP/IP implementations for Macintosh and PC-class computers as well as for other multiuser computers. The use of the TCP/IP protocol suite is widespread outside the Internet; simply running TCP/IP does not guarantee an Internet connection.

From your perspective as a user, any TCP/IP-based local area network is like a miniature version of the Internet. Many of the tools available on the Internet (mail, `telnet`, and `ftp`) are packaged with the basic networking software on UNIX systems. Applications developed by the Internet community could also be moved to a TCP/IP-based LAN, and there is no reason why an Internet application such as gopher could not be used to manage local resources.

Internet Addresses

For the Internet Protocol to do its job, there must be some way to identify the places or sites that will exchange messages. The physical network (the cable) is largely undifferentiated. Computers are attached to it at various points, but the points of attachment are arbitrary and changeable. Under the Internet Protocol, each network and each computer attached to the physical network has a fixed address. This address allows computers on the Internet to continue receiving messages even if the physical location of the computer changes.

An Internet address is a 32-bit number, just the sort of thing computers were invented to deal with. To make things easier on the human beings who occasionally need to read these numbers, Internet addresses are usually written as four numbers separated by periods:

130.214.50.59

Each number represents eight bits of the Internet address. (For most Internet users, this fact is largely insignificant, but it does mean that none of the four numbers can be larger than 255.)

The 32-bit IP address has two components. One identifies the individual computer, and the other identifies the network of which that computer is a member. The network component is assigned when the local network registers for an Internet connection with the Internet Network Information Center (InterNIC, also known as "the NIC"). The InterNIC supplies the portion of the address that identifies the local network and gives the local network's administrator a range of addresses that can be assigned to individual hosts within the local network.

An Internet address is a powerful thing. It uniquely identifies a host on the Internet, and it is the key to interacting with that computer and any applications installed on it. For example, some of the agricultural market information used by farmers can be found on a host whose address is `129.8.100.15`. Using the command `telnet 129.8.100.15`, you can connect to the computer at this address and use the database containing this information. Although you can reach many of the information resources available on the Internet through menu systems, many others will be identified only by IP address, so it's a good idea to become comfortable with these numbers.

Numbers Are Not Enough: The Domain Naming System

An IP address uniquely identifies a host on the Internet, but even in its more-nearly-readable format (four numbers separated by periods), an IP address can be hard to work with. The numeric addresses don't have much personality, and are difficult to remember. The IP address `128.114.143.4` isn't particularly memorable, but you won't quickly forget the name `infoslug` (which refers to the computer at that address). Moreover, the one-to-one correspondence of IP addresses and computers doesn't provide the flexibility that is sometimes needed in managing the placement of resources on the Internet.

Because each IP address refers to one and only one network host, it was relatively easy for the Internet to establish a naming system for network hosts. A well-defined set of conventions for naming computers on the network has evolved along with a directory service for looking up names. These conventions and the directory service are known collectively as the Domain Name System (DNS). A *domain* is just a named group of network hosts, and if you know a computer's name (host name) and the domains it belongs to, you'll have a better picture of where it is on the Internet than if you have only its IP address.

NOTE –

The local network administrator is responsible for establishing local domains and registering them with the NIC, which maintains a database of domains and their members. This process is similar to network registration, but the two are completely independent of each other: registering a network does not automatically create a domain for that network. Some sites register domain names well before they have Internet access, to simplify the exchange of electronic mail between the site and the Internet.

Domain-style names consist of a series of names separated by periods. A Fully Qualified Domain Name (FQDN for short) represents the name of a computer and the hierarchy of domains in which it is nested. An FQDN looks a little like an IP address, but there is no correspondence between the fields in the two names. The fully qualified domain name for the computer that contains the agricultural database consulted above looks like this:

```
caticsuf.csufresno.edu
```

We can use this name in place of an IP address. The command `telnet caticsuf.csufresno.edu` would connect us—telnet allows you to log onto a remote computer—to the computer that maintains the agricultural database.

Let's dissect this name. The leftmost field (`caticsuf`) is the host name, the name assigned to the computer by its administrator. Following the host name are names of domains the host belongs to, in order of increasing generality. The computer named `caticsuf` is a member of the `csufresno` domain (a domain at California State University in Fresno) which in turn is a member of the `edu` domain—the domain for educational institutions.

The name `caticsuf.csufresno.edu` is an *organizational* domain name: it tells us what sort of organization the named computer belongs to. As listed in Table 1.1, there are seven top-level organizational domains in the Internet's hierarchy, and every computer that registers an organizational name must fit into one of these top-level domains.

There are also geographically based top-level domains. These domains (listed in Table 1.2) have two-letter names representing a country. The lower-level domains beneath the "country-based" domains are a mixture of geographical and non-geographical names. For example, the name `well.sf.ca.us` indicates that the computer named `well` is in the San Francisco area, in California, in the United States. On the other hand, `info.anu.edu.au` identifies the host

Table 1.1: Top-Level Organizational Domains

DOMAIN NAME	CATEGORY
com	Commercial Organizations
edu	Educational Institutions
gov	US Government Organizations
int	International Organizations
mil	US Military Organizations
net	Network Backbone Systems and Information Centers
org	Nonprofit Organizations

named info at the Australian National University, an educational institution, in Australia. Note that geographical codes are unique only within fields, not across them. For example, Canada's country code is ca. California's state code is also ca.

Table 1.2:   A Selection of Top-Level Geographical Domains

au	Australia
at	Austria
ca	Canada
cl	Chile
dk	Denmark
ec	Ecuador
fi	Finland
fr	France
de	Germany
is	Iceland
it	Italy
jp	Japan
kr	Korea
nz	New Zealand
es	Spain
se	Sweden
tw	Taiwan
uk	UK/Ireland
us	United States

66

> **NOTE** –
>
> Whenever you refer to a host on the Internet by name, the software you're using will translate the name into an IP Address and use that. This translation always starts with the most general domain. Consequently, the rightmost field in a domain name is always assumed to be a top-level domain—either one of the organization types or a country code. A reference to `well.sf.ca` will be assumed to be a computer in Canada, and the translation will fail. To be translatable, domain names must always end with the name of a top-level domain.

On the Internet a host is known by an IP address, but it may have several names (all of which map to its IP address). Unlike IP addresses, names can be reassigned or reused, and this makes them more versatile than IP addresses.

When, for example, the agricultural database at Cal State Fresno outgrows the computer it's on now, it will be moved to a different computer, with a different IP address. If you use the old computer's IP address, you will be routed to that computer and there will be no database there. However, when the database is moved, the administrator of the local network at Cal State Fresno will be able to reassign the name (`caticsuf.csufresno.edu`) so that it refers to the IP address of the new computer. References to the name will then be routed automatically to the new computer.

The Human Touch: Networked Applications

The protocols and cabling that make up the Internet give us a network over which messages can be transmitted from one place to another. The Internet's ability to move messages around has a great

HOW DO CLIENTS FIND SERVERS? – – – – – – – – – –

By now you're probably wondering how clients connect to servers. When a server is running, it listens for client connections at a particular address that was programmed into it. On the Internet this address is called a `port number`. Port numbers are always relative to the IP address of an Internet host. To connect to a server, a client program must know which host the server is running on and what port number the server monitors for connections.

For example, the `finger` command we discussed earlier is a client/server application. When you issue a `finger` command, a connection is made to a `finger` server (named `fingerd`) on the computer you specify. By convention, the `finger` server monitors port 79 for connections, and this port number has been programmed into the `finger` client.

Earlier, in the sidebar on troubleshooting the `finger` command, we used `telnet` as a substitute for `finger`. That was possible because both `telnet` and `finger` use the same application protocol. `Telnet` is programmed to use port 23, but you can override this by supplying an alternate port number on the `telnet` command line. The command

```
telnet xi.uleth.ca 79
```

directs `telnet` to connect to the port monitored by the `finger` server at `xi.uleth.ca`. Once the connection is made, you must provide the name of the user you want the `finger` server to look up for you.

deal in common with other familiar networks (the postal service, the telephone system, tin cans connected by string) whose main purpose is to allow people to communicate with each other. How people interact with each other through these other networks is perfectly clear: the letter carrier hands you a stack of mail and you read it. We all know to pick up the phone when it rings and begin talking.

On the Internet, getting people in touch with the network and each other is the job of software applications, the programs that enable us to communicate with others and to access data of all sorts throughout the Internet.

Using these programs is not particularly difficult, but they aren't yet as familiar as telephones or tin cans. Some of the applications you will encounter on the Internet (`mail`, `telnet`, and `ftp`, for example) are practically universal because they are bundled with the network portion of the UNIX operating system and are very likely to be included with networking packages for other operating systems as well.

Other Internet tools (`gopher`, `WAIS`, `WWW`, and `archie`, for example) are not part of any operating system. They were developed within the Internet community to simplify access to worldwide resources. These programs are generally not commercial software in the usual sense, but they are not hard to find on the Internet. In later chapters we'll talk about finding and using these applications.

As diverse as they are, most of the applications in use on the Internet today share a common structure that is different from that of conventional, stand-alone applications. Understanding this structure and how it differs from that of stand-alone programs will simplify learning how things work on the Internet.

Stand-Alone Programs and Their Limits

Conventional, stand-alone computer programs are able to get all resources they need from local sources, usually one or more files located on a disk on the computer where the program is run. Such programs work well in an environment where everything (the user, the computer, the program, and the data) is private and nothing needs to be shared.

However, when data needs to be shared among a group of users (or a group of computers), stand-alone programs lose some of their usefulness.

Trying to use a stand-alone program to share data among several users will require one of two things: either the data must be replicated on many machines, or everyone must run the program on the one machine that holds the data. Imagine ten (or a hundred, or a thousand) spreadsheet users who must all use data from the same worksheet. Copying the same data everywhere wastes disk space, and forcing all the interested users to run on one computer is likely to create performance problems (as well as interpersonal conflicts). Simply introducing a network in which to run stand-alone applications will not solve this problem. The underlying program architecture needs to change.

The Network Application Alternative

To overcome these limits, network applications are built on the "client/server" model. Tools based on this architecture distribute the work of one application across two programs, a client and a server, that carry on a dialog with each other over the network. Virtually all of the applications that are used to reach resources on the Internet use the client/server model. The client/server approach to networked applications is also what enables the Internet to be more than a vehicle for personal communication. Many networks provide person-to-person communication; what the Internet provides beyond this is access to information on everything from agriculture to astrophysics. Client/server applications make it possible for anyone with Internet access to use much of this data "anonymously," that is, without having to know someone (or be known by someone) at the institution that publishes the data. Thanks largely to client/server architecture (and the broadmindedness of the many people who administer data sources on the Internet), your ability to access data on the Internet does not depend on whom you know.

The Dialog between Clients and Servers

The basic structure of a client/server application is fairly simple. A diagram of this structure appears in Figure 1.7. When you need information or access to some resource, you start up a program (a "client") that collects details about what you need. The client program makes a connection (usually over the network) to a server program that controls the information requested.

The dialog between client and server takes place using application protocols. The client formats your request in an application protocol it shares with the server and then dispatches the request by handing it to program that will format the message in the appropriate protocol to be transmitted across the network to the server.

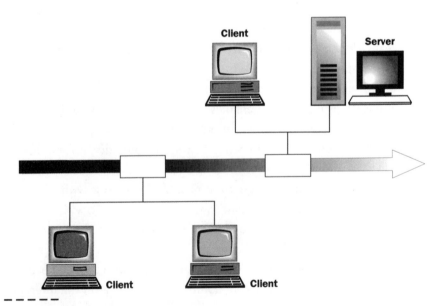

Figure 1.7 Client/server architecture.

NOTE -

Here, the term server also refers to a program. In other contexts you may be familiar with, it is common to describe a computer as a server when it provides some resource (disks or file systems, printers, and so forth) for other machines on a network. Software servers can be designed to manage almost any kind of resource. We usually think first of database servers, but there are servers for other resources as well.

The server receives the client's request, evaluates it, finds the desired resource or information, formats the result in an application protocol, and passes the response to the appropriate protocol handler to begin a network transmission back to the client.

When the client receives the requested information, it provides an interface through which you can either look at the information or direct it elsewhere. When you are through with the results and have no further requests, you simply exit the client program.

Client programs are always run ad hoc. You start a client when you have a question or need some information. You use the client to make specific requests and then stop the program when you've received the needed information or resources. Server programs, on the other hand, run continuously. When there are no active clients, the server continues to run, waiting for clients to submit new requests.

Client/server applications are extraordinarily versatile. The client and server programs can be run on the same computer or (given a sufficiently robust network) on different computers thousands of miles apart. A client/server dialog can occur between programs on computers of wildly different operating systems.

Clients can be built to maintain multiple, simultaneous connections to a server or even to connect to more than one server at a time. Servers can be programmed to open connections to other servers.

 **HUNTING THROUGH THE INTERNET** ---------

The `Internet Hunt` is a scavenger hunt for information from Internet sources hosted by Rick Gates. Each month 10 new questions appear, and anyone who wants to play downloads the questions and sets off to find the answers using only Internet resources. Points are awarded not just for getting the correct answer, but for doing so in a way that is intuitively satisfying, easy to figure out, and instructive about the Internet. Throughout the rest of this book, we'll have a Hunt of our own with questions (and answers) to get more familiar with the Internet and its resources. The question below is an example of what's coming up in later chapters. (We haven't talked about finding things on the Internet yet, so this installment consists of a question and its answer. Future hunt questions will focus more on search strategy.)

Question 1   Chapter 1 mentioned some statistics about the growth of the Internet. Is there any place on the Internet where you can read more about its history and get more detailed information about its growth?

Clients and servers can be built to support multiple network protocols.

Interface Issues

The Internet itself does not really have a user interface. Instead, each client program provides an interface that is appropriate for the services to which it gives access. Predicting what sort of workstations will be used to run a client program is difficult, and so client programs are often distributed in different versions for different interfaces.

Answer   With no tools, this is going to be tough, but we did mention something called the Network Information Center (NIC, or InterNIC), and there were a couple of references to `telnet` connections. The NIC will accept `telnet` connections to let you browse through their collection of Internet Information. Try this command:

```
telnet rs.internic.net
```

Once you're connected, follow the instructions for using the InterNIC's `gopher` interface. (We'll look at `gopher` in detail in Chapter 6.) Look for Robert Hobbes Zakon's Internet Timeline, a compact history of the Internet with a nifty table of statistics showing its growth.

Remember the InterNIC! It's a place you'll want to visit often as you start working with the Internet. The InterNIC seems to have just about everything of interest to the Internet explorer.

The ASCII (character-based) version of a client has the least extravagant hardware requirements; all you see is text. This is particularly helpful if you don't have access to a graphical user interface (GUI) or if your only access to Internet is indirect, that is, through `telnet` or through a dial-up connection. (You'll learn more about types of connections in Chapter 2.) It's important to remember that the client program must run on a computer on the Internet in order to connect to a server. In addition to ASCII versions of client programs, there may also be versions for different GUIs (MS-Windows, Macintosh, and Xwindows versions are all popular). The examples used throughout this book will show either Windows 3.x user interfaces or ASCII terminal-based interfaces.

Detecting and Responding to Errors

Along with the data you asked for, the client program may also deliver messages when things go wrong during the client/server dialog. The important thing to remember is that the client program is not necessarily the source of the errors it reports. It may be relaying messages originating in the server or anywhere along the path between client and server. Knowing the general structure of the client/server interaction can be helpful in figuring out what to do next. (Specific error messages are covered in Chapter 2.)

The Next Step: From Practical Perspective to Practice

You now have a high-level view of what the Internet is and a rough notion of how it works. By developing this understanding, you have already taken the first step in learning how to work with the Internet and what you can use it for. The next step is to sit down at a computer and begin using the Internet itself to build on what you already know.

CHAPTER

2

**Getting to
the Internet
by Phone**

There was one light on in the computer lab at Sherman Peabody High School. Two kids, the Duke of Url and El Ron, hunched over a PC keyboard.

- "Man, this is so much jive!" El Ron whined. "These guys are the C-I-A, man. They are not gonna put anything real up on some computer network where any bozo can get to it."

- The Duke of Url stared at him. "We aren't bozos, man, and the way I see it, you've got a civics paper due tomorrow and the only way you're gonna get it in on time is if we hustle one or two factoids off of this net and into your brain. Just the facts, man. We don't need any secrets."

- The Duke of Url dispatched another command to the gopher server. Lights blinked on the modem beside the computer, and a second later, the screen filled with a menu. The Duke picked the item labeled "Libraries" and another menu appeared. One entry near the bottom of the screen was titled "Reference Works," and the Duke chose that.

- "Now watch this," the Duke said. The menu that appeared now had an entry for the 1993 CIA World Factbook. The Duke selected that and turned to El Ron. "Okay. What country do you want to write a paper about?"

- Ron thought for a minute. "Liechtenstein."

Connecting to the Internet by Telephone

The way you connect to the Internet is changing. A few years ago, most people who used the Internet got their network access at work or at school. Their point of contact with the Internet was likely to be a dedicated computer or workstation with a permanent network connection.

Today, more and more people are connecting to the Internet from home using a personal computer, a modem, and an Internet access provider to establish a temporary point of contact with the Internet.

There are two ways to get Internet access via phone, and it's worth considering each in detail so you can choose the alternative that is best for you. The two choices are *conventional* dialup and *protocol* dialup. Most access providers offer conventional dialup service; some offer both service types. With conventional dialup, you establish an interactive session with another computer that is an Internet host. (Figure 2.1 is a schematic representation of a conventional dialup connection.) The remote computer becomes your home base

INTERNET ACCESS PROVIDERS - - - - - - - - - - -

What's an access provider? Any commercial service that provides its subscribers with access to the Internet. Some access providers (Northern California's Netcom, for example) specialize in Internet access. Others (America Online, or the WELL, for example) offer Internet access along with other on-line or conferencing services. At a minimum, an access provider should supply you with: a secure account of your own with a login name and password, a directory in which you can store files, and the opportunity to run network applications (`ftp`, `telnet`, mail, `gopher`, and WorldWideWeb) to contact Internet sites.

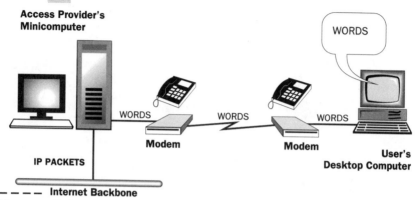

Figure 2.1 A conventional dialup connection.

for working on the Internet. Your desktop computer assumes the role of an ASCII terminal. Protocol dialup, on the other hand, uses one of several serial line protocols (like the Point-to-Point Protocol, PPP, or the Serial Line Internet Protocol, SLIP) to extend the Internet Protocol to the computer sitting on your desk. SLIP is the older of the two protocols and may someday be rendered obsolete by PPP. Many commercial networking software packages support both protocols. (Figure 2.2 is a schematic representation of a protocol dialup connection.) You still establish a phone connection to a computer attached to the Internet, but in this case, your home computer exchanges protocol information with the remote computer to become a full-fledged Internet host while you're dialed in. With protocol dialup connections, your desktop computer becomes your base of operations for using the Internet, and you can use all of its graphical capabilities when running network applications. Let's take a quick look at each of these alternatives and see how they work. Further on we'll look at each type of connection in detail.

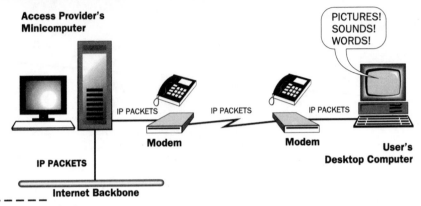

Figure 2.2 A protocol dialup connection.

How It Works: Conventional Dialup

Conventional dialup connections are similar to the connections you use when you dial up a bulletin board. You use your computer, a modem, and communications software (a terminal emulation program) to place a call over your home phone to your access provider's computer. When the modem on the other end answers, it puts you directly in contact with the computer at that site. Your computer acts like a terminal (essentially, a monitor and keyboard) that is attached directly to the remote computer, rather than the self-contained computer you're familiar with. Anything you type at your keyboard is sent straight to the remote computer, which treats it just like the input it collects from its own local users.

When you establish a conventional dialup connection to a computer on the Internet, you'll have to supply a user name (or login name) and a password that lets the Internet host know you're an authorized user. (See Appendix C for general information about logging in.) Once you're dialed in to a computer on the Internet, you can use that computer as a home base for exploring the Internet. Of course, you'll have to learn something about that computer to use it (and your Internet access provider should provide some documentation to help you get acclimated), but you'll be able to run any client programs installed at that site. Even though you're using your home computer to establish a connection to a machine on the Internet, your computer isn't an Internet host: it has no IP (Internet Protocol) address of its own.

How It Works: Protocol Dialup

Protocol dialup connections start out the same way: a call is placed from your computer and modem to another modem and computer. The difference is that protocol dialup connections require special software that understands how to send and receive information in the TCP/IP protocol's format over the serial line that connects your computer to the phone. When the remote computer answers, this software sends your login and password information to the remote computer. After logging in, your computer and the remote one begin exchanging messages using the Internet protocol. The computer on your desktop becomes a genuine Internet host and a base from which you can explore the Internet. This means you can run client programs for Internet applications on your own computer; files or other data you requested are delivered directly to your machine.

Making the Right Choice

Choosing which kind of connection to use can be a complicated decision. Here are some of the things you should consider.

Availability

First of all, you can't choose something that's not available. Not all Internet access providers offer protocol dialup service. As you shop around for an Internet access provider, inquire about the different kinds of service they provide. Many access providers use the term "shell account" for their conventional dialup services. (A shell account gives you a user ID, a home directory to store files, and the privilege of running programs from the system's normal command line interpreter or "shell.") Protocol Dialup services are usually identified by the name of the protocol the system uses. Look for the services based on PPP (Point-to-Point Protocol), SLIP (Serial Line Internet Protocol), and CSLIP (Compressed Serial Line Internet Protocol).

NOTE

PPP, SLIP, and CSLIP are all slightly different protocols, and they're not interchangeable. Don't buy your network protocol software until you know which protocols your Internet access provider supports.

Special Equipment

In general, protocol dialup access requires some equipment that conventional dialup does not. Protocol dialups require software to implement the protocol on your computer, and SLIP or PPP software is not yet the mainstream product that ordinary communications software has become. Protocol dialup access requires a high-speed modem. It's probably unwise to attempt protocol dialup access with anything slower than 9600 bps, and the faster your modem, the more enjoyable protocol dialups are. (Of course, all this is limited by the speed of your access provider's modems: it won't do you any good to buy a modem faster than the modems you call. That is, a 14,400 bps modem communicates with a 9600 bps modem at the slower rate.)

Expense

Conventional dialup access is usually a less expensive service than Protocol dialup access. Generally, Internet access providers charge higher rates for protocol dialup service, but the rates vary a great deal from one carrier to the next. High-speed modems and network protocol software also add to the initial cost for protocol dialup users.

Ease of Use and Performance

Protocol dialup connections let you use your home computer's user interface (for example, Windows) to run Internet client programs. Conventional dialup connections restrict you to clients that use an ASCII terminal interface. If your home computer uses a graphical user interface (like the Macintosh operating system or Windows), protocol dialup connections will make it easier for you to work with Internet resources that use graphics or sound. The newer Internet application clients (like Cello or the Windows gopher, both discussed in later chapters) can display graphic images as you encounter them. The ASCII terminal interface doesn't support in-line display of graphics images: with an ASCII client, your only choice is to download the graphics files and display them later, using graphics software.

On the other hand, displaying graphics in-line is very resource intensive: the graphics file must still be downloaded to your computer to be displayed. You may find that using GUI-based client programs taxes your patience and that the ASCII clients enable you to cruise the Internet more efficiently.

Downloading Procedures

Collecting information is one of the main attractions of the Internet, and it helps to be able to download things efficiently from the Internet to your computer. Protocol dialup connections allow you to retrieve information from the Internet directly to your home computer. Conventional dialup connections require an extra step: you first retrieve information to your Internet access provider's computer and then download that information to your computer. This can be complicated and tedious.

A Cookbook for Conventional Dialups

Let's take a look at how you go about getting a dialup connection up and running. We'll first work through a checklist of the things you need for a conventional dialup connection and then walk through the procedure of setting things up and getting dialed in.

What You Need

To establish a conventional dialup connection to the Internet, you'll need the following:

- ☐ a home telephone
- ☐ a computer with a serial port (for external modems) or an expansion slot (for internal modems)
- ☐ a modem (and if it's an external modem, a cable to connect it to your computer)
- ☐ communications (or "terminal emulation") software
- ☐ an account with an Internet access provider

Modems have become a mass-market item, but a few words about telephone lines, computers, cables and modems are in order. We'll also describe the information your Internet access provider will give you. Let's talk about each of these.

A Phone of Your Own

You should use the simplest phone line available for your dialup connections. For most home users, this is fairly straightforward. There are a few items you should be aware of, however. In general, modems for home computers are designed for use with single-line, voice phones. They aren't, unless otherwise noted by the modem manufacturer, intended for PBX (Public Branch Exchange) phones or digital phones. Phone lines that have additional features (such as call waiting) may cause problems for your modem connections.

NOTE –

If you plan to do a significant amount of dialup work on your computer, consider having a separate phone line installed exclusively for your modem. (Your friends will thank you for this!) If you don't want to add a second line, you'll need to remember to plug the phone line back into your phone or answering machine after you've finished a dialup session.

Your Computer

It doesn't make much difference what sort of computer you use to establish your dialup connection. The main requirement is that you can connect your computer to a modem. Depending on your preferences and the kind of computer you have, the modem can be either internal or external. Internal modems require a free slot inside the computer. External modems need to be attached to one of the computer's serial ports (most computers come equipped with at least one serial port). You should be aware that serial ports may have any of several different kinds of connectors. Check the serial port on you computer before you go modem shopping so you'll know what kind of connectors are needed for your modem cable.

Modems and Cabling

Modems are the devices that translate between the digital format for information that computers use and the analog signal used over phone lines. Your modem will determine the speed at which you interact with computers over the phone. When you place a call to another computer, your modem and the answering modem at the remote site will negotiate a speed when they connect. Check with your Internet access provider and find out what speeds their modems support. Shop around for the fastest modem you can afford. If you're buying an external modem, make sure the vendor has the cable you'll need to connect it with your computer (find out ahead of time what kind of serial connector your computer has). The modem should come with a cable to connect it to the phone line. Communications software comes bundled with many modems. When buying a modem, ask about any terminal emulation software that comes with the modem.

Terminal Emulation Software

The only software you need to establish a conventional dialup connection to the Internet is a communication or "terminal emulation" program. This software lets your computer behave like a terminal passing input to the remote system and displaying any output that comes from the remote computer. (As mentioned above, terminal emulation software is frequently bundled with modems. You can also purchase it separately. In general, your access provider won't supply either your modem or the communication software.) From most terminal emulation programs, you can give commands directly to the modem, watch the modem's progress in connecting to the remote system, and finally work interactively with the computers you connect to. Beyond these basic features, some communications programs offer dialing directories, special "error checking" protocols for file transfers, or logging features (that allow you to capture an entire session with a remote computer in a file). If software was bundled with your modem, it should already be configured to work with that modem. If you purchase communications software independently, you may have to configure it for your modem manually.

Your Internet Account

Finally, you'll need an account with an Internet access provider. When you sign up for your account, the access provider will give you some basic information: the phone number you must use to connect, the login name and password for your account, and possibly some basic documentation for the system.

If there is more than one Internet access provider in your area, it may be worthwhile to do some comparison shopping. Internet access is a service that the providers charge for, but there are likely to be different levels of service. Some service providers bill at a flat rate (usually monthly); others bill according to the amount of time you spend using the service or the number of characters you download. Some providers offer limited-use accounts (e-mail and USENET News only). In any case, be sure you understand what services you're buying from the provider and what those services cost before you sign up. In addition to the provider's charges for a login account, you should also consider any phone costs. Is the access number for the provider's system a local call or will you have to pay toll charges (or long distance charges)?

Cost is not the only factor to consider in signing up with an access provider. You should also take into account what software the provider makes available. (For example, does the provider's system have client programs for gopher or the World Wide Web? What programs are available to read e-mail or USENET News?) Some Internet access services provide documentation for their systems. You will, after all, be dialing in to a computer that is very likely to have a different operating system from anything you're accustomed to. Some documentation would be helpful.

You should also be aware of any support services the provider offers. If you have questions about the system or problems using it, is there anyone you can call for information? (Support services are particularly important for users who are new to the whole business of dialup access.)

If you travel and want to have Internet access while traveling, you should ask your provider about "points of presence": local phone numbers in different areas of the country that will give you access to your Internet account.

Finally, you should take into account the access provider's policies about the proper uses of the system and the network.

Conventional Dialup: Getting Connected

Getting set up for a conventional dialup session is relatively straightforward. Do your shopping first! Plan ahead: figure out what modem you want and which Internet access provider you'll subscribe to before you buy anything. Pick out the Internet access provider that makes sense for your needs. Choose a modem and software that will work with your computer and take advantage of the fastest speeds your access provider supports.

Next, buy the modem, and if need be, communications software and cable. Follow the instructions that came with the modem for attaching it to the phone line and your computer. Install (and, if necessary, configure) the communications software. Many modem manufacturers maintain bulletin boards that you can use to test your newly installed modem. Test your modem by calling a local bulletin board or your modem manufacturer's BBS.

Once your modem connection works, register for an account with the Internet access provider you selected. If your Internet access service provides documentation, take the time to read it and become familiar with the system's basic commands. An important command to learn early is how to log *off* the computer to end a session, so that you won't be charged for more "connect time" than necessary. (Many Internet access systems use the UNIX operating system, and the common commands to quit a session are `logout` and `exit`.)

You're ready to start using the Internet. All you need to do is dial the local point of presence for your Internet service's computer and log in using your user name and password. Later in this chapter we'll discuss some commands you can give in this first session to take stock of what Internet applications are available to you. When you've finished a dialup session, don't forget to log off the remote computer and instruct your modem to hang up the phone.

A Cookbook for Protocol Dialups

If you want to use a protocol dialup for your Internet access, you'll need some additional software, and your configuration procedures will be a little more complicated.

Protocol Dialups: What You Need

Here's a checklist of things you'll need to set up your computer for protocol dialup sessions:

- [ ] A home telephone

- [ ] A computer with a serial port (for external modems) or an expansion slot (for internal modems)

- [ ] A modem (and if it's an external modem, a cable to connect it to your computer)

- [ ] Communications (or "terminal emulation") software

- [ ] Software for the PPP or SLIP protocols

- [ ] A SLIP or PPP account with an Internet access provider

The telephone line, modem, and computer requirements are essentially the same for protocol dialups as they are for conventional dialups. (PPP or SLIP connections can be made at modem speeds below 9600 bps, but they are frustratingly slow. Use a 9600 bps or faster modem for protocol dialup connections.) Strictly speaking, a terminal emulation program is not necessary for protocol dialup connections, but it is helpful to have one around for testing your modem configuration. SLIP and PPP protocols don't require any unusual hardware, but you should shop carefully.

Protocol Software

To establish a protocol dialup connection, you'll have to install on your home computer an implementation of the protocol that your Internet access provider supports. Protocol implementations are specialized communications software packages. Some Internet access providers (Netcom in California and Pipeline in New York) have begun to provide integrated

Internet clients with serial line protocol software. You can also purchase network protocol software from other sources.

When you buy a version of PPP or SLIP for your computer, you should get several things: a program that handles all communications in that protocol (a *protocol driver*), some supporting utilities to manage the business of connecting to the modem and dialing the right number, and several client programs capable of using the network connection that the protocol driver will establish.

To use your protocol dialup connection effectively, you will definitely need clients for telnet and ftp. Many protocol packages also include utilities like finger, whois, or ping. These are helpful, but not necessary. Your protocol package may also include client programs for electronic mail or USENET News or for some of the Internet community's newer applications like gopher or the World Wide Web.

Before you buy a package, check with the vendor to determine what client programs are included and whether or not you can add clients later. There is a great deal of free client software for network applications available through the Internet. Pick a PPP or SLIP package that allows you to install your own client programs.

You should also inquire about the protocol software's hardware and operating system requirements. For example, a protocol implementation may require more than the default amount of memory, or it may require that you run Windows in 386 Enhanced mode. Verify the protocol software's requirements ahead of time and make sure your computer can satisfy those requirements before you buy.

Implementations of the SLIP/PPP protocols are becoming less obscure than they were even a year ago. Today you can find implementations of SLIP or PPP from several different sources. Protocol implementations are available from conventional network software vendors (for example, FTP Software's PC/TCP product or NetManage's Chameleon products) as well as from some Internet access providers (for example, the NetCruiser product from Netcom). Serial line network protocols are relatively new products, and the manufacturers are just beginning to figure out how to package this software effectively. Don't hesitate to shop around for the features you want.

SLIP or PPP Internet Accounts

Protocol dialup connections use a different kind of login account from that used by conventional dialup connections. When you sign up for a SLIP or PPP account, your access provider will assign you a login name and password and will also give you the phone number your modem should use when establishing a connection. Unless your access provider says otherwise, you should not use your PPP or SLIP account for a conventional dialup session. In general, the login accounts used for SLIP/PPP connections can't be used interactively: these accounts don't expect a human being trying to log in. They expect a protocol implementation sending instructions for setting up a network connection.

Along with the other account information, your access provider may give you some important local network addresses to use in setting up your protocol software. You may get:

- your own IP address (although many access providers prefer not to assign IP addresses permanently to SLIP/PPP connections)

- the name of the domain your computer will be part of

- the IP address for domain name servers

- the address for a USENET News (NNTP) server

- the address for an electronic mail server

Note this information carefully and have it handy when you install and configure your PPP or SLIP software.

Protocol Dialups: Getting Connected

Getting connected to the Internet via SLIP or PPP is a little more complicated than just pulling your modem out of the box, plugging it in and dialing into Cyberspace.

As with conventional dialup access, it's best to plan ahead. If this is your first venture into using a modem, make all your decisions about what to buy before you actually purchase anything. Buy your modem first and test it with local bulletin boards or other conventional dialup services. Next get the information about your SLIP or PPP account from the Internet access provider. (Remember to ask your access provider about calling in for help while you're getting everything set up.) Finally, install and configure the SLIP or PPP software of choice. It helps to have the account information already in hand before you begin to install the network software.

The configuration procedures vary from one software vendor to the next, and it is important to read and follow the vendor's instructions carefully. The basic procedure will require you to provide the connection information (your access provider's phone number, and your login name, and your password) and identifying information for the Internet Protocol (your IP address, the address for a domain name server, and your domain name). For some PPP/SLIP products, you'll have to edit configuration files using your favorite editor. Others provide a configuration program to collect this information. When you've finished configuring the software, you're ready to test your ability to connect to the Internet.

Protocol dialup sessions usually use a script to place the call to the access provider and log in. A template for this script should accompany your network protocol software. All that's needed to complete the script is the phone number for your access provider's modem and some information about the modem you use. After a successful login, the protocol driver controls the modem. The connection, once it's made, will slip into the background. At that point, you can run Internet client software to access the network.

`Telnet` is a helpful program to test your connection. Consult the documentation that accompanied your PPP software for information about starting a `telnet` session after you have started the PPP protocol driver. You'll need a conventional login name and password to use `telnet` to connect to an Internet host. (Many Internet access providers include a conventional login ID as part of the protocol dialup account.) `Telnet` is essentially a terminal emulation program that runs across the network. When you use `telnet`, your session will look very much like a conventional dialup session: you will log in to another machine and have access to any ASCII client programs installed on that machine. In later chapters, we'll discuss interesting network application clients you can run with a PPP or SLIP connection. For the time being, if you can run `telnet`, you'll be able to test your Internet connection and do the exercises in the next section.

When you're through working with the Internet in a PPP or SLIP session, remember to exit from all the clients you've started and signal the protocol driver to drop the connection. Different manufacturers of PPP and SLIP software do this in different ways. Consult the manual that came with your network software to learn how to disconnect at the end of a session.

The Internet Applications Toolkit

Regardless of how you access the Internet, it's a good idea to take an inventory of the network applications that are available on the machine that puts you in touch with the Internet. Here are some exercises to see which Internet applications are available to you.

This inventory was taken using a conventional dialup connection to an Internet access provider (Netcom) using the login name "bkf". Netcom uses UNIX computers, and the exercises illustrate the UNIX versions of some of the basic Internet applications. The tools we look for in this inventory will be discussed only briefly here. Detailed discussions of the various tools appear in Parts 2 and 3. These exercises assume that you've already established a conventional dialup connection or that you've started a protocol dialup session and are running `telnet` to connect to an Internet host.

You will find two types of networked applications on Internet hosts. Some applications come bundled with the TCP/IP network software. `Telnet` and `ftp` are nearly universal regardless of operating system. In addition to `telnet` and `ftp`, UNIX systems will almost always have `mail`, `finger`, and a utility named `whois`. Mail programs are not usually included in the TCP/IP package for personal computers, and the availability of `finger` and `whois` is spotty at best. Other applications, developed and maintained by the Internet community (`archie`, `gopher`, World Wide Web, and many others), must be installed voluntarily.

The easiest way to see if an application is available is to try starting it. The applications we test may not start in the way we want, but if they fail, they will do so in predictable ways. The common errors that you might encounter are those discussed in Chapter 1 ("When Finger is Fickle"):

- Command not found

- Host unknown

- Connection refused

- Connection timed out

Since we're browsing to see what commands are available, "Command not found" is the most ominous failure indicator. Executing any of the bundled utilities (telnet, ftp, and so on) should not produce this message. The community-developed applications can be installed wherever the local system administrator prefers. By convention, software outside the standard UNIX distribution is usually installed in the directory /usr/local/bin.

If you try to execute any of the commands discussed below and get a "Command not found" message, first check that you have typed the command properly. If so, and you still get a "Command not found" response, try executing the command by full pathname (for example, /usr/ucb/telnet or /usr/local/bin/gopher). If executing the commands by full pathname fares no better, it is time to consult your Internet access provider's help desk.

Remote login using telnet

Telnet is a program used to start a login session on any computer on the network. Many databases on the Internet are accessible only through telnet. For example, the agricultural database at California State University in Fresno (discussed in Chapter 1) can only be reached by a telnet request to caticsuf.csufresno.edu. The login prompt for that computer provides instructions for logging in and registering to use the database.

When you're using `telnet` to access some service, you will need a valid login name and password for the computer you're connecting to. All that we need to test `telnet`, however, is a host name. We'll test `telnet` by using it to connect to `well.sf.ca.us`, the host name for the Well. Figure 2.3 shows our test session.

```
┌─────────────────────────────────────────────────────────────┐
│ ▒                    Win100 Terminal Emulator on COM1    ▼ ▲ │
├─────────────────────────────────────────────────────────────┤
│ File  Edit  Setup  Kermit  Help                             │
│ netcom11% telnet well.sf.ca.us                              │
│  Trying...                                                  │
│  Connected to well.sf.ca.us.                               │
│  Escape character is '^]'.                                  │
│                                                            │
│  UNIX(r) System V Release 4.0 (well)                       │
│                                                            │
│  This is the WELL                                          │
│                                                            │
│  Type    newuser   to sign up.                             │
│  Type    trouble   if you are having trouble logging in.   │
│  Type    guest     to learn about the WELL.                │
│                                                            │
│  If you already have a WELL account, type your username.   │
│                                                            │
│  login:                                                    │
│  telnet> quit                                              │
│  Connection closed.                                        │
│ netcom11%                                                   │
│                                                            │
├─────────────────────────────────────────────────────────────┤
│ ←□                                                        →│
└─────────────────────────────────────────────────────────────┘
```

Figure 2.3 Testing telnet by connecting to the Well.

A `telnet` command consists of the word `telnet` and a host name (or IP address). You should see two informational messages as `telnet` starts. The first message reports the host that `telnet` will attempt to reach. Some versions of `telnet` identify the host by IP address; others identify the host by name. The second message notes what the "escape" character is. Since you're starting an interactive session with another host, most of what you type will just be passed directly to that host. Typing the escape character (in this case Ctrl-[) will interrupt the interactive session and let you give commands directly to `telnet`.

In this case the connection was made and we received a login prompt (along with some instructions) from `well.sf.ca.us`. Rather than log in, we typed the escape character (it doesn't show up on the screen) and issued the `quit` command to close the interactive session.

Transferring Files with ftp

`Ftp` is a generic file transfer program. It can be used to connect to another host specifically to move files between the two computers. Like `telnet`, `ftp` expects a host name (or IP address) on its command line and requires a valid login name and password. Figure 2.4 shows an `ftp` connection to the host `rtfm.mit.edu`.

`Ftp` opened the connection to `rtfm`, a host at MIT, and prompted for a login name and a password. `Ftp` suggested the current username ("bkf") as a default. In this case, we don't have a login account on `rtfm.mit.edu`, so we used the guest user id "anonymous." After the login succeeded, `ftp` prompted for further activity with the `ftp>`

```
                        Win100 Terminal Emulator on COM1
 File   Edit   Setup   Kermit   Help
netcom11% ftp rtfm.mit.edu
 Connected to BLOOM-PICAYUNE.MIT.EDU.
 220 rtfm ftpd (wu-2.4(21) with built-in ls); bugs to ftp-bugs@rtfm.mit.edu
 Name (rtfm.mit.edu:bkf): anonymous
 331 Guest login ok, send your complete e-mail address as password.
 Password:
 230 Guest login ok, access restrictions apply.
 ftp> quit
 221 Goodbye.
netcom11%
```

Figure 2.4   An ftp test session.

prompt. Since we're just checking that ftp is available, we can quit.

Internet Community Tools: archie

Archie is a program to help you locate files that are accessible through ftp on the Internet. Information about the availability of files is kept on several servers, and the archie program you run is a client that can query these servers with a keyword you specify.

If you just want to see whether archie is available on your system, type archie and press ↵. If the archie client is installed, you will get a summary of the options the archie command allows. We'll discuss those in detail in Chapter 3.

Archie is one of the tools that might be of help in locating the CIA World Factbook. Since all we know about it is its name, we can try using "factbook" as a search string for archie. Figure 2.5 shows this command and some of the results it returned. Interpreting archie results and actually transferring files are topics that we'll cover in

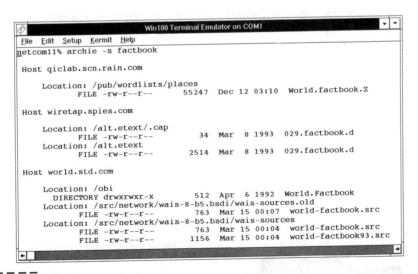

Figure 2.5 An archie test session—searching for "factbook."

Chapter 3. For the time being, however, we know at least one place where we can find a copy of the CIA World Factbook should we need it.

Internet Community Tools: gopher

The Internet gopher is a program that provides menu-driven access to many of the facilities of the Internet. When you give the gopher command, you are starting a client program connected to a gopher server (by default a gopher server at the University of Minnesota, where gopher was developed). Gopher can be started by simply typing the word gopher and pressing ↵. On UNIX systems this will start a "terminal-based" gopher client. Gopher is a full-screen client program, and it needs to know what kind of terminal you're using. (For information on setting terminal types, see Appendix D, "Just Enough UNIX.") If a gopher client is installed on your machine and the default server is running, you will see a menu like that shown in Figure 2.6.

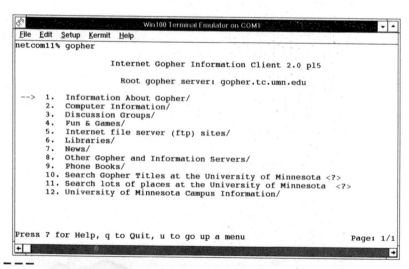

Figure 2.6 Connecting to the default gopher server at the University of Minnesota.

Gopher clients have good error-handling facilities and will generally tell you if something goes wrong in the connection procedure.

If a gopher client has paused for what seems an unreasonable time waiting to connect to a server, you can abort the gopher client by typing Ctrl-C (^C).

At the beginning of this chapter, the Duke of Url and El Ron found the CIA World Factbook through gopher. Gopher offers a slightly different perspective on this resource from that offered by ftp. From the menu above, select the "Libraries" item. That selection produces a menu of things related to libraries, and one item on that menu is Reference Works. This selection brings up a menu with an entry for the CIA World Factbook. That item in turn displays a menu with entries describing the Factbook and its contents and a series of items for the letters of the alphabet. Selecting a letter will bring up a menu of Factbook articles for countries beginning with that letter. Simply select the country name from this menu to view its article.

Internet Community Tools: WWW

The World Wide Web provides a hypertext interface to many things on the Internet. *Hypertext* is a system for cross-referencing and retrieving related documents. Using a special viewer (called a "browser") you can read a hypertext document as you would any other. However, the browser will also highlight any elements of the current document that are cross-referenced to other documents. When you select a cross-reference, the browser will retrieve the referenced document for you to read (and that, of course, may lead to other documents in turn).

Www is a hypertext browser. It is a screen-oriented tool (like go-pher) that provides an orderly set of choices for navigating through Internet resources.

You start the WorldWideWeb application by typing www and pressing ↵. Normally this will present a hypertext "home page" on your screen. The www command and a "home page" are shown in Figure 2.7. As you'll see in Chapter 7, each Web site has a home page from which to begin exploring. Which home page you get depends on how your Internet access provider has configured the Web software. The Web browser at your site may bring up a different home page from that shown.

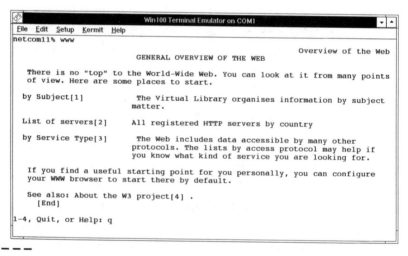

Figure 2.7 A world wide web "home page."

As with gopher, testing the www client program requires connecting to a www server. If this connection fails or appears to hang, type Ctrl-C to abort the session.

Further into the Internet

This chapter has shown you two ways to connect to the Internet by phone. We've also introduced some of the applications for reaching resources over the Internet. In Part 2 we will begin to use the essential network application tools in earnest: `ftp`, `telnet`, and mail. We'll also provide some pointers for finding and installing Internet clients you can use with PPP or SLIP connections.

HUNTING THROUGH THE INTERNET – – – – – – – – –

This chapter talked quite a bit about shopping for PPP or SLIP software. The Internet is the sort of tool that ought to make it easier to collect the information you need to do that shopping. As with the Hunt question in Chapter 1, this episode of the hunt will focus on identifying a resource, not on a strategy for finding things.

Question   Where can you find out more about the SLIP/PPP software packages that are available for personal computers?

Answer   One of the Internet's institutions is a document called an "FAQ": a compilation of frequently asked questions (and their answers) about some topic. The forum in which the frequently asked questions appear is usually a USENET news group, (Chapter 8 will discuss USENET News in detail.) The FAQs are of general enough interest that they have been collected in a separate newsgroup named `news.answers`. FAQs have been compiled from questions asked in all sorts of subject areas, some technical, some not. We're looking for information about commercially available PPP software. This is just the sort of thing for which there should be an FAQ, and there is. The PPP FAQ is generated from the newsgroup `comp.protocols.ppp` and is posted there and in `news.answers`. The procedures for starting a newsreader, navigating to a newsgroup and then selecting an article or group of articles is discussed in Chapter 8. The FAQ for the Point-to-Point Protocol is divided into eight articles in `news.answers`. Article 7 discusses commercially available PPP software.

First Generation Internet Applications: ftp, telnet, and E-Mail

- There are three fundamental application services on the Internet that everyone should master: transferring files, remote login, and electronic mail.

- In Chapter 3 you'll learn how to use ftp (the Internet's file transfer program) and the related archie database to find and copy files from sites with public archives.

- Telnet (the Internet's remote login program) is discussed in Chapter 4. Remote login brings Bulletin Board Services and Library Card Collections within any user's reach.

- Electronic mail offers an unparalleled ability to interact with people and information resources. In Chapter 5 you'll discover the basics of sending and receiving e-mail. Protocol dialup users will learn about the Eudora mailer.

CHAPTER

Using ftp, the Internet File Transfer Program

"This is too much," he said, pounding on the keyboard. "It's more than I can stand. There are two million computers at my fingertips, I don't know where to start or what to do, and any minute now somebody's going to walk in here and fire me. Arghh!"

- A paper airplane sailed into his cube, passed silently over his shoulder and crashed into the screen in front of him. He would have crumpled it up and thrown it away except for the message composed of big letters cut from the morning paper and pasted in plain view along the wing:

```
ftp ftp.csd.uwm.edu
anonymous
pub/inet*
```

- Here was a puzzle. `Ftp` rang a bell; it was an Internet file transfer command. The second `ftp`, however, seemed to be the name of a computer. It was, after all, part of what looked like a fully qualified domain name. The computer named `ftp` was located in domains named csd (Computer Science Department, perhaps?), uwm (probably a university somewhere), and edu (uwm was definitely an educational institution of some kind).
- He poked at the keyboard and found that he could execute the `ftp` command. On his screen was a prompt for a user name. He looked at the paper and typed in the word `anonymous`. In a second, he was in!
- The next line looked something like a directory name. He tried the only directory commands he knew (`cd` and `dir`) and they worked: he was in a directory named "pub" and it contained files named `inet.services.something`. With a little fidgeting, he figured out how to copy one of them to his computer. That done, he typed `quit`, and `ftp` went away.
- He skimmed through the file and realized that he had just downloaded something called the Internet Services List. It appeared to be a kind of quick reference card put together by someone named Scott Yanoff, and it contained information about all sorts of things available on the Internet. There were brief instructions for reaching dozens of bulletin boards and databases. It listed sites with files available for copying with `ftp`. It described `archie` servers and where to get up-to-the-minute baseball scores and stock quotes. It even told him how to use the `finger` command to monitor a soft drink machine in the computer science department at MIT.
- "Well, I suppose it's better," he thought with a smile, "to get fired for using this thing than for just sitting here."

Information to Go

The problem with libraries is that sooner or later, you have to return the books you borrow. In a lot of ways, the Internet is like a global reference library. A big difference, however, is that many of the Internet's resources are available for you to copy onto your computer free of charge, and these resources go far beyond the resources of most libraries. On the Internet, you will have access to files containing information, source code, and even compiled, ready-to-run programs. Many Internet sites publish files in directories that are accessible to anyone who can connect to the Internet, and these files can be freely copied using the Internet file transfer program (ftp). The contents of these directories are then publicized so people on the Internet can find files of interest. One vehicle for publishing information about what is available at ftp sites is Yanoff's List. Yanoff names at least forty sites providing information on various topics available via ftp.

Copying files quickly and accurately from computer to computer over the Internet is a technological achievement that we often take for granted. If you think about it, the odds against successful file transfers are impressive. To begin with, a file can contain just about anything: plain text, source code for some program, data in goodness knows what format, or binary stuff to be executed by some chip somewhere. Clearly not all files are the same. Add to that the complexity of copying files between computers that have different operating systems, different processors, and even different ways of sequencing bytes, and the task of transferring files accurately seems even more daunting. Nevertheless, ftp provides just such a service, transferring any sort of file between any pair of computers on the Internet. In the following pages we'll discuss:

- Getting ready to use ftp
- How anonymous ftp works

- Basic `ftp` commands

- Using `archie` to find files available for `ftp`.

If you access the Internet via a conventional dialup connection, you'll use a version of `ftp` that has a simple command-line interface. If you're using PPP or SLIP to connect to the Internet from a computer with a graphical user interface, you may have an implementation of `ftp` with a "point-and-click" style interface. If you have a protocol dialup connection to the Internet, you can still use the command-line version of ftp from your Internet access provider's computer, and there may be times when that is just what you want to do. In this chapter, we'll use the command-line version of `ftp` to get familiar with the basics of Internet file transfers. The command-line version lets you see clearly how `ftp` works and what its features are. After we've explained what `ftp` can do, we'll show some examples of the point-and-click style of `ftp`.

Getting Ready to Use ftp

Using `ftp` requires a little preparation. Before you can copy files around on the Internet, you need to be aware of a few basic facts about files you intend to copy. For any file, you'll have to know the file's location, what kind of file it is, and if you're extra-cautious, how big it is.

Where the Files Are

The hardest part of using `ftp` may be finding out where the files you want to copy are located. The location of a file on the Internet (Yanoff's list, for example, or the CIA World Factbook mentioned in Chapter 2) consists of two things:

- the name (or the IP address) of the computer the file is on

- the full pathname of the file (the file name and the path to the directory that contains the file).

Fortunately, you're not on your own to find these things. The Internet offers a number of tools to help you find the files you're interested in. The list of Internet Services mentioned above is a good starting point for locating files to transfer. The USENET newsgroups (discussed more fully in Chapter 8) are another helpful source of information concerning publicly available files. And finally, there's archie, an Internet application that maintains an index of files available via ftp. Archie lets you do keyword searches of this index to find files to copy with ftp. Later in this chapter, we'll work with archie in greater detail.

Fun File Facts

When you're looking for files to download with ftp, you may need to be aware of both the type and the size of files you intend to transfer. Everyone knows about file size. If you have only 1 MB of disk storage space available, you won't be able to download a file as large as the complete CIA World Factbook. Later on, we'll demonstrate how to use ftp's dir command to check file sizes.

File types are not so widely understood. You need to be aware of file type for two different reasons. First, ftp recognizes two very general kinds of files: ascii and binary. When you're copying files with ftp, you'll need to tell ftp which kind of file you're copying, and of course, ftp does different things for each file type.

In addition to ftp's file type requirements, you have some requirements about file type as well, and your needs are likely to be a lot more restrictive than ftp's. File type is determined by two things: the kind of computer that produced the file, and the kind of program the file is intended for. Being aware of file types will ensure that the files you download will be useful. You can, for example, copy Macintosh program files to an IBM PC, but that won't make them usable. Similarly, if you run across a file that was compressed with PKZIP, downloading the file won't do you much good if you don't have some way to decompress the file.

Unfortunately, there is no simple program to tell you what kind of file you're working with. Distinguishing one kind of file from another is mostly a matter of knowing how to interpret file names and trusting that whoever named the files followed a few simple rules.

A File Name Primer

In the ftp archives on the Internet, you will encounter files for all sorts of computers. Some of these files will be plain text which can be displayed on almost any kind of computer with little or no modification. Others will be intended for a particular computer architecture or for a particular program. These are binary files. The line between text and binary is not always very clear. For example, you'll run into text files that have been compressed to conserve space at the site that has published the file. Compressed files are almost always binary, no matter what the original file's contents were. Similarly, some binary files (such as files in the GIF image format) may be encoded into a "text" format. If you know the most common file naming conventions, you will be able to find the files you want more quickly.

Table 3.1 lists the naming conventions you are most likely to run into on the Internet. Extensions are divided into ASCII (or text) and binary, the two file types that matter most to ftp.

Classifying files according to these conventions can sometimes be a problem. For example, the BinHex format used on Macintosh changed from ASCII to binary between release 4 and release 5.

Table 3.1: Common ASCII and Binary File Name Extensions

CATEGORY	EXTENSION	MEANING
ASCII	.c	C programming language source code
	.h	C programming language header file
	.txt	Text (ASCII) file
	.uu	ASCII file produced by uuencode
	.bat	DOS Batch file
	.shar	UNIX Shell archive
	.ps	PostScript file
	.hqx	Macintosh BinHexed file release 4.0 or earlier.
Binary	.EXE	Executable binary file (DOS or VAX/VMS)
	.COM	Executable binary file (DOS)
	.Z	Binary file created by compress
	.sit	StuffIt file for Macintosh
	.gz	File compressed with GNU gzip
	.hqx	Macintosh BinHexed file release 5.0 or greater

Similarly, the .COM extension designates a binary file under MS-DOS and an ASCII file under other operating systems.

In the personal computer world there has been a proliferation of programs to archive and compress groups of files, and this complicates the task of figuring out which ftp files you can use. Downloading a compressed file requires that you have the correct software to decompress it on the target computer. Fortunately, you can get a comprehensive list of file compression utilities and their naming conventions via anonymous ftp (which will be explained below). This list is in the file /doc/pcnet/compression at a machine named ftp.cso.uiuc.edu. This file is updated when new tools for file compression become available. By getting this information from the Internet itself, you can be sure that you're getting the most up-to-date information available.

Using ftp

Ftp makes an Internet connection between two computers for the purpose of exchanging files. When you use ftp, the Internet host from which you issue the ftp command is the "local" computer. Your ftp command starts a client program that connects to an ftp server on the "remote" computer. You should tell ftp which remote computer to connect to by including its name or IP address on the ftp command line:

```
ftp name.domain.qualified.fully
```

When you use ftp to connect to another computer, the remote computer will ask you to identify yourself with a login name and a password before it gives you access to any of its files. You can use ftp to make a connection to any computer on the Internet on which you have an account or any computer that allows anonymous ftp connections. The login name and password you provide must be valid on the remote computer. The login information that you use on your local computer will not automatically be usable on the remote system.

With more than 2 million computers on the Internet, you can be sure that most Internet users do not have accounts on all the machines from which they want to copy files. Therefore, the Internet sites that publish files to be copied via ftp usually offer a special login name, anonymous, that anyone on the Internet can use to log in via ftp. When you log in as anonymous, the remote system may prompt you with instructions for what to enter in place of a password. Frequently, you will be asked to supply something (for example, your electronic mail address) that identifies who you are and how you can be reached. The sample session for downloading Yanoff's list of Internet resources in Figure 3.1 illustrates this prompting.

Connecting to another computer via ftp is very much like logging in to the remote computer. Not only do you use a login name and

GETTING YANOFF'S LIST - - - - - - - - - - -

Scott Yanoff's instructions for getting the Internet Services List via ftp are terse, but they tell you everything you need to know:

```
ftp ftp.csd.uwm.edu (available in pub/inet.services.txt).
```

By now you probably recognize ftp.csd.uwm.edu as a fully qualified domain name. The file you want to transfer is named inet.services.txt, and it is located in a directory named pub. The .txt suffix indicates that the file is a text or ASCII file. The only additional piece of information you might want is the login name and password to use when ftp prompts you for these things. As a general rule, use anonymous to log in to machines on which you have no personal account. Ftp will tell you if a password is required, and often you will be asked to enter your electronic mail address (for example, bennett@wsqpd.com) as the password. By default ftp provides status messages about every command you execute. You'll see a three-digit number preceding each message. You can suppress these messages with the verbose command. An ftp session to download the list to your computer should look something like the session shown in Figure 3.1.

```
┌──────────────────────────────────────────────────────────────────────┐
│ ⬙              Win100 Terminal Emulator on COM1              ▼ ▲ │
├──────────────────────────────────────────────────────────────────────┤
│ File  Edit  Setup  Kermit  Help                                       │
│ netcom% ftp ftp.csd.uwm.edu                                           │
│ Connected to alpha2.csd.uwm.edu.                                      │
│  220 alpha2.csd.uwm.edu FTP server (Version wu-2.1c(2)) ready.        │
│ Name (ftp.csd.uwm.edu:bkf): anonymous                                 │
│ 331 Guest login ok, send your complete e-mail address as password.    │
│ Password:                                                             │
│ 230-University of Wisconsin-Milwaukee FTP server                      │
│ 230-Local time is Thu Jun  9 22:57:22 1994                            │
│ 230-                                                                  │
│ 230-If you have any unusual problems, please report them              │
│ 230-via e-mail to help@uwm.edu.                                       │
│ 230-                                                                  │
│ 230-If you do have problems, please try using a dash (-) as the       │
│ 230-first character of your password -- this will turn off the        │
│ 230-continuation messages that may be confusing your ftp client.      │
│ 230-                                                                  │
│ 230-Please read the file Policy                                       │
│ 230-  it was last modified on Mon Jan 24 12:49:58 1994 - 136 days ago │
│ 230 Guest login ok, access restrictions apply.                        │
└──────────────────────────────────────────────────────────────────────┘
```

```
┌──────────────────────────────────────────────────────────────────────┐
│ ⬙              Win100 Terminal Emulator on COM1              ▼ ▲ │
├──────────────────────────────────────────────────────────────────────┤
│ File  Edit  Setup  Kermit  Help                                       │
│ 230-  it was last modified on Mon Dec  6 08:06:40 1993 - 185 days ago │
│ 230 Guest login ok, access restrictions apply.                        │
│ ftp> cd pub                                                           │
│ 250-This directory contains public files for anonymous users.  Files may │
│ 250-be read, but not written (use "/incoming" for writing new files). │
│ 250-                                                                  │
│ 250 CWD command successful.                                           │
│ ftp> dir i*                                                           │
│ 200 PORT command successful.                                          │
│ 150 Opening ASCII mode data connection for /bin/ls.                   │
│ -rwxr-xr-x 1 4494      -2           48244 Jun  1 14:58 inet.services.txt │
│ ftp> get inet.services.txt                                            │
│ 200 PORT command successful.                                          │
│ 150 Opening ASCII mode data connection for inet.services.txt (48244 bytes). │
│ 226 Transfer complete.                                                │
│ local: inet.services.txt remote: inet.services.txt                    │
│ 49151 bytes received in 0.86 seconds (56 Kbytes/s)                    │
│ ftp> quit                                                             │
│ 221 Goodbye.                                                          │
│ netcom%                                                               │
└──────────────────────────────────────────────────────────────────────┘
```

Figure 3.1 Using ftp to copy Yanoff's List.

password to make the connection, once the login completes, your ftp session will be assigned a working directory from which you can copy files or navigate to other directories. If you use a regular login account to make the connection, your ftp session will start from that account's home directory, and you can work directly with the files there or move to another directory. When you connect to another system anonymously, ftp also gives you a working directory at the top of a special tree of directories and files that has been set up both to ensure the security of the remote system and to make it easy for you to move from directory to directory and find the files you want to copy.

If you're using a command-line version of ftp, you'll receive an ftp> prompt after the login sequence has completed. From this prompt you can issue simple commands (get and put, discussed below) to move files between the two computers. The sidebar showing how to copy Yanoff's list illustrates this process.

GETTING HELP WITH FTP ‒ ‒ ‒ ‒ ‒ ‒ ‒ ‒ ‒ ‒ ‒ ‒

You should be aware that ftp has a built-in help facility that can be invoked by typing help or ? in response to the ftp> prompt. The default help is a list of all the available commands:

```
ftp> help
Commands may be abbreviated. Commands are:
!           cr          ls          prompt      runique
$           delete      macdef      proxy       send
account     debug       mdelete     sendport    status
append      dir         mdir        put         struct
ascii       disconnect  mget        pwd         sunique
bell        form        mkdir       quit        tenex
binary      get         mls         quote       trace
bye         glob        mode        recv        type
case        hash        mput        remotehelp  user
cd          help        nmap        rename      verbose
cdup        image       ntrans      reset       ?
close       lcd         open        rmdir
```

All of these commands are discussed in the on-line documentation for ftp. On UNIX systems, you can display this information at any time by typing man ftp.

CHAPTER **3**

Taming ftp

Ftp is not the world's friendliest program, but it's far from hostile. You can use ftp perfectly well knowing only five commands: ascii, binary, get, put, and quit. However, using get and put is much simpler if you have learned a few additional commands to set up some features of your ftp session and to move to the directory that contains the files you want to transfer. The most important commands to control an ftp session are:

ascii	Treat transferred files as text (default).
binary	Treat transferred files as binary (image).
cr	Toggle stripping of carriage returns from ASCII files.
hash	Print hash marks to controlling terminal during transfers.
prompt	Toggle prompting on or off during multiple file transfers.
status	Display current status of all options you can set.
user	Set login name and password.
verbose	Toggle verbose messages on/off.

ASCII AND BINARY   The single most important decision you will need to make in working with ftp concerns the type of file transfer you want ftp to make: ascii or binary. This choice will determine whether the files you retrieve with ftp are usable or not, and unfortunately, there is no universally correct choice. (Table 3.1, earlier in this chapter, lists common ASCII and binary filename extensions.) The default transfer type is ascii, but it is always a good idea to check

SUMMARY: ASCII OR BINARY? - - - - - - - - - - -

Choosing ASCII or binary depends on both the file's contents and on how you intend to use it. There are two rules of thumb that will be helpful in making this choice:

- If the file you're going to download will ultimately be used on another computer with a different architecture or operating system, use binary representation for the download. (This happens to conventional dialup users all the time: you use ftp to copy a file to your access provider's computer, which is not at all like your home machine where you'll probably use the file. Files that you download to an access provider's computer for use elsewhere should be downloaded as binary files.)

- If you expect to read the file with the local machine's generic program for displaying files (such as the DOS command TYPE or the UNIX command cat), use the ASCII type of transfer. If you don't expect to view the file on the local machine, you should probably choose binary representation for your file transfer.

this setting (with the status command) before transferring files.

With the file type set to ascii, ftp will make adjustments to the file being transferred to compensate for differences between the local and remote machines that affect the readability of text files. Thus, for ascii transfers, ftp will adjust the end-of-line sequence to whatever is appropriate for the receiving machine. When the file type is set to binary, ftp produces an exact byte-for-byte image of any file it must copy.

CR   The cr command controls the way ftp handles the carriage return characters that occur as part of the end-of-line sequence in ASCII files on some computers. On UNIX systems, the end-of-line is marked by a linefeed character (Control-J). On many other systems (DOS, for example) the end-of-line sequence is carriage-return/linefeed (Control-M/Control-J). Like many other `ftp` commands, `cr` toggles between two states. When `cr` is on (the default setting), `ftp` will strip carriage returns from text files. To preserve carriage returns, toggle `cr` off.

HASH   The command-line version of `ftp` is usually silent during file transfers. Most `ftp` transfers are completed in a matter of seconds, but if very large files are being moved or if the network is sluggish, a transfer can take several minutes. The `hash` command provides a way to monitor `ftp`'s progress during a file transfer. When `hash` is toggled on, a "hash mark" (#) is printed to your screen for each block of data transferred.

The `hash` command has another important use. Some systems on the Internet automatically disconnect users who are inactive for some period of time. During a long file transfer, when you aren't typing on the keyboard, your login session on the local machine may appear to be idle. Setting `hash` on sends a steady stream of characters to your screen during the file transfer, and this will signal the system that your login session is still active.

PROMPT   The `prompt` command controls how `ftp` behaves when you're transferring a group of files. By default prompting is on, and you will be asked to confirm each file transfer. If you want to transfer multiple files without interruption, use the `prompt` command to toggle prompting off.

STATUS   The `status` command displays the current setting of all `ftp`'s optional features. Use this command if you're unsure about which options are currently enabled. A typical `ftp` status report is show in Figure 3.2.

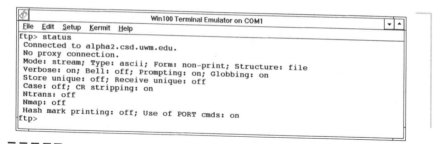

```
                          Win100 Terminal Emulator on COM1                    ▼ ▲
 File   Edit  Setup  Kermit  Help
ftp> status
 Connected to alpha2.csd.uwm.edu.
 No proxy connection.
 Mode: stream; Type: ascii; Form: non-print; Structure: file
 Verbose: on; Bell: off; Prompting: on; Globbing: on
 Store unique: off; Receive unique: off
 Case: off; CR stripping: on
 Ntrans: off
 Nmap: off
 Hash mark printing: off; Use of PORT cmds: on
ftp>
```

Figure 3.2   Output from the ftp status command.

USER   The user command allows you to specify the user name and password that ftp will use in making a connection to a remote computer. It lets you recover from failed logins when you first start ftp.

FAQS, FTP, AND YOU ----------------

Many systems on the Internet collect Frequently Asked Questions (and their answers). FAQs have become an Internet institution, and often this supplemental documentation is more helpful than the official manual because it addresses questions that have come up in the course of actually using the Internet.

There is no standard way to access FAQs. Some systems have a special utility that can be used to query specific topics or keywords. Other systems keep their FAQs in files that anyone can browse.

Even If your local Internet system doesn't maintain FAQs, you may still be able to get FAQs from other sources. For example, much of the Internet lore regarding ftp originates in the USENET newsgroups where ftp is a frequent topic of discussion, and FAQs about ftp can be found as a regular part of the archives for these newsgroups. USENET is the subject of Chapter 8. Later in this chapter, we'll use archie to locate these FAQs.

VERBOSE By default, ftp is very verbose: all the responses from the ftp server along with their message numbers are printed on your screen during an ftp session. (These messages are also illustrated in the Yanoff sample session.) The verbose command lets you suppress these messages when you want.

Working with Directories

Whenever you connect to a remote computer with ftp, the ftp server on that computer will assign a current or working directory to your session. If you have logged in as a regular user, the working directory will be the login directory for that user. If you have logged in anonymously, the working directory will be the top directory of a directory hierarchy reserved exclusively for anonymous ftp. In either case, ftp provides some commands for moving around among the directories on the remote machine. These commands are similar to the directory navigation commands for both UNIX and DOS. Examples of these commands in use appear in Listing 3.1.

pwd	Print working (current) directory for remote system.
cd	Change directory on remote system (requires directory name).
cdup	Change directory on remote system to the parent of the current directory.
dir	List the contents of a directory on the remote system including name, permissions, owner, and size.
mdir	List the contents of the multiple directories on the remote system including name, permissions, owner, and size.

<dl>
<dt>ls</dt>
<dd>List the contents of a directory on the remote system by name only.</dd>

<dt>mls</dt>
<dd>List the contents of multiple directories on the remote system by name only.</dd>

<dt>lcd</dt>
<dd>Change the working directory on the local system (requires directory name).</dd>
</dl>

Listing 3.1:
Examples of FTP Directory Navigation

```
ftp> pwd    Print the name of the current directory.
257 "/" is current directory.
ftp> dir    List contents of current directory.
200 PORT command successful.
150 Opening data connection for /bin/ls  (0 bytes).
----------  1 root    system         0 Oct 29 1993   .notar
----------  1 root    system         0 Oct 29 1993   .rhosts
-r--r--r--  1 root    users       2148 Jan 24 12:49 Policy
d--x--x--x  2 root    system       512 Mar 25 08:29 bin
d--x--x--x  4 root    system       512 Mar 25 08:29 etc
d-wxrwxrwx  2 ftp     system       512 Jun 09 16:39 incoming
dr-xrwxrwt 14 ftp     system       512 May 26 17:28 pub
d--x--x--x  2 root    system       512 Mar 25 08:29 sbin
d--x--x--x  5 root    system       512 Mar 25 08:29 usr
226 Transfer complete.
556 bytes received in 0.3 seconds (1.8 Kbytes/s)
ftp> dir pub/i*    List names of files in pub dir beginning with
"i".
200 PORT command successful.
150 Opening data connection for /bin/ls  (0 bytes).
-rwxr-xr-x  1 4494    system     59741 Jun 01 14:58
pub/inet.services.html
-rwxr-xr-x  1 4494    system     48244 Jun 01 14:58
pub/inet.services.txt
lrwxr-x---  1 wls     system        17 May 06 15:05
pub/inetserv.txt-> inet.services.txt
226 Transfer complete.
remote: pub/i*
248 bytes received in 0.0047 seconds (52 Kbytes/s)
```

```
ftp> cd    What happens if you give a cd command with no target
directory?
(remote-directory) pub   ftp prompts for target!
250 CWD command successful.
ftp> ls i*   list files beginning with "i" again.
200 PORT command successful.
150 Opening data connection for /bin/ls  (0 bytes).
inet.services.html
inet.services.txt
inetserv.txt
226 Transfer complete.
remote: i*
53 bytes received in 0.005 seconds (10 Kbytes/s)

ftp> cdup   change to parent directory
250 CWD command successful.

ftp> ls   list contents of new working directory
200 PORT command successful.
150 Opening data connection for /bin/ls  (0 bytes).
Policy
bin
etc
incoming
pub
sbin
usr
.notar
.rhosts
226 Transfer complete.
61 bytes received in 0.0069 seconds (8.6 Kbytes/s)
ftp> quit
221 Goodbye.
```

Pwd and cdup are relatively simple to use. Neither command requires you to provide any further information. You simply type pwd, and ftp reports the current directory on the remote system. Similarly, when you type cdup, ftp moves you to the parent of the current directory and makes that the new working directory.

The cd command must include the name of a directory on the remote machine. If this name is left out, ftp will prompt you for a directory name.

The dir and ls commands both list the contents of a directory, but differ in the amount of information they show. Dir produces the long form of the listing, and ls lists names only. If you just type dir or ls, you'll get a listing of the current directory on the remote machine.

TIP –

Directory listings can be long. If you get a listing that is longer than you expected, use Control-C (^C) to abort the listing. The dir and ls commands also recognize asterisk (*) as a wildcard character if you want to restrict the listing to a range of files.

If you want a listing of some directory other than the current one, you can include its name on the command line. To restrict the listing only to certain files, you can include a suitably wildcarded filename to indicate those files.

TIP –

The ftp commands mls, mdir, and get (described below) expect the name of a local file to hold the command's output. Occasionally you will want to review the output of your commands on the screen rather than store it in a file. There are two ways to redirect output of ftp commands directly to the screen: (1) When prompted for a local file name, enter a hyphen (–). This will send the ftp output to the screen in an uninterrupted stream. (2) To control the flow of output from ftp with one of the UNIX commands for viewing a file one page at a time (pg or more, for example), enter ¦ more or ¦ pg (depending on which pager is available) when prompted for a local file name. This will redirect the ftp output to the command you specify.

Ftp uses a special pair of commands (mdir and mls) to list the contents of multiple directories. Both mdir and mls expect two command-line arguments: the remote directory to be listed, and the name of a local file in which to store the command's output. (Ftp expects this output to be so long that you won't want to browse through it on the screen.)

Copying Files

Once you have set up your ftp session and maneuvered to the appropriate directory, you will need relatively few commands to do the work of moving files back and forth across the Internet:

get	Move a file from remote to local.
recv	Synonym for get.
put	Move a file from local to remote.
send	Synonym for put.
mget	Move several files from remote to local.
mput	Move several files from local to remote.

Because we're interested chiefly in anonymous ftp, we'll concentrate on the commands for downloading files (get, mget, and recv). Get copies files from the remote computer to the local one. Send does exactly the same thing in the opposite direction; it copies files from local to remote. Sending files to other sites via anonymous ftp requires a directory on the remote computer in which the anonymous user has permission to store files. Many anonymous ftp sites do not allow files to be uploaded anonymously. If you want to send a file to a site via anonymous ftp, you should first check with the administrator of the receiving site to find out what the local conventions are for uploading files.

The get Command

The get command must always include the name of the file to be
copied (the source file) and may include a name for the destination
file. The simplest form of the get command looks like this:

```
ftp> get inet.services.txt
200 PORT command successful.
150 Opening data connection for inet.services.txt (29474 bytes).
226 Transfer complete.
local: inet.services.txt remote: inet.services.txt 30043 bytes
received in 0.85 seconds (35 Kbytes/s)
```

This command copied the file named inet.services.txt from the
remote computer to the local computer. After a get command, ftp
reports the number of bytes transferred and the elapsed time for the
transfer.

This simple version of the get command depends on a series of as-
sumptions. It assumes that the file to be copied is in the current directory on the remote machine, that the local machine's copy should
also be named inet.services.txt, and that the local copy should be
created in the current directory for the ftp session on the local machine. You must have permission to create files in the current directory of the local computer for this command to succeed. If you don't
have such permission, you'll get a "permission denied" message like
the following:

```
ftp> get inet.services.txt
inet.services.txt: Permission denied
```

If you want to specify either the source or destination files by
pathname, you can do so, but it takes a little extra care. The general
syntax is this:

```
get source destination
```

where *source* and *destination* each specify a pathname. For example, the following command gets a remote file named `faq` from a directory named `pub/ftp-list` and creates a local copy of it called `ftp.faq` in the `/tmp` directory of the local machine:

```
get pub/ftp-lis/faq /tmp/ftp.faq
```

The destination filename must be a complete path that includes the file name. If you provide a destination name that consists only of a directory path (/tmp, for example), `ftp` will tell you that /tmp is a directory and not legal as a name for the destination file.

TIP –

On UNIX systems (like those used by many Internet access providers), /tmp is a directory in which any user can create files. If you have problems with directory permissions and `ftp`, you can place destination files in /tmp. Remember to include both the path and the file name (/tmp/*filename*) when specifying the destination file. As its name implies, /tmp is used for temporary storage. Many UNIX applications put their temporary files in this directory. It is not a good practice to put large files in /tmp, and because /tmp is periodically purged, you shouldn't use it for permanent storage. However, it is a handy directory into which you can copy small files to be moved to other directories later. If you copy files into /tmp, don't forget to delete them or move them to your own directory as soon as possible.

When your `get` command does not include a destination name, `ftp` assumes that you want your copy of the file to have exactly the same name as the source file, including any directories you listed as part of the source file name. However, `get` doesn't create directories as part of copying files. If you omitted the destination file name and included directories in the source file name (pub/ftp-list/faq, for example), those directories must already exist at the destination site for the get command to succeed. The following example shows what happens when a get command fails because the pathname it needs at the destination site doesn't exist.

```
ftp> get pub/ftp-list/faq
pub/ftp-list/faq: no such file or directory
```

Using mget to Work with Groups of Files

The get command works with individual files only. To transfer multiple files with a single command, use mget. The mget command allows you to specify several source files on a single command line. If, for example, you wanted to copy all the files in the current directory whose names end in .c or .h, you could do so with the command

```
mget  *.c *.h
```

 MLS–TESTING WILDCARD FILE SPECIFICATIONS – – – – –

When you use wildcard characters like * and ? with mget, it is always a good idea to check that the wildcards will match the filenames you're interested in. Use the mls command to do this:

```
ftp> mls *.c
```

Mls simply lists the filenames that match, so you can adjust any wildcard specifications that don't find the files you want without first transferring either too many or too few files. Mls will expand only one wildcard at a time, and so a command like the following will fail:

```
mls *.c *.h
```

This command will copy the all the files ending in .c or .h from the current directory on the remote machine. (The asterisk is a wild-card character that matches any string of characters in the file name. Thus, *.c matches all the filenames with a .c extension.)

Note that mget accepts only the names of files to be copied: you can't specify a target file name with mget. (Among other things, this means that the trick of using a hyphen to send a file to the screen can't be used with mget.) As with the get command, any directories in the source file name must already exist at the destination site for the transfer to succeed.

Beyond Yanoff: Using archie

The Internet Services List that we retrieved earlier will provide a starting point for browsing Internet resources of many kinds. It also offers signposts to a few Internet sites that have extensive archives of files you can retrieve through anonymous ftp. It's relatively easy to connect to one of these sites and meander among the directories looking for files of interest. But this sort of browsing is time-consuming, and if you depend on chance encounters to find interesting files, you probably won't use ftp very much.

Fortunately there's a database that contains the names of files and directories that are available via anonymous ftp. There are also tools that let you query this database with keywords. The database and the tools that access it are collectively called archie.

Archie is a project of the McGill University School of Computer Science. The heart of archie is a database containing directory list-ings of what is available through anonymous ftp at several hundred Internet sites. The database is compiled by a program that over the course of a month or so makes an ftp connection to each site and produces a listing of what the site has to offer. This database is then published to various `archie` servers and made available for anyone to query. The following servers host the `archie` database:

`archie.ans.net`	(USA [NY])
`archie.rutgers.edu`	(USA [NJ])
`archie.sura.net`	(USA [MD])
`archie.unl.edu`	(USA [NE])
`archie.mcgill.ca`	(Canada)
`archie.funet.fi`	(Finland/Mainland Europe)
`archie.au`	(Australia)
`archie.doc.ic.ac.uk`	(Great Britain/Ireland)
`archie.wide.ad.jp`	(Japan)
`archie.ncu.edu.tw`	(Taiwan)

The `archie` service has become so popular that there are several ways to query these servers. The preferred ways of submitting `archie` queries are through an `archie` client program or, if your site doesn't have an `archie` client, via electronic mail. `Archie` client programs are not usually included among the utilities that come with the network software used for protocol dialup connections. Most Internet access providers have installed `archie` clients, however, so you're most likely to find (and use) `archie` on your access provider's computer. To tell whether your access provider's machine has this client, just type `archie` at the command line prompt. If you do have it, the archie client will print a help message and exit. If not, you'll get a message that the `archie` command can't be found. In Chapter 2, we used the archie client to locate the CIA World Factbook with the command:

```
% archie factbook
```

This command found a directory named factbook that contained several versions of the file we were looking for. When archie is given a keyword like factbook, it queries the database for the names of files or directories that contain that keyword. Many of the ftp archives on the Internet are duplicated at numerous sites, and it's important to choose keywords carefully to get results that are manageable. Archie has several options that make its keyword querying more flexible:

-c   Case-sensitive search for names containing the keyword.

-s   Case-insensitive search for names containing the keyword.

-o*file*   Put the results of the search in the named file.

-m#   Limit the search to no more than # results (the default is 95).

-h*server*   Query the archie database at the named server.

Earlier it was mentioned that FAQs often originate from USENET newsgroups. An archie query to find FAQs about ftp, for example, could take this form:

```
% archie ftp-list
Host procyon.cis.ksu.edu
              Location: /pub/mirrors/news.answers
        DIRECTORY drwxr-xr-x        512 May 3 11:04 ftp-list
<Listing truncated.>
```

Responses to archie queries are sorted first by host name, then by directory location or path. For each location that contains an entry satisfying the query, archie provides a listing that shows the permissions, size, date and name of each file or directory that matches your keyword. In this case archie found many more hits than we have room to illustrate here.

Notice that we queried for the keyword `ftp-list`. We chose this keyword because many of the USENET newsgroups maintain their archives in the form of a mailing list to which users can subscribe. (Mailing lists are discussed in Chapter 5.) A query for `ftp-list` is much more specific than a query for simply `ftp` or `faq`.

Even if the `archie` client program is not installed on the system that provides your Internet access, you can still submit `archie` queries via electronic mail. For information on the mail interface to `archie`, pick the `archie` server nearest you from the list presented earlier and send a message to `archie` at that site. For example, there's an `archie` server at the University of Nebraska at Lincoln. To reach it by mail, use this command:

```
% mail archie@archie.unl.edu
Subject: ...
help
```

The user name `archie` in this mail address is an automated mailbox, not a human user. Archie is also the host name in this case, and that host is in the `unl` and `edu` domains. The body of your message should contain the word *help*. You'll get back a short user guide for the e-mail interface to archie.

Point-and-Click ftp

If you're using a protocol dialup connection (PPP or SLIP) to access the Internet, you may have a version of `ftp` that uses the Graphical User Interface of your computer. (GUI versions of `ftp` are often packaged with network software like PPP and SLIP.) Using a GUI version of `ftp` over a protocol dialup connection will enable you to browse conveniently through directories at `ftp` sites and copy files from the Internet directly to your computer.

The appearance of these point-and-click ftp clients (or browsers) will vary from vendor to vendor, but they all offer essentially the same features as the command-line version of ftp. Figure 3.3 shows the ftp client program for Windows (WFTP) that accompanies FTP Software's PC/TCP software.

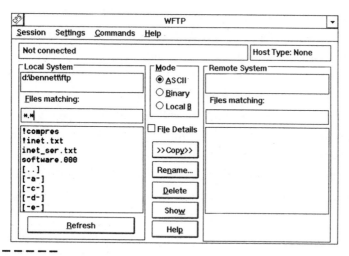

Figure 3.3 The Wftp Browser.

Getting Connected with WFTP

Just under the menu bar at the top of the browser's screen are a couple of fields that tell you the current status of the ftp connection. Beneath the status bar, you'll see information about the local machine (the current directory and its contents) on the left side of the screen. The right side of the screen displays the same information for the remote system. (In Figure 3.3, we haven't connected to anything yet.) Between these two displays are buttons for four basic commands you may want to execute. Above the commands are buttons that allow you to select what kind of file transfer to do. ASCII and binary have already been discussed. The browser shown

95

also has a mode named "local 8" that is not offered by all ftp implementations. (Local 8 mode is useful for the very rare occasions when you must download files from a computer that stores data in something other than multiples of 8 bits. You probably won't encounter this on the Internet without some warning from the remote site.) The Commands menu item at the top of the screen leads to a pull-down menu of additional directory navigation commands for both systems.

The first step in using a GUI ftp browser is to connect to a remote system. As with the command-line version of ftp, you'll need to know the full domain name of the system you want to copy files from. To start an ftp session from WFTP, click on the Session item in the menu bar. A pull-down menu will appear. When you select New from this menu, a dialog box will prompt you for the remote system's name and the login name and password you wish to use. After you've entered this information, you can instruct WFTP to connect to the other system immediately. Figure 3.4 shows the dialog box for a connection to ftp.csd.uwm.edu.

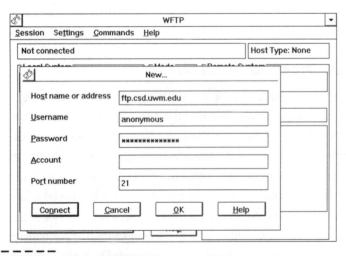

Figure 3.4 Entering connection information for the WFTP browser.

Browsing and Copying

Once connected to a remote system, you can use the directory navigation commands to move to the directory that contains the files you want to copy. Figure 3.5 shows the WFTP browser after a connection has been established. (Notice that the window's title bar now shows the name of the remote system.) Figure 3.5 also shows that /pub has been made the current directory on the remote system. Notice that we've entered the pattern "inet*" to restrict the listing of this directory's contents to the files that we're interested in. You can change directories and filename matching patterns as often as you like.

To copy a file with WFTP, first select ASCII or Binary mode and then click on the file name (this will cause it to be highlighted). Click the Copy button located in the center of the screen. When you issue the copy command, WFTP checks the name of the file you're copying. WFTP runs on DOS computers, which restrict filenames to an eight-dot-three format: a file name of up to eight characters, a dot, and a

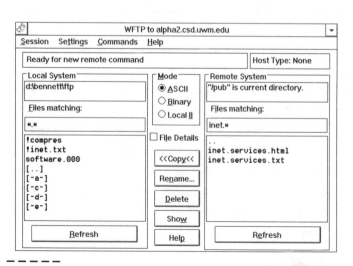

Figure 3.5 Getting ready to copy a file with WFTP.

three-character file name extension. Other systems support different conventions for naming files. In this example, we're copying inet.services.txt from a UNIX computer, and that name is illegal on the local computer. WFTP will prompt for a destination filename and suggest "inet_ser.txt". You can override this name if you like.

When you've finished a WFTP session with one computer, you should disconnect before exiting WFTP or trying to connect elsewhere. The Disconnect command is an entry on the Session pulldown menu.

Where We've Been

You now know the basics of using ftp. We've discussed how to use ftp to connect to another computer and transfer files from that computer to the Internet host you usually use. Along the way, we touched on how to move around in a directory hierarchy and how to interpret filenames. You should find many uses outside of ftp for these skills. We've looked at how the archie application can be used to locate files available by anonymous ftp, and we've pointed to some other sources of information about archie servers. Above all, we've used ftp to get the Internet to tell us something about itself. You can now get a copy of Scott Yanoff's Internet Services List whenever you want (the list is updated every two weeks). This list contains access information for ftp resources all over theare shown Internet. You can get to some of these resources with your new-found ftp skills. Other resources on the list will be accessible through other tools we'll discuss here: telnet, gopher, electronic mail, or finger. No matter what your interests are or what Internet tools you feel most comfortable using, you'll find something of value in the Internet Services List.

HUNTING THROUGH THE INTERNET – – – – – – – –

Question 1   We mentioned in Chapter 1 how to use gopher to get information about the Internet Hunt. We won't learn about gopher in detail until Chapter 6. How would you find the real Internet Hunt if you couldn't use gopher?

Answer   An archie query will help you locate information about the Hunt if you can come up with a keyword or file name that identifies the Internet Hunt uniquely. Both hunt and internet would match file names for many, many archives. Try putting both words together. These days it is fashionable to add a placeholder character to separate words in a filename. Common placeholders are the dash (–), dot (.), and underscore (_). Using *internet-hunt* found what we wanted right away:

```
% archie -s internet-hunt

Host nic.cic.net

    Location: /pub
    FILE lrwxrwxrwx   21 Feb  4 17:33  internet-hunt
```

The next step is to connect to nic.cic.net with ftp and look at what's there to be sure we're on the right track:

```
% ftp nic.cic.net
Connected to nic.cic.net.
220 nic.cic.net FTP server (Version 5.60+UA) ready.
Name (nic.cic.net:bennett): anonymous
331 Guest login ok, send ident as password.
Password:
230- Guest login ok, access restrictions apply.
230 Local time is Mon Aug  9 11:18:02 1993
ftp> cd pub
ftp> dir internet-hunt
lrwxrwxrwx  1 0       1            21 Jun 14 12:19 internet-
➥hunt -> ./nircomm/gopher/hunt
```

```
ftp> cd internet-hunt
ftp> dir
total 7
-rwxr-xr-x  1 0        0                207 Aug  9 15:12 .cache
-rwxr-xr-x  1 0        0                310 May 31 01:12
➥ .cache.html
drwxr-xr-x  2 1002    20                512 Feb 19 18:14 .cap
drwxr-xr-x  3 1002    20                512 Jul 13 17:56 about
drwxr-xr-x  3 1002    20                512 May  7 15:56 comments
drwxr-xr-x  3 1002    20                512 Jul 31 08:04 questions
drwxr-xr-x  5 1002    20                512 Jul 11 21:00 results
ftp> cd about
ftp> dir
total 22
-rwxr-xr-x  1 0        0                594 Aug  9 15:12 .cache
-rwxr-xr-x  1 0        0                785 May 24 20:12
➥ .cache.html
drwxr-xr-x  2 1002    20                512 Feb  8  1993 .cap
-rw-r--r--  1 1002    20               2472 Feb 21 16:05
➥00readme.txt
-rw-r--r--  1 1002    20       2458 May  8 19:22 distrib.txt
-rw-r--r--  1 1002    20       2762 Feb  8  1993 history.txt
-rw-r--r--  1 1002    20       1442 Jul 13 17:53 individ.txt
-rw-r--r--  1 1002    20       2649 May  5 20:52 intro.txt
-rw-r--r--  1 1002    20       1345 Feb  8  1993 rules.txt
-rw-r--r--  1 1002    20       1313 Feb  8  1993 scoring.txt
-rw-r--r--  1 1002    20        943 Jul 13 17:54 team.txt
ftp> get intro.txt
local: intro.txt remote: intro.txt
ftp> quit
%
```

Reading the intro.txt file will lead you to other files in this directory.
The file distrib.txt describes the usual channels for distributing the
Internet Hunt.

Navigating the Internet by Hand: Working with telnet

The phone rang on Bernice's desk.

- "Wittgenstein, Sellars, Quine, Putnam, and Davidson. How can I help you?" she said.

- "Bernice? Bernice?" The caller's faint and crackly voice had a distinctly anxious edge.

- "Mr. Simon, is that you? What are you doing on the phone? You're supposed to be in Paris meeting with Barthes, Sartre, Descartes, and Pascal. Is something wrong?"

- "Terribly wrong. I'm lost in the Paris Metro. Can you call BSD&P and tell them I'll be late?"
- "Oh dear, yes. Would you like some help with directions?"
- "Have you ever been to Paris, Bernice?" Mr. Simon's anxiety gave way to sarcasm.
- "Well, no, but I have my sources. Where are you and where do you need to go?"
- "I'm at the Montparnasse train station, Gare Montparnasse." Mr. Simon sounded as though he were talking through clenched teeth. "I need to get to Montmartre in less than 45 minutes. Please hurry."
- Bernice tapped away at a computer terminal at her desk. "Well, Mr. Simon, the number 13 metro line runs through the Montparnasse station. Take a train on that line toward Gabriel Peri or St. Denis Basilique. Go four stops to the Invalides metro station and transfer to a train on the number 8 line headed for Creteil-Prefecture. The fifth stop will be Rue Montmartre. It will take you about 25 minutes. Did you get all that?"
- "Yes, I got it. Uh, Bernice, how did you, uh, um, oh, never mind, I don't want to know."
- The line suddenly went dead. Bernice shook her head. She had just used `telnet` to connect to the subway navigator, a database in France that has route information for two dozen subway systems around the world. She hoped Mr. Simon would calm down a bit before he arrived at his meeting.

A Delicate Balance: Resources and Applications

There are thousands of information resources on the Internet. Yanoff's Internet Services List is basically a quick reference card for the Internet, and it summarizes several hundred resources. An encyclopedia of Internet resources would be truly huge. There are millions of people using the Internet to reach these resources, and there are only a dozen or so client/server application tools to make the connection between people and resources. The Internet's information resources, applications, and users make up a delicate ecology unlike any other in the world. The Internet would be far more difficult to use if every information source had its own application. Publishing information on the Internet would be a nightmare if each publisher had to build and distribute a client/server application for its resources.

Hundreds of Internet resources (bulletin boards, library card catalogs, and databases of every sort) are implemented as conventional, stand-alone programs running on individual computers that happen to be attached to the Internet. These resources don't have network accessibility built into them. The tool that puts a network-wide audience in touch with such stand-alone resources is telnet.

Telnet is a network application that you can use to log in to one computer on the Internet from another. This is a lot like establishing a conventional dialup connection between two computers, but instead of using modems and voice phone lines, telnet connections use the Internet and exchange data between the two connected computers much faster than conventional dialup connections would allow. With telnet you can navigate through the Internet manually.

Unlike ftp (which makes a connection strictly for the purpose of transferring files), telnet connections are general-purpose. The use you can make of a telnet connection depends more on what the remote computer has to offer than on any of telnet's features. You can use telnet to reach applications of any kind (stand-alone as well as client/server) that are installed on other computers. Telnet usually requires a login name and password, but many applications that are available through telnet use special login names (similar to the "anonymous" login name often used with ftp). Some telnet-accessible applications use no login name at all. You can also use telnet from any computer on the network to connect to any other machine for which you have a login.

If you access the Internet through a conventional dialup connection, you'll use telnet on your Internet access provider's computer. The version of telnet that is available for conventional dialup users has a simple command-line interface. Most of the examples in this chapter will illustrate this interface.

If you connect to the Internet via a protocol dialup connection like PPP or SLIP, your network software should include a version of telnet that will run on your home computer. Some versions of telnet packaged with PPP and SLIP networking software will use the "point-and-click" style of user interface. Telnet is essentially a network-based terminal emulation program, and it doesn't gain as much from graphical user interfaces as some other Internet applications do. Let's take a look at what telnet does.

How telnet Works

The telnet command itself is quite simple: you need only a host name or an IP address to identify the computer to which you want to connect. Once the telnet connection is established, you should be prepared to enter a login name and password that are valid for the computer you've reached. Don't expect that the login name and password from your home computer will be valid elsewhere. A minimal telnet session is shown in Figure 4.1. In this illustration, a user connected to Netcom (`netcom.com`) via PPP is using `telnet` on Netcom to connect to the WELL (`well.sf.ca.us`). Notice the login instructions that are displayed when the connection is established. Internet sites that want to be accessible via `telnet` often explain the login procedure when a connection is first established.

The computer from which you execute the `telnet` command (a client program) is the local computer. The computer to which a connection is made is the remote computer. In Figure 4.1, the remote computer is `well.sf.ca.us`, and we're using a login account named

Figure 4.1 A simple telnet session.

"rosebody" on that host. The name of the local computer and your local user name don't play any role in making a `telnet` connection. Once you've connected to the remote computer, you can use it interactively. Here, we simply wanted to show the similarity between normal logins and logins through `telnet`; more often, you'll use `telnet` as Bernice did: to get access to a program or a database like the metro information service in France. Examples of the different kinds of services you can reach with `telnet` are shown throughout this chapter.

INPUT MODE: SEEING THROUGH TELNET – – – – – – –

For `telnet` to make a connection, the remote computer must be running a `telnet` server that listens for connection requests from `telnet` clients. (When `telnet` was developed, server programs running continuously in the background were referred to as daemons. The `telnet` server is usually named `telnetd`, a shortened form of `telnet daemon`.) On most Internet hosts, the `telnet` daemon is started automatically as part of the system's boot procedure. Once a `telnet` client has connected to the server on a remote machine, it acts as a "virtual terminal" that enables you to work directly with programs running on the remote computer. Even though you can't see them, the `telnet` client and server are still there. They have become "transparent." Telnet creates the appearance that the terminal you're working on is connected directly to the remote computer.

The terminal connection may be simulated, but the interaction is certainly real. When you make a `telnet` connection to a UNIX computer, for example, your `telnet` session will show up among the currently logged-in users reported by the `who` command, as illustrated in Figure 4.1. (An `ftp` connection, for example, does not show up in the output of `who`.) However, `telnet` connections are not as direct as they appear. After making a connection, the `telnet` client program passes anything you type across the network to the `telnet` server. The server on the remote computer starts a program (usually the same program used to prompt native users on the remote computer for login information). Any input the server receives from you via the `telnet` client is passed on to this program. Any output from the program is handed to the `telnet` server, which pushes it across the network to the `telnet` client, which finally passes the output through to you.

Your input and the program's output are passed back and forth by client and server until you log out of the remote computer. Logging out signals the `telnet` server that the session is over, and it closes the connection with the client. The client sees the closed connection, cleans up, and exits—returning you to the program (usually a shell or command interpreter) from which you called `telnet`.

Anything that can be done over a terminal connected directly to the remote computer can also be done through a `telnet` connection. From within a `telnet` session, you can even `telnet` from the remote computer to a third computer elsewhere on the network.

telnet's Command Mode

Once you've made a connection via `telnet` (as discussed in the accompanying sidebar), you will be working with programs on the remote computer. The commands you issue will be executed by the remote computer, not by your `telnet` program. You may occasionally need to issue a command to telnet itself. (The telnet commands are discussed below.) If you're using a point-and-click version of telnet, there will be menu buttons at the top of your telnet window to give you access to telnet's commands. If you're using a telnet program with a command-line interface, you can put telnet in "command" mode by typing the telnet escape character. Control-] is the default, but (as you'll see in a moment) you can change this if need be. The command-line version of telnet displays a reminder about the escape character at the start of each telnet session (see Figure 4.1 for an example). The signal that you're in command mode is the telnet> prompt. If you have an open connection to a remote computer, you can exit telnet's command mode (and return to input mode) by just pressing the Enter or Return key in response to the telnet> prompt.

Telnet provides commands to manage the connection you have to the remote computer. Telnet only connects two computers at a time, but you can "nest" telnet sessions. For example, a user at Netcom can telnet to the WELL, log in there and then telnet from the WELL to a third computer. If you use "nested" telnet sessions, it is a good idea to assign a unique escape character to each of the sessions. The frequently-used telnet commands are summarized below, and an annotated telnet session illustrating the use of these commands appears in Listing 4.1. This listing illustrates commands available in the command line version of telnet.

? [*command*]   The ? command prints telnet's help messages. With no arguments, it prints a summary of all telnet commands. If you specify a command, telnet will display the help information for that command only.

open *hostname* The open command attempts to make a connection to the named host. *Hostname* can be either a fully-qualified domain name or an IP address. Note that a telnet client can support only one open connection at a time.

close The close command closes the current connection. If you provided a host name on telnet's command line, close will also exit from telnet. If you started telnet without a host name, close returns to telnet's command mode.

quit The quit command closes the current connection and exits telnet. This is the graceful way to leave a telnet session.

status The status command displays the current status of telnet, including the name of the remote computer you're connected to. After a status command, you are returned to input mode if your telnet session has an open connection.

set escape The set escape command can be used to
value change the character that triggers command mode.

Listing 4.1:
Using Telnet Commands
- - - - -

```
netcom3% telnet Note no host name. Telnet will start in command
mode.
telnet> status From command mode, issue status command.
No connection.
```

110

```
Escape character is '^]'.
telnet> set escape ~   Change the escape character to '~'
escape character is '~'.
telnet> open well.sf.ca.us  Open a connection to well.sf.ca.us
Trying...
Connected to well.sf.ca.us.
Escape character is '~'.


UNIX(r) System V Release 4.0 (well)


This is the WELL


Type   newuser   to sign up.
Type   trouble   if you are having trouble logging in.
Type   guest     to learn about the WELL.


If you already have a WELL account, type your username.


login: rosebody    Normal login sequence
Password:    Password not echoed
Last login: Sun Jun 12 07:39:49 from netcom3.netcom.c
Sun Microsystems Inc.   SunOS 5.3   Generic   September 1993


You own your own words. This means that you are responsible for
the words that you post on the WELL and that reproduction of
those words without your permission in any medium outside of the
WELL's conferencing system may be challenged by you, the author.


Checking new mail...


TERM = (ANSI)  This terminal type is okay, so press RETURN.
Erase is Backspace
Kill is Ctrl-X
well% who  "who" shows the telnet login
rosebody   pts/17     Jun 12 07:44     (netcom3.netcom.com)
well%            Escape character (~) is not echoed!
telnet> status
Connected to well.sf.ca.us.
Operating in character-at-a-time mode.
Escape character is '~'.   Telnet returns to input mode after
status.


well%    Press Return for prompt.
telnet> close   Escape to command mode and close the connection.
Connection closed.
telnet> status
```

```
No connection.
Escape character is '~'.
telnet> quit    Exit the telnet client
netcom3%
```

Doing Things with telnet

Telnet comes in handy any time you want to use a program (or any other kind of resource) that resides on another computer. Some typical circumstances in which you might want to use telnet are:

- When you have a login on a remote computer and want to do some work on that host.

- When you want to use one of the Internet's client/server applications but don't have a client program installed on your machine.

- When you need access to a stand-alone application that is installed on another computer.

Telnet is the only way to get in touch with the Internet's stand-alone applications, and we'll concentrate on those in the pages that follow. There are three distinct kinds of stand-alone programs on the Internet, and we'll look at an example of each kind of service:

- Bulletin Board Services: Internet BBSs are similar to the dialup BBSs you may already have encountered—they provide access to files about some topic and occasionally offer the opportunity to exchange messages with other BBS users. We'll look at the BBS run by the US Food and Drug Administration below as an example of this service.

- Databases: Internet databases are collections of information about some topic, like the metro database that Bernice used at the beginning of this chapter. When you connect to a database on the Internet you'll be able to query the database for specific information. We'll look at the subway navigator database and the telnet interface to archie. (Archie is technically not a stand-alone application, but you may have difficulty finding client programs to query the archie database. If you use SLIP or PPP to connect to the Internet, you probably will *not* have an archie client program for your home machine.)

- Programs that integrate Internet services and provide menu-driven access: These are stand-alone programs that give you a convenient way of reaching many of the Internet's resources. We'll look at one of the sites that runs the LIBS program and show how to use that program to contact other Internet applications.

In any list of Internet services, you will find stand-alone services and resources of all these types. To use telnet to reach these resources, you need to know the name (or IP address) of the computer that hosts the resource you're interested in and a valid login name and password for that computer. Most services that rely on telnet access provide a special login name that anyone can use to connect to the service. This is similar to the "anonymous" login with ftp, but each service available through telnet assigns login information independently.

Internet Bulletin Board Services

Internet bulletin boards are a lot like bulletin board services elsewhere. They are designed to be easy to use without a lot of preparation. A good

BBS will provide—on-line—all the information you need to use the service. Many BBSs require users to register, and you should be ready to provide some information about yourself. Registering helps the BBS operators to know their audience, and it helps the BBS stay secure.

The US Food and Drug Administration (FDA) maintains a bulletin board that is typical of interactive services on the Internet. You can reach the FDA BBS with this command:

```
telnet fdabbs.fda.gov
```

Figure 4.2 shows how you would connect to the FDA BBS using a Windows version of telnet with a protocol dialup connection. (The telnet client shown is from the Chameleon Software by NetManage. Telnet client programs are usually packaged with other network

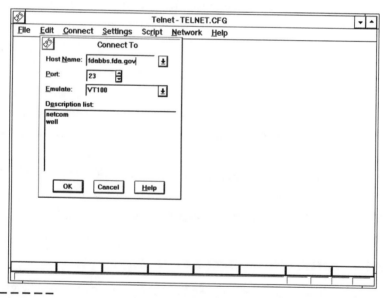

Figure 4.2 Connecting to the FDA bulletin board service.

access software, and you'll find also find `telnet` clients in FTP Software's PC/TCP package or Netcom's NetCruiser Internet software.)

When you connect to the FDA BBS, you will be presented with a login prompt from the computer that hosts the bulletin board. When you log in as *bbs*, the bulletin board software will start and you will be asked for your first and last names. If you're new to the system, you will be asked to register and select a password. After registering, you will be presented with a list of topics the system has information on. (A list of topics is shown in Figure 4.3.) Each topic represents a collection of files. Once you've selected a topic, you can get a table of contents for that topic, read any documents posted there, or perform a keyword search. The FDA BBS doesn't allow its users to post documents or to send and receive messages.

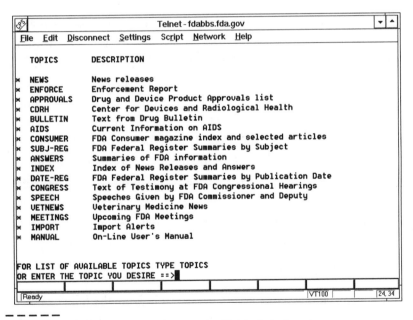

Figure 4.3 Topics available on the FDA bulletin board service.

Internet Databases

A database is just a searchable collection of information, and the Internet is home to hundreds of these collections covering all sorts of subjects, everything from library catalogs to subway routes. As with any other stand-alone resource, Internet databases are mostly self-explanatory. We'll look at two examples: the subway navigator database and archie's `telnet` interface.

The Subway Navigator Database

The subway navigator service mentioned at the beginning of this chapter is an example of the kind of special-purpose databases you can find on the Internet. (Others, like the geographic names server at the University of Michigan, are listed in Yanoff's Internet Services List.) The subway navigator uses a feature of `telnet` not previously discussed—the ability to open a `telnet` connection on a specific port. As you may remember from Chapter 1, a port is a public address on an Internet host at which two programs can make a network connection. The default port reserved for ordinary `telnet` connections on all Internet hosts is port 23. The subway navigator uses port 10000 on a machine named `metro.jussieu.fr`. (If an Internet resource uses a nonstandard port number, this information will be included in any directory that describes the resource. Scott Yanoff's Internet Services List contains listings for several resources that use nonstandard port numbers.) You can reach the subway navigator with this `telnet` command:

```
% telnet metro.jussieu.fr 10000
```

In this command, the number 10000 following the fully qualified domain name is a port number. When you don't specify a port number on your `telnet` command line, `telnet` uses its default port. The telnet server that monitors connection requests over port 23 starts up a login procedure for any incoming connections on that port. If you want to telnet to the subway navigator, don't forget to specify the port number.

When you use the telnet command above, your connection is made directly to the subway navigator database, bypassing the standard login process entirely. (Note that you can't pick any port at random for a telnet connection. The port you choose must be monitored by a program that knows how to interpret the telnet protocol.)

A connection to the subway navigator is shown in Figure 4.4. When you first connect to the subway navigator, you'll get a set of instructions

Figure 4.4 The subway navigator's opening screen.

in both French and English. You'll be asked to choose which language you'd like to use for this session, and the default is English.

After you've chosen a language, the subway navigator presents a menu of roughly two dozen cities for which it has subway information. Figure 4.5 shows the menu of subway systems that the subway navigator knows about. Select the city you're interested in. Your city selection will lead to a prompt for a starting point and destination. You should enter these items as the names of stations in the subway system you choose. Figure 4.6 shows a query for the time and route from Hyde Park in London to the suburb of Highgate.

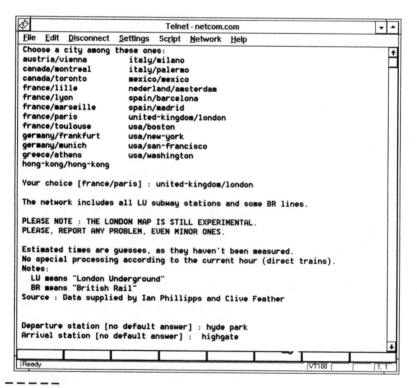

```
Telnet - netcom.com
File  Edit  Disconnect  Settings  Script  Network  Help

Choose a city among these ones:
austria/vienna          italy/milano
canada/montreal         italy/palermo
canada/toronto          mexico/mexico
france/lille            nederland/amsterdam
france/lyon             spain/barcelona
france/marseille        spain/madrid
france/paris            united-kingdom/london
france/toulouse         usa/boston
germany/frankfurt       usa/new-york
germany/munich          usa/san-francisco
greece/athens           usa/washington
hong-kong/hong-kong

Your choice [france/paris] : united-kingdom/london

The network includes all LU subway stations and some BR lines.

PLEASE NOTE : THE LONDON MAP IS STILL EXPERIMENTAL.
PLEASE, REPORT ANY PROBLEM, EVEN MINOR ONES.

Estimated times are guesses, as they haven't been measured.
No special processing according to the current hour (direct trains).
Notes:
  LU means "London Underground"
  BR means "British Rail"
Source : Data supplied by Ian Phillipps and Clive Feather


Departure station [no default answer] : hyde park
Arrival station [no default answer] :  highgate

Ready                                          VT100        1, 1
```

Figure 4.5 The subway navigator's menu of metro systems.

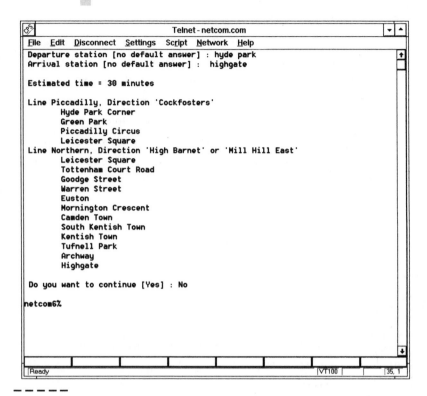

```
┌──────────────────────────────────────────────────────────────┐
│ ⚏             Telnet - netcom.com                      ▼  ▲  │
├──────────────────────────────────────────────────────────────┤
│ File  Edit  Disconnect  Settings  Script  Network  Help      │
│ Departure station [no default answer] : hyde park          ↑ │
│ Arrival station [no default answer] :  highgate              │
│                                                              │
│ Estimated time = 30 minutes                                  │
│                                                              │
│ Line Piccadilly, Direction 'Cockfosters'                     │
│         Hyde Park Corner                                     │
│         Green Park                                           │
│         Piccadilly Circus                                    │
│         Leicester Square                                     │
│ Line Northern, Direction 'High Barnet' or 'Mill Hill East'   │
│         Leicester Square                                     │
│         Tottenham Court Road                                 │
│         Goodge Street                                        │
│         Warren Street                                        │
│         Euston                                               │
│         Mornington Crescent                                  │
│         Camden Town                                          │
│         South Kentish Town                                   │
│         Kentish Town                                         │
│         Tufnell Park                                         │
│         Archway                                              │
│         Highgate                                            │
│                                                              │
│ Do you want to continue [Yes] : No                           │
│                                                              │
│ netcom6%                                                   ↓ │
├──────────────────────────────────────────────────────────────┤
│ │Ready                          │VT100 │        │35, 1       │
└──────────────────────────────────────────────────────────────┘
```

– – – – –
Figure 4.6 The subway navigator's route from Hyde Park to Highgate.

The subway navigator is typical of Internet databases. It's a resource that you can use anonymously, without identifying yourself or registering. It has an easy-to-use interface that gives you relatively few options at each prompt and it delivers just the information you asked for.

Using Archie through telnet

The archie application, introduced in Chapter 3, has a great deal in common with the other databases on the Internet. Unlike other databases, however, archie is a tool to help you find out more about the

Internet itself. Archie databases manage information about files that are published through anonymous ftp sites. These databases can be queried through archie client programs, via electronic mail, and by using telnet to log in to any of the computers on which archie servers are running. (See Chapter 3 for a list of computers hosting archie servers.) Telnet connections to archie servers are helpful if you need to run a batch of archie queries. A telnet session using archie is shown in Figure 4.7. In the session shown, we've used a PPP connection and telnet to log in to netcom.com. From there, another telnet command

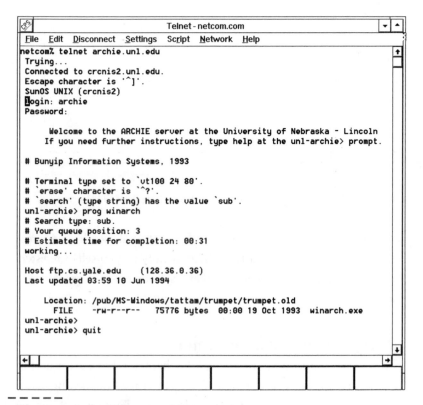

```
Telnet - netcom.com                        ▼ ▲
File  Edit  Disconnect  Settings   Script  Network  Help
netcom% telnet archie.unl.edu                              ↑
 Trying...
 Connected to crcnis2.unl.edu.
 Escape character is '^]'.
 SunOS UNIX (crcnis2)
 login: archie
 Password:

     Welcome to the ARCHIE server at the University of Nebraska - Lincoln
     If you need further instructions, type help at the unl-archie> prompt.

# Bunyip Information Systems, 1993

# Terminal type set to 'vt100 24 80'.
# 'erase' character is '^?'.
# 'search' (type string) has the value 'sub'.
unl-archie> prog winarch
# Search type: sub.
# Your queue position: 3
# Estimated time for completion: 00:31
working...

Host ftp.cs.yale.edu    (128.36.0.36)
Last updated 03:59 10 Jun 1994

    Location: /pub/MS-Windows/tattam/trumpet/trumpet.old
        FILE    -rw-r--r--   75776 bytes  00:00 19 Oct 1993  winarch.exe
unl-archie>
unl-archie> quit                                          ↓
←|                                                         →|
```

Figure 4.7 Using telnet to connect to an archie server.

was issued to connect to archie.unl.edu (the host for the archie database at the University of Nebraska at Lincoln).

The Internet sites running archie servers are set up to include the host name archie as an alias for the host that runs the archie database at that site. When you telnet to a host name that is an alias, don't be surprised if the machine you connect to identifies itself by its "unaliased" name. For example, one of the sites running an archie server is the University of Nebraska at Lincoln (unl.edu). When you telnet to archie.unl.edu, as in Figure 4.7, telnet gives you the computer's unaliased name (in this case crcnis2). To make things simple, the archie servers also recognize the login name archie. To query the archie database via telnet, connect to an archie server site and log in as archie (the archie account has no password).

When you log in to an archie server, you should see a message describing the service you're about to use. Read the opening message carefully. It will describe how to get help during the current session and how to report any problems you encounter. Archie's on-line help for telnet users is extensive.

The telnet version of archie uses the command prog to request a search. The query shown in Figure 4.8 is part of a quest for an archie client program to use with Windows. The ever-so-patient user in this session made up the key word "winarch" (a combination of "Windows" and "archie" that is short enough to be a DOS filename). To search the archie database for filenames and directory names containing the keyword "winarch," for example, use the following command in response to the archie prompt:

```
unl-archie> prog winarch
```

Archie will respond to your queries with a progress report indicating the number of entries that satisfy your query and the percentage of the database searched so far. The query for *winarch* produced one hit, a program named winarch.exe at `ftp.cc.yale.edu`. (Unfortunately winarch.exe is in a directory named `trumpet.old`, which does not inspire confidence. This program was downloaded and tested, and was judged not ready for prime time. It's a good example for how to use `telnet` to talk to `archie`, but not a particularly useful file to download.)

Traffic Jams   `Archie` is a very heavily used Internet service, and `telnet` connections (unlike the connections of `archie` clients or the e-mail interface) are open-ended. They aren't closed until you deliberately close them. If, while connected via `telnet` to an `archie` server, you are interrupted and called away suddenly, leaving your `telnet` session in place would accidentally tie up resources that other people are eager to use. Consequently, the `archie` servers will accept only a limited number of `telnet` connections. Don't be surprised if you encounter an `archie` server that cannot accept a new connection. When this happens, the `archie` server that can't accept your connection will provide a list of `archie` servers and then break the `telnet` connection. You can either wait a while and try again or query a different server.

Internet on the Menu

`Telnet` can put you in touch with lots of different services, but finding them one at a time is not very efficient, and remembering all the resources you've found can be a burden. Providing some kind of integrated interface to a large number of the Internet's resources is clearly a good thing (and we'll see a lot of this kind of integration in Chapters 6 and 7 when `gopher` and the WorldWideWeb are introduced). Before we get to `gopher` and the Web, however, you should know about the stand-alone applications that provide a convenient interface to many of the services the Internet has to offer. The examples below come from the LIBS application running at nessie.cc.wwu.edu (a computer at Western Washington University). Scott Yanoff's List has pointers to several other computers running LIBS as well as similar services (the "services" application that runs at library.wustl.edu and the Launchpad BBS that runs at launchpad.unc.edu).

All the resources for which LIBS provides an interface can be reached independently of LIBS. However, packaging access to dozens of Internet services in a single menu system is so convenient that you may prefer to use LIBS rather than memorize the procedures for connecting to services that you don't use often.

You can connect to LIBS with this command:

```
telnet nessie.cc.wwu.edu
```

When you receive a login prompt, use the user name LIBS, and the LIBS programs will start automatically. The top-level LIBS menu has entries for several categories of Internet services. It also provides instructions for exiting from the program. When you exit from LIBS, you will be logged out of the remote computer (nessie in this example), your telnet session will end, and you will be returned to your local computer. The top-level LIBS menu is shown in Figure 4.8. This figure shows what a conventional dialup user would see after issuing the telnet command above and providing the LIBS user name.

Further into the Internet with LIBS

Once you have reached the LIBS application, you have the opportunity in a single telnet session to branch out easily and quickly to other Internet resources. LIBS will handle the details of making connections, so you won't be forced to trust your memory or hunt around for a list of Internet services, and telnet will work discreetly

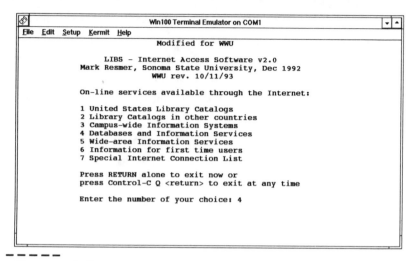

```
┌─┬──────────────────────────────────────────────────────────────┬───┬─┐
│⟨§⟩│                Win100 Terminal Emulator on COM1              │ ▾ │▲│
├───┴──────────────────────────────────────────────────────────────┴───┴─┤
│ File  Edit  Setup  Kermit  Help                                         │
│                          Modified for WWU                               │
│                                                                         │
│                  LIBS - Internet Access Software v2.0                   │
│             Mark Resmer, Sonoma State University, Dec 1992              │
│                        WWU rev. 10/11/93                                │
│                                                                         │
│             On-line services available through the Internet:           │
│                                                                         │
│             1 United States Library Catalogs                           │
│             2 Library Catalogs in other countries                      │
│             3 Campus-wide Information Systems                           │
│             4 Databases and Information Services                        │
│             5 Wide-area Information Services                            │
│             6 Information for first time users                          │
│             7 Special Internet Connection List                         │
│                                                                         │
│             Press RETURN alone to exit now or                          │
│             press Control-C Q <return> to exit at any time             │
│                                                                         │
│             Enter the number of your choice: 4                         │
│                                                                         │
└─────────────────────────────────────────────────────────────────────────┘
```

Figure 4.8   Connecting to LIBS via telnet.

in the background maintaining your connection to LIBS. Let's look at a simple example of how LIBS executes commands for you within a telnet session.

A Simple Example: The Time Service

Once LIBS starts, you can browse through the various menus it displays without actually using any of the services it describes. Whenever you select a menu item that will connect to some resource outside of LIBS itself, LIBS displays a short description of the resource and hints for using it. Figures 4.9 through 4.11 show the sequence of LIBS menus that lead to the National Bureau of Standards Time service. (All this service does is accept incoming connections, display the current time as reported by the National Bureau of Standards reference clock in Colorado, and disconnect.) This dialog begins after we've selected item 4, Databases and Information Services, from the main LIBS menu shown above in Figure 4.5.

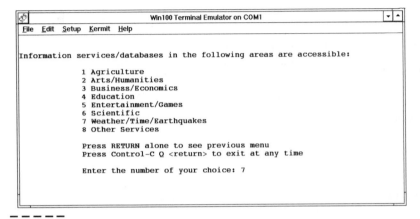

Figure 4.9 The LIBS Database/Information Services menu.

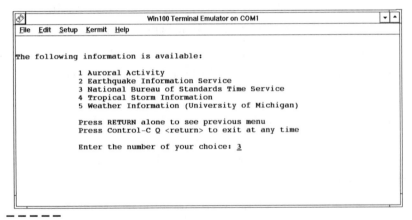

Figure 4.10 The LIBS menu for Weather/Time/Earthquake Information.

Here's a summary of the steps:

1. From the LIBS top-level menu, we chose the Databases/ Information item.

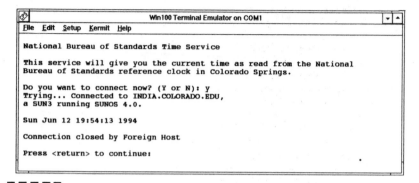

Figure 4.11 Using the National Bureau of Standards Time Service.

2. The submenu for databases (shown in Figure 4.9) contains an item for weather, time, and earthquake information, and that menu (Figure 4.10) contains an item for querying the National Bureau of Standards Time Service.

3. When you select this item, LIBS explains briefly what kind of service is offered and asks for confirmation before connecting.

4. When you confirm that LIBS should connect to the time service, a telnet connection is opened between the machine LIBS is running on (nessie) and a machine named india at the University of Colorado.

5. On the remote machine, a program is run that sends the current time and immediately closes the connection. This nested telnet session does its work and exits without disturbing the original connection to nessie. (Figure 4.11 shows the last three steps of the dialog.)

As you explore the LIBS menus, you'll find entries for many of the items on Yanoff's Internet Services List. For example, the FDA BBS is accessible through LIBS' menu of Scientific Information Sources (item 6 on the LIBS main menu).

Ecological Considerations

At the beginning of this chapter, telnet was introduced as a tool to give an Internet-wide audience access to stand-alone information resources. Telnet is a necessary part of anyone's Internet toolkit. It is relatively easy to use, and many Internet resources would not be accessible at all without it. As you can see from the example of LIBS, telnet can be made even more convenient when it is embedded within a menu-driven application. The application frees the user from having to remember machine names and login information for resources of interest.

But telnet also needs to be used with some care. In most cases, a connection established with telnet will remain open until it is closed by the user who initiated it. The accumulation of open but inactive connections can ultimately put a resource out of reach for anyone trying to make a new connection. Special-purpose client/server applications (such as archie) tend to manage their connections more efficiently than telnet does, and these clients should be preferred over telnet as a vehicle for launching database queries.

Where We've Been

We've now covered the basic uses of telnet, and seen how to make interactive connections to other computers on the Internet. We've discussed some features of telnet's command mode so you can customize the escape character and manage some features of your telnet connections.

The real value of `telnet` is the world of information that it brings within reach. We've seen how to use `telnet` as an alternate way of accessing the `archie` database. We've also used `telnet` to connect to the stand-alone LIBS application, which is a useful stepping stone to other Internet resources.

HUNTING THROUGH THE INTERNET – – – – – – – –

Question 1   What Illinois county contains the town of Amboy and how many people live in Amboy?

Answer   Amboy is located in Lee County, and the town's population is 2377.

To find this information, you can start with either LIBS or with Yanoff's list. Yanoff cites the Geographic Names Server at the University of Michigan. You can reach this server directly via `telnet`:

```
telnet martini.eecs.umich.edu 3000
```

Don't forget the port number (3000)! Once you get connected, the dialog for entering your query will look like this:

```
# Geographic Name Server, Copyright 1992 Regents of the
➥ University of Michigan.
# Version 8/19/92. Use "help" or "?" for assistance, "info"
➥ for hints.
amboy, il
0 Amboy
1 17103 Lee
2 IL Illinois
3 US United States
F 45 Populated place
L 41 42 51 N   89 19 43 W
P 2377
E 743
Z 61310
quit
```

The Geographic Names Server labels its output. Item 1 contains the county name, and the item labeled P is the population.

You can reach the same server via LIBS by selecting the Databases and Information Services item from the LIBS main menu. From the Databases menu, select "Other Information Services," and you'll see a menu that contains the Geographic Names Server. When you select this item, LIBS will make the `telnet` connection for you and your database query will be identical to the one shown above.

Question 2   The name of the LIBS application comes from its use as a tool for reaching library catalogs on the Internet. There is an obscure book named *From Fish to Philosopher*. Who wrote it and what is it about? For extra credit, who directed the movie made from this book?

Answer   The author of *From Fish to Philosopher* is William Homer Smith. The book is a natural history of the kidney. The film was directed by Norman Laden.

To find the author's name and the book's subject, use this strategy:

1. `Telnet` to `nessie.cc.wwu.edu` and login as `libs`.

2. Select U.S. Libraries from the menu of topics.

3. Select a state from the menu of states.

4. Select a library from the menu of school libraries.

5. When connected to the library of choice, perform a title search for *From Fish to Philosopher*.

6. Use the Display Item command to see the complete card catalog entry, which includes the subject classification for the book.

Procedures for searches by title will vary from library to library. You'll have to use the on-line help at the library you connect to for tips on how to search by title.

An alternate method (which will also score bonus points for finding the director of the film version) is to use **telnet** to connect to the Library of Congress database (Yanoff's list has a reference for this site).

```
--<Menus and query results edited for readability>--
% telnet locis.loc.gov
Trying...
Connected to locis.loc.gov.
Escape character is '^]'.
  L O C I S :  LIBRARY OF CONGRESS INFORMATION SYSTEM


        To make a choice: type a number, then press ENTER


    1   Library of Congress Catalog   4   Braille and Audio

    2   Federal Legislation           5   Organizations

    3   Copyright Information          6   Foreign Law


    7   Searching Hours and Basics
    8   Documentation and Classes
    9   Library of Congress General Information


    12  Comments and Logoff


        Choice:  1      Select item 1 for card catalog searches.

CHOICE   LIBRARY OF CONGRESS CATALOG FILE

    1       BOOKS: English language books 1968-,  LOCI

    2       BOOKS earlier than the dates above.   PREM

    3       Combination of files 1 and 2 above    (LOCI and PREM).
```

- -

```
4        SERIALS cataloged at LC .            LOCS

5        MAPS and other cartographic items    LOCM

6        SUBJECT TERMS and cross references    LCXR

12       Return to LOCIS MENU screen.


  Choice: 3   We're unsure of the publication date, so select item
3 to search for entries before and after 1968.


MONDAY, 08/09/95  10:58 A.M.
***You are now signed on to LOCI and PREM.
   READY FOR NEW COMMAND:
READY LOCIS:
find from fish to philosopher   query for the title.
PAGE from fish to philosopher
NUMBER OF HITS=2   FIND  MUMS   SEQUENTIAL RECORDS    1 TO 2


1  From fish to philosopher.
       Smith, Homer William, 1895-1962.
          From fish to philosopher.    1953
             LC CALL NUMBER: QH369.S58                  53-7332
2  Fish to philosopher motion picture / Merck Sharp & Dohme
 ➥ International ;
   produced by Norman Laden & Associates ; producer, director,
 ➥ and screenwriter, Norman Laden.
       Fish to philosopher...    1982    A/V
          NOT IN LC COLLECTION                       82-700391


READY LOCIS:
display item 1


53-7332                    ITEM 1 OF 2 IN SET 1         (LCCC)


Smith, Homer William, 1895-1962.
  From fish to philosopher. [1st ed.]  Boston, Little, Brown
 ➥ [1953]   264 p.
```

```
illus. 21 cm.
LC CALL NUMBER: QH369 .S58

SUBJECTS:
    Evolution (Biology)
    Kidneys.
    Consciousness.

DEWEY DEC:  575.6

NOTES:
  Includes bibliography.

LCCN:  53-7332 L r91

READY LOCIS: quit
```

CHAPTER 5

The Electronic
Post Office

Dear Ms. Propriety,

- I do not make a habit of writing to etiquette columnists, but I recently attended a dinner party at the home of a friend and witnessed an alarming trend in modern manners. Throughout the evening, from cocktails and appetizers right on through to after-dinner coffee, the guests could find no more fit topic for conversation than their most recent experiences with *electronic mail*. People whom I know to lead perfectly fascinating lives rattled on interminably about the programs they use to read and send e-mail. Their conversations were littered with the worst sort of jargon, strange names (Eudora and Uuencode), a blizzard of onomatopoetic acronyms (SMTP, POP, and PPP) and long, pointless stories.

- At one point, the hostess, whom I know to be a woman of great social sensitivity, told a lengthy story about typing one of these messages until the program she was using "froze." When I asked what that meant, she glowered at me and explained that the program would accept no more input. Pressing any key, she said, simply caused the computer to beep at her. Eventually she discovered that the back-space key did not cause the terminal to beep, which led her to hypothesize that she'd entered too long a line or too many characters without pressing Return. I hadn't the slightest idea what she was talking about, but everyone else seemed to take this as some sort of great revelation. I believe electronic mail is undermining our ability to think, and I'm sure you agree that it is not an appropriate topic for polite conversation in mixed company.

- Sincerely,
- rosebody@well.sf.ca.us

- Ms. Propriety replies:

- Gentle Reader: Ms. Propriety sympathizes with your uneasiness on this topic, but sees nothing wrong with conversation about electronic mail. Perhaps you should lighten up and cut your friends some slack.

E-Mail: the Message and the Medium

Electronic mail (or e-mail) is the ability to send and receive messages via computer. It has become a staple of modern business life and is rapidly finding a place in the home. E-mail is not a service found exclusively on the Internet, and its potential as a medium for communication extends far beyond the resources that the Internet offers. This chapter will discuss:

- the basics of sending and receiving e-mail,
- how to reach Internet resources that have an e-mail interface
- how to exchange e-mail between the Internet and other computer networks.

An Overview of E-Mail

E-mail is different from the other network applications examined here. Client/server applications like `ftp` and `telnet` create an "end-to-end" connection between you and an Internet resource. This is a little like using the telephone: if you want to talk with someone, you have to establish a connection and get the attention of the person you want to talk to. They have to listen while you talk and vice versa, or you won't communicate.

E-mail, on the other hand, is a "store-and-forward" service that works very much like the regular postal service. E-mail lets people communicate asynchronously: you can send mail messages whenever you want, and the people who receive mail from you can read the messages whenever they want. You and your audience don't have to connect to communicate. When you send e-mail, your message is forwarded from one computer to another until the destination is reached. At the destination, your message goes to the recipient's system mail box, a file that holds that user's incoming messages.

Of course, the technology behind the Internet can do quite a bit to streamline the delivery of e-mail. The presence of a high-speed network speeds things up considerably. Mail between Internet users will usually get to its destination within seconds regardless of the distance. The Internet Domain Name Service (DNS, discussed in Chapter 1) vastly simplifies both addressing and routing of e-mail. Before DNS, mail had to be routed directly to the machine that hosted the recipient's mailbox. With domains, mail can be addressed to the recipient's domain without the sender having to know the specific machine that the recipient uses. Each domain has an e-mail server (using the Simple Mail Transfer Protocol, SMTP) that distributes incoming mail and lets users read their mail from any computer in the domain. Mail that must travel between networks that aren't permanently connected or that don't share a common protocol for handling mail will take a little longer. Before you can send anything, however, you have to get connected to a computer that can act as a base for your e-mail communications, and there is no shortage of ways to get e-mail access.

Access To E-Mail

The path of least resistance is to use e-mail at work or at school if it's available. If you do this, please be careful to distinguish your personal messages, opinions, and the like from the official business of your school or employer. You can also get e-mail access at home by subscribing to an e-mail provider. Most e-mail providers offer dialup access. (See the discussion of conventional dialup connections in Chapter 2 for details about this sort of access.) To use an e-mail subscription service, you will need a computer (or a terminal of some kind), a modem, and a telephone line on which you can call the subscription service. In general, e-mail subscriptions don't provide home delivery of your e-mail; you will have to log in to the service's computer to send and read mail. The subscription service will provide:

- information about getting connected

- your e-mail address, the name other people should use to send mail to you

- a login name and password for you to use when connecting to the service (your login name will probably also appear as part of your e-mail address)

- a system mailbox

E-mail access providers charge for their services. Some charge a flat rate, others charge by volume (either by the message or by the size of your messages). Many e-mail providers allow you to store messages you've already read on the provider's computer. Be aware that using disk space may be a billable service. Before subscribing to any e-mail service, be sure that you understand what your subscription includes and what the charges are.

There are several kinds of e-mail access providers. Virtually all of the commercial Internet access providers include e-mail access with their Internet accounts. Most of the "on-line" services (America On-line, CompuServe, Delphi, Genie, The WELL) and many Bulletin Board Systems, whether they're connected to Internet or not, provide e-mail along with bulletin board and conferencing facilities. And of course, telecommunications companies like MCI and Sprint offer e-mail–only subscriptions.

138

In choosing an e-mail access provider, think about the cost of the service and the audience you want to exchange messages with. Some services offer e-mail within their own network only. Others allow you to send mail to other networks. The number of people with whom you can exchange messages depends entirely on how well connected your computer (or your subscription service) is. If you have an Internet account or an e-mail access provider that exchanges mail with the Internet, you can choose your e-mail correspondents from among the millions of people worldwide who use the Internet. You can also use the Internet to relay mail to users on other networks. (The networks that can be reached from the Internet via mail are sometimes called "the outernet." We'll talk about how to exchange mail with those networks below.)

Mail Programs

When you connect to an e-mail service (or when you send and receive mail through your Internet access provider), you'll use a program called a "mailer." If you've subscribed to an e-mail–only service (like MCIMail or SprintMail) you probably won't have a choice of mailers. If you've subscribed to an Internet access provider or to a conferencing system (like the WELL, for example), the computer where you send and receive mail may offer a choice of mailers, though there should be a default program. Choosing a mailer is a matter of personal preference, and without looking very hard, you'll encounter a wealth of opinion about the advantages and disadvantages of different mailers. For details about any particular mailer, there is no substitute for reading the documentation. Mailers differ dramatically in user interface and in strategies for storing received messages, but the basic sending and receiving capabilities should be common in all of them.

If you're using a protocol dialup connection or a PC connected directly to a local network connected to the Internet, you have some additional choices. You can either `telnet` to the computer that has your system mailbox and use that computer's mailer, or you can install a mailer on your home computer and work with mail there.

This chapter will present examples using two different mailers: the UNIX `mail` program for conventional dialup users and the `eudora` mailer available in Windows and Macintosh versions for protocol dialup users. (Note that the `eudora` release contains just the mailer and no networking software. To use `eudora`, you should already have installed and tested your network protocol software.) Eudora is written and maintained by Qualcomm, Inc. which distributes two versions of the program: an unsupported freeware version that you can download from the Internet, and a commercial version with more advanced features and help desk access. Examples in this chapter will use the freeware version. See the accompanying sidebar for information about downloading and installing this version of `eudora`.

 DOWNLOADING AND INSTALLING EUDORA - - - - - - -

You can get a copy of the freeware version of Eudora via anonymous `ftp`. (A detailed discussion of `ftp` appears in Chapter 3.) Eudora, originally developed at the University of Illinois Urbana-Champaign, is now published by Qualcomm for both Macintosh and Windows environments. The steps for obtaining the freeware version of Eudora are as follows:

1. You should have at least 1 megabyte of free disk space to download and install Eudora. If you're just downloading, but not installing, you'll need about 300K of disk space on the machine you're downloading to. Qualcomm publishes Eudora in a "self-extracting" archive. When you get ready to install Eudora, the 300K file you

downloaded will have to be unpacked, and its contents take up
nearly 700K.

2. Use `ftp` to connect to `ftp.qualcomm.com`. Log in as anonymous
   and, as the password, use your mailing address (in the format
   `username@fully.qualified.domain.name`).

3. Once you've connected, look at the README file for the most
   current information about the location of the files you need to
   download. `Ftp` sites frequently rearrange their files, so you may
   need to navigate to a different directory from the one shown in
   Figure 5.1. In our example, the file to be downloaded is
   `eudora14.exe` and it is kept in `quest/windows/eudora/1.4`.

4. In your `ftp` session, change to the correct directory with the `cd`
   command. `Eudora` archives are numbered according to version. In
   our example, `Eudora 1.4` is being downloaded, and the file to be
   copied from Qualcomm is named `Eudora14.exe`.

5. Tell `ftp` you're downloading a binary file and issue the `get`
   command.

6. After the transfer succeeds, quit from `ftp`.

7. After you've downloaded the `Eudora` archive, you need to extract
   the `Eudora` files from the archive. From the Windows File Manager, navigate to the directory containing `Eudora14.exe`. To execute this file, you can either double-click its name in the File
   Manager display or select File ➤ Run from the File Manager
   menu bar and enter the name of the archive in the command field
   of the Run dialog box. The self-extracting archive is a DOS program and does not use the Windows user interface. The extrac-
   tion will momentarily return your display to DOS mode. When it
   completes, your Windows session will resume.

8. The directory containing the Eudora archive should now also contain weudora.exe. Use the standard Windows commands to create a new file and associate weudora.exe with that file. Now you can execute Eudora by double-clicking on its icon.

9. Start Eudora and select the menu bar item labeled Special. Select Configure from the pull-down menu. The dialog box for configuring Eudora is shown in Figure 5.1 with entries filled out for monitoring mail for rosebody@well.sf.ca.us. You need to supply a fully qualified domain name for the Internet host on which you receive your mail and your login name. See the on-line help that accompanies Eudora for more information about configuration options.

10. Some additional options for controlling Eudora are located in the Special ➤ Switches dialog box.

11. To test your newly installed mailer, make sure you've established a network connection (via PPP or SLIP), and then click on Eudora's File menu button. Select Check Mail from the pull down menu. Eudora will make a connection to the network server on your Internet host a retrieve any new mail from your system mailbox. If eudora fails to connect, try another network application (ftp or telnet, for example) to test your Internet link.

E-Mail Basics

Once you've gotten access to e-mail and selected a mailer, you're ready to send and receive mail. The basics of using mail are more or less the same regardless of which mailer you use. We'll discuss sending mail,

Figure 5.1 is represented by the following UI layout:

```
PC Eudora                                    ▼ ▲
File  Edit  Mailbox  Message        Special  Window  Help

                        Configuration

   ┌─ Network Configuration ──────────────────────────────┐
   │  POP Account:     rosebody@well.sf.ca.us             │
   │  Real Name:       Bennett Falk                       │
   │  SMTP Server:                                        │
   │  Return Address:  rosebody@well.sf.ca.us             │
   │  Check For Mail Every  [30]  Minute(s)               │
   │  Ph Server:                                          │
   └──────────────────────────────────────────────────────┘

   ┌─ Message Configuration ──────────────────────────────┐
   │  Message Width: [80]   Message Lines: [20]   Tab Stop: [8] │
   │  Screen Font: [Courier New ▼]  Size: [10]            │
   │  Printer Font: [Courier New ▼]  Size: [12]           │
   │  ☒ Auto Receive Attachment Directory:  [D:\ROSEBODY] │
   └──────────────────────────────────────────────────────┘

   [■]                              [ Cancel ]  [ OK ]
```

Figure 5.1 Configuring Eudora.

reading your messages, managing your mailbox, and working with mailing lists.

Sending Mail

Sending mail messages is a three-step process. You compose the message, address it, and finally send it on its way. In practice, most mailers ask you to provide an address before you've written the message. Addressing e-mail is a matter of identifying the person (or group of people) to whom you're sending mail. Names alone should be adequate to send mail to other local users. Some systems, such as CompuServe, use numbers rather than names to identify users, but the principle is the same. If you're not sure whether a user is local or not, follow the instructions below for mailing to users elsewhere.

To send mail to users outside your local area, include in the address the name of the domain where the addressee receives mail. Addresses for sending mail between the Internet and other networks will be discussed below. The addressing convention for sending a message from one Internet user to another is:

```
username@name.domain.qualified.fully
```

or, for example,

```
rosebody@well.sf.ca.us
```

Username is just the recipient's login name. The fully qualified domain name (FQDN) you specify routes the mail to the Internet domain for that user.

Composure and How to Maintain It

After addressing your message, you're ready to write it. What you say in your messages and how you compose them are almost entirely up to you. You'll discover, however, that communicating accurately with someone else through the medium of e-mail may be as much of a challenge as mastering the features of the mailer you use. It's easy to write something that your audience might misinterpret. The best defense against miscommunication is to proofread everything you write before you send it. Avoid sending e-mail hastily or when you're angry or upset. The etiquette of sending electronic mail is similar to the etiquette of posting articles to USENET Newsgroups. The "Summary of USENET Etiquette" in Chapter 8 describes good practices for any electronic communication.

Of course, composing a message does have a technical side as well. Most mailers provide very limited built-in text editing capabilities for composing messages. Many mailer programs provide a way for you to use a separate text editor to compose messages. If your message is more than a few lines long, you'll want to take advantage of this feature. You may also want to compose your message in an editor ahead of time and save it in a file that the mailer will import to form the body of your mail message. (The ability to import files is a feature that may vary quite a bit from one mailer to another.)

Unless your mailer explicitly supports sending and receiving binary files, you should avoid sending files that are not text (or ASCII) files. There are two reasons for this. Text files can be read by virtually any mailer. If you send a binary file of some kind, the addressee will need the appropriate software to read your message. In addition, because mail is a store-and-forward service, you can't predict what programs will handle your message along the way. If you send binary-formatted mail, intermediate programs may not be able to transmit your messages accurately.

The ASCII-only limitation for mail messages is a serious one. Much of the interesting material on the Internet is not ASCII, and there's a great demand for tools to convert binary files into something that can be mailed safely. There are lots of tools that meet this need. (We'll discuss uuencode/uudecode, one of the most widely used conversion tools, below.) However, converting files manually is time-consuming and it requires that the sender and the receiver reach some kind of agreement about which tools to use. To ease this burden, a standard has been established for encoding binary information for Internet e-mail. The standard is called MIME, Multi-purpose Internet Mail Extensions. MIME is not something you use directly. If you're interested in exchanging binary information with other Internet users, look for a mailer that implements the MIME standard. (The eudora mailer is "MIME-aware," and its ability to handle binary attachments will be discussed below.) Mailers that support MIME can decide what sort of encoding your outbound messages need and do the encoding of binary files for you automatically. Inbound messages from other MIME-compliant mailers will be decoded automatically as well.

When you tell the mailer that the message is ready to send, it will compare the address with addresses it knows. If the mail is going to a local user, your message will be routed to that user's *mailbox*, a file that holds messages arriving for a particular user. If your mail must be handed off to another computer or network, the mailer will check the computer portion of the address, make some decisions about routing your message to its destination, and send the message on its way. When your message arrives at its destination, a mail server at the destination computer will put it in the appropriate mailbox, where it will stay until the recipient logs in and issues a command to read mail.

Sending Mail: A Sample Session

The standard mailer on UNIX systems is named `mail`, and a sample dialog for sending mail is shown in Figure 5.2. In this example, the user sending mail is connected to an Internet host over a conventional dialup connection, and mail is being sent to a user named `rosebody` at a computer named `well.sf.ca.us` (Whole Earth 'Lectronic Link, the WELL). The address `rosebody@well.sf.ca.us` is all that is needed to send mail from anywhere on the Internet to the user `rosebody` at the WELL.

The UNIX `mail` command is used for both sending and receiving mail. If you just type `mail` and press ↵, the mailer will let you read your system mailbox. To send mail, your `mail` command should include the username of the person you're sending to.

The UNIX mail command first prompts for a subject. In this example, the subject is "What's in a name?" (A good rule of thumb is to limit the subject line to 45 characters or less.) If you don't want to

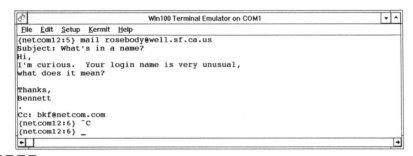

Figure 5.2 Sending mail with the UNIX mailer.

enter a subject, just press Return, and you can begin entering the text
of your mail message. Note that there is no prompt for this; you simply begin typing. There are practically no editing capabilities built
into the UNIX mailer. You can use the erase character (usually either
Backspace or Delete) to back up one character at a time within a line,
but that's about it. It's a good idea to use relatively short lines in mail
messages. Don't expect the mailer to wrap lines for you. At any point
if you want to stop editing the message and throw the text away, just
type Ctrl-C. The mailer will ask you to confirm that you want to quit
by typing Ctrl-C a second time.

When your message is complete, type Ctrl-D or a period (.) on a
line by itself to send the message. In Figure 5.2, the mailer has been
configured to prompt for any users who should receive a carbon
copy of the message. In this case, we've requested that a carbon copy
be sent to the sender, bkf@netcom.com.

When this message is sent, a copy will go to the system mailbox
for the user bkf. This message (and any others in a user's system mailbox)
can be read using the UNIX mailer. To read mail with this program,

simply type `mail` and press Return. See Figure 5.3 for an example of using the UNIX mailer to read mail. You'll see information about your version of `mail`, and about the messages in your system mailbox. The > symbol indicates the current message, and the letter N shows that this message is New. The number following that is the sequence of the message in the mailbox. These items are followed by the sender's name, the time the message was sent, the size of the message, and the subject. The ampersand (&) is the `mail` command prompt; the program is now ready for your input. To read the current message, simply press Return. You can read any message by typing its sequence number. After you've read a message, use the d command to delete it and then quit the mailer by typing q. If you're using the UNIX mailer and want a summary of its commands, type ? at the & prompt. A full description of the UNIX mailer's features can be found in the UNIX on-line manual. (See Appendix D for more information on using the on-line documentation for UNIX systems.)

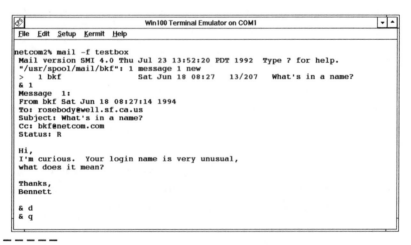

Figure 5.3 Reading mail with the UNIX `mail` program.

Reading Rosebody's Mail

A few seconds after the message is sent, it will arrive in rosebody's mailbox at well.sf.ca.us. Rosebody uses a protocol dialup connection to reach the Internet and has installed the eudora mailer. After establishing the phone link to an Internet access provider, rosebody starts the eudora program to check mail. Eudora first prompts for the password of the rosebody account, then connects to well.sf.ca.us and downloads new messages from rosebody's system mailbox at the WELL. Eudora does not need to maintain an Internet connection the whole time rosebody reads mail. Eudora connects to the Internet only to check for new mail and to send rosebody's outbound messages. Programs that batch mail operations in this way are sometimes called "off-line" readers, and using an off-line reader can help keep the cost of your Internet access down. While Eudora is running, it will check rosebody's system mailbox for new mail periodically. You can also initiate a check for new mail at any time during a eudora session.

Eudora organizes mail into mailboxes. There are three default mailboxes: *In* for new messages, *Out* for outbound messages, and *Trash* for messages that have been deleted. You can also create mailboxes of your own to organize messages that you want to save. A Eudora mailbox corresponds roughly to a file. Each mailbox can contain a number of messages. Mailboxes can be organized into folders, which correspond to directories. The screen rosebody sees is shown in Figure 5.4.

To use eudora to read mail, you simply open the *In* mailbox. (Eudora can be set up to open this mailbox automatically.) A table of contents for the mailbox will be displayed with one message per line, and you can scroll through the table of contents to find the message you want to read. Clicking on the table of contents entry will bring up a window with the full text of a message. Unlike the UNIX mailer, eudora allows you to look at several messages simultaneously.

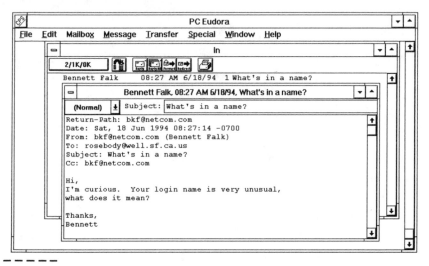

Figure 5.4 **Figure 5.4** Using `Eudora` to read mail for `rosebody@well.sf.ca.us`.

When you're reading a message, you can reply to the sender by clicking the Message button on the `eudora` menu bar and selecting the Reply entry on the pull-down menu that appears. `Eudora` will create a new window containing an address template and the text of the original message. By default, your response will be addressed to the sender of the original message. You can change this address or add to it if you wish: use the mouse to select the address field you want to change. You can also use the Tab key to move the cursor through the fields in the address header. When you've finished composing the address and text, click the Send button to dispatch your reply.

TIP -

Know your correspondents! Always check the "To:" and "Cc:" lists when replying to electronic mail to be certain your response is going to the audience you intend.

Forming Attachments

Like other mailers that adhere to the MIME standard, eudora allows you to attach documents to mail messages. The attached document can be just about any kind of file. Figure 5.5 shows the dialog for attaching a document to a mail message. In this case, both the sender (bkf) and the receiver (rosebody) are using the eudora mailer. Bkf composed the mail message as usual, but before sending it selected the Message menu button and the Attach Document item on the pull down menu that appeared. This brought up the file browser shown in Figure 5.5. The bigsur.doc file was selected and its name was added to the Attachments field in the message header.

Reading this mail, rosebody will see the screen in Figure 5.6. Notice that a status message has been appended to the message text, reporting that the document was successfully converted and is stored

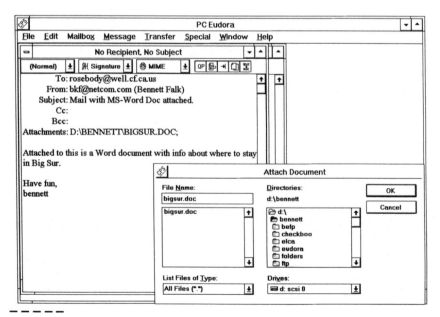

Figure 5.5 Attaching a document to a mail message in eudora.

in the directory configured for eudora attachments. In transit this file was converted to an ASCII form and then restored to its usable format on arrival.

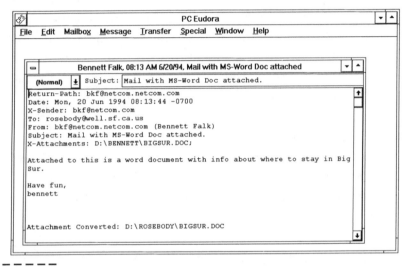

Figure 5.6 Reading a message with an attached document.

Mailbox Management

Managing your mailbox is one of those important things no one tells you about until it's too late. When you receive new mail, it will be stored in your system mailbox. This file should be kept relatively small. Mail messages take up disk space. If everyone lets them accumulate in system mailboxes, there is some risk of running out of space for new messages. In addition, the more messages your mailbox contains, the harder your mailer must work when you read mail. When software works hard, it usually also works more slowly.

Some mailers automatically move mail messages from the system mailbox to a local mailbox after the message has been read. This protects the system mailboxes from running out of space, but at the cost of creating a local file that must also be managed.

The UNIX `mail` program, for example, by default puts messages that have been read but not otherwise disposed of in a file named mbox in your home directory. If you don't get into the habit of deleting messages (or saving them elsewhere), your mbox file will happily keep growing. If you're sure there's nothing you want to preserve in this file, it can be deleted. You may, however, want to delete messages from it selectively. The UNIX `mail` program can be used to browse through the mbox file with the following command:

```
% mail -f mbox
```

The mailer will provide a summary display of the messages in mbox, and you can read, reply to, delete or save messages just as you do when working with your system mailbox.

When you're reading your mail with the UNIX mailer, you can tell the mailer to keep unread messages in your system mailbox instead of moving them to your mbox file. Just before quitting the mailer, issue the `pre` command (an abbreviation for "preserve") to keep unread mail in your system mailbox.

If you use a mailer like eudora, you still need to manage your system mailbox, but the procedure will be a little different. When you first start eudora, it checks your system mailbox and downloads any new messages it finds. When you read your mail with eudora, you're working with a local copy of the message in a eudora In folder. Eudora can be configured either to delete messages from your system mailbox after it has downloaded them or to leave messages in your system mailbox. (If you set up eudora to leave messages in your system mailbox, you'll need to manage your system mailbox using the technique described above.)

When you use eudora, you'll have local mailboxes to manage as well. Eudora has commands for deleting messages (individually or in groups), transferring messages from one mailbox to another, compacting mailboxes, and taking out the trash. (When you delete messages, they are moved to the Trash mailbox, and if you deleted a message accidentally, you can recover it by simply reading the Trash mailbox. Taking out the Trash empties this mailbox.) See eudora's Help facility for information on these commands.

Mailing Lists and How to Find Them

If all you could do with e-mail was send personal communications to other users, its usefulness would depend on who you know well enough to send messages to. In fact, there is a lot more to e-mail than sending messages to your friends. One of the main attractions of the Internet is access to mailing lists. A mailing list is a discussion group that communicates entirely by e-mail. There are mailing lists for all sorts of interest groups and discussion topics: aeronautics, bread baking, the latest operating system from Sun Microsystems, theology, vampires and much more. Some mailing lists are discussion groups to which any of the list's subscribers can contribute. Discussion-oriented mailing lists can be either moderated or unmoderated. Other mailing lists are used to broadcast announcements from some source to interested parties. Most mailing lists are open for anyone to subscribe.

The first step in joining a mailing list is finding out about it in the first place. Fortunately, much of the information about mailing lists is centralized in a few resources that you can easily reach from the Internet.

Quite a few mailing lists of interest to Internet users are developed and maintained on BITNET, a sister network to the Internet. (BITNET is an acronym for "Because It's Time Network", or sometimes, "Because It's There Network".) Some BITNET sites feature servers that provide mailing list information and administrative services (like subscribing and unsubscribing). These are known as LISTSERV sites. If you know the address for a LISTSERV site, you can get information about mailing lists by sending e-mail to that site. Scott Yanoff's Internet Services List has an entry for mailing lists related to music at `listserv@vm.marist.edu`. To find out about the mailing lists that a LISTSERV site knows about, you should first send mail to the list server requesting help. Simply send a message to LISTSERV with the word "help" on a line by itself. Here's how you'd do this from the UNIX mailer on Netcom:

```
netcom% mail listserv@vm.marist.edu
Subject:
help
```

The dot on a line by itself is not part of the message, but a signal to the UNIX mailer that you're through entering the body of your message. LISTSERV will respond with a list of the commands that it recognizes. A portion of the response is shown in Figure 5.7.

Each LISTSERV site is home to some mailing lists. You can get information about a single LISTSERV's mailing lists by sending it the command `list short`. You can also get information about all the mailing lists known to all the LISTSERVs by sending the command `list global`. You'll get back e-mail with the names of more than 5000 mailing lists. If you'd like more information about a particular list, send the LISTSERV a message with the command `info` and the name of the list you're curious about. Other LISTSERV commands will let you subscribe to or resign from a list. Once you've subscribed to a list, you'll receive all the mail traffic that is sent to the list, and this will vary from a few messages a week to dozens of messages a day, depending on the list.

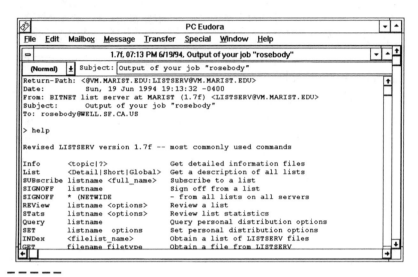

Figure 5.7 E-mail from LISTSERV showing its commands.

Following the lead of the BITNET LISTSERV sites, many Internet sites also publish mailing lists as well. Mailing lists at Internet sites are often managed by a program called `majordomo` that performs very much like LISTSERV. To find mailing lists at an Internet site, send mail to `majordomo` at that site (for example, `majordomo@netcom.com`) with the `lists` command on a line by itself. `Majordomo` manages the mailing lists at one site only, and there is no way to query for all the mailing lists managed by `majordomo` throughout the Internet. Apart from this, `majordomo` provides essentially the same features as LISTSERV.

In addition to these mailing list servers, there is a catalog of more than 1200 mailing lists (the "list of lists") that you can obtain via anonymous `ftp`: the file is named INTEREST-GROUPS in the NET-INFO directory at `crvax.sri.com`. This list identifies each mailing list by name and includes a short description of the list and its subscription procedure. The file is updated quarterly.

TIP —

If you find a list you're interested in and want to subscribe, don't send your request directly to the mailing address for the list. Instead use LISTSERV or majordomo to subscribe. Many lists have a separate address for administrative issues. Check the "list of lists" for subscription information. By convention, many administrative mailboxes use the suffix –request appended to the mailing list address. For example, if you're interested in a mailing list named salamanders@wsqpd.com, your subscription request should be sent to salamanders-request@wsqpd.com.

Using Services through E-Mail

On the Internet, electronic mail is more than a medium for communicating with other people. It is also a general-purpose tool for querying databases and transferring files. We hinted at these more adventurous applications of mail by introducing the e-mail interface to archie in Chapter 3. Now we need to consider in more detail what happens when you use e-mail to interact not with other users, but with programs.

We'll look at three representative services:

- **Almanac** is an e-mail-based bulletin-board system for general information, agricultural issues, and market news. Almanac mail servers can be reached at a number of Internet sites. The example below will use the almanac mail server at cce.cornell.edu.

- The **archie e-mail interface** enables mail-based querying of the database of ftp archives at any archie server. We'll send mail to archie@archie.unl.edu.

- The **ftpmail** service (at `decwrl.dec.com`) provides an e-mail interface for file transfers via `ftp`.

We'll discuss how to contact each of these services via e-mail, how to request its documentation (at least a list of its commands), and what sort of e-mail you should expect in response. These and other e-mail services can be found in Scott Yanoff's Internet Services List. (Detailed instructions for retrieving this list via `ftp` are in Chapter 3.)

Mail-Based Bulletin Boards: The Almanac Service

The `almanac` service is an electronic bulletin board that users access via e-mail. It was developed at Oregon State University under a grant from the Kellogg Foundation, and there are at least six `almanac` installations around the continental U.S.

To get started with `almanac`, send mail to the user `almanac` at one of the server sites. Each site's BBS is unique, and you may want to shop around to find topics of interest. The body of the mail message should contain the command `send guide` to retrieve documentation for `almanac`. To reach `almanac` at Cornell University send a message to `almanac@cce.cornell.edu`. The message should contain two commands:

```
send guide
send catalog
```

In response to the `send guide` command, `almanac` will send you a message containing the manual (about 10 pages when printed). The manual describes `almanac` commands and how to use them, but it doesn't tell you what topics are available for discussion on this `almanac` server. The command `send catalog` returns a list of topics being discussed on this server. When you send both commands together, their combined output comes back in a single return message from the almanac server.

Almanac servers offer a diverse range of services. The Cornell almanac server includes a home buyer's guide, a seminar on coping with change, an Internet exploration guide and an information exchange group about pesticides. The catalog of primary topics also contains instructions for getting more detailed information about individual topics. For example, to get more detail on the home buyers guide, mail almanac the command

```
send home-buyers-guide overview
```

Almanac will respond with an overview of the guide and instructions for getting further information.

Each almanac server also contains a mail-catalog in which you'll find topic-oriented mail groups. Like other Internet mailing lists, the mail groups distribute messages about some topic to subscribers. Some almanac mail groups are forums inviting subscribers to participate in a discussion of some issue. Others are used to broadcast newsletters and reports to interested parties.

The Archie E-Mail Interface

Archie is one of the most versatile applications on the Internet, offering access via archie clients, telnet, and electronic mail. The basic service that archie provides is a database of anonymous ftp archives throughout the Internet. Anonymous ftp archives are files available for anyone to copy via an ftp client. (You'll find a detailed explanation of anonymous ftp in Chapter 3.) The archie database accepts queries containing keywords, and it returns the locations and names of files whose titles contain the specified keyword. The archie database is published to at least 10 sites, any of which can support queries via e-mail. (See Chapter 3 for a list of `archie` server sites.)

E-mail queries of the `archie` database should be addressed to the user `archie` at the computer named `archie` at one of the `archie` sites. For example, the e-mail address for the `archie` server at the University of Nebraska at Lincoln is `archie@archie.unl.edu`. To get usage information for the `archie` e-mail interface, send a message containing the `help` command on a line by itself.

If you send an `archie` server a `help` command, it will ignore any subsequent command the message contains. Unlike LISTSERV and `major-domo`, the `archie` e-mail interface merges the Subject line of incoming messages with the rest of the message text, so you could send the `help` command as the subject of your message. Finally, the `help` command must begin at the left margin. If you indent the `archie` commands in your message, the server won't recognize them. If you send an `archie` server a message that contains no legal `archie` commands, you'll receive the `archie` server's help message in reply. The commonly used commands for `archie`'s e-mail interface are listed below:

`help`

Returns usage information about `archie`'s e-mail interface.

`find` *pattern1* [*pattern2,* ...]

`Find` is the basic search command used by `archie`. The arguments to the `find` command are words or portions of words you expect to find in filenames at some `ftp` site. Archie will search for each pattern independently. If you use multiple patterns in a single `find` command, all the results will be returned in a single `mail` message. If you use multiple `find` commands, `archie` will return a separate response for each command. Earlier versions of `archie` used the command `prog` to execute searches. `Find` is a synonym for `prog`.

`site` *fqdn* ¦ *IP address*

The `site` command requests a listing of the `ftp` archives at the specified site. You should use either a fully qualified domain name or an IP address for the site.

```
quit
```

The `quit` command tells the `archie` server to stop interpreting the input message.

Submitting An Archie Query by E-Mail

Let's test the e-mail interface to `archie`. Someone named John Chew is rumored to have created an e-mail address guide that summarizes how to address mail messages going from one network to another. This mail guide is supposed to be available through anonymous `ftp`, and if we can find it and download a copy of it, we can find out some things about exchanging mail with networks outside.

The first problem is to pick a keyword or pattern to submit in an `archie` command. *Internetwork, mail,* and *guide* are all promising candidates, but any of them alone will probably match many filenames in the `ftp` archives that we have no interest in; so we need to be more specific. The pattern we specify has to fit in one file name. On UNIX systems, file names frequently consist of two or more words, separated with dots (.), dashes (–), or underscores (_). Let's submit a mail query to `archie` using the pattern *mail-guide*:

```
find mail-guide
quit
```

An edited version of the response to this query is shown in Figure 5.8.

The `archie` query returned a total of 25 references to sites having a file satisfying the *mail-guide* query. Most of the matches for this query were named either *inter-net-mail-guide* or *inter-networking-mail-guide*. Many of the sites reported were quite remote, and several had

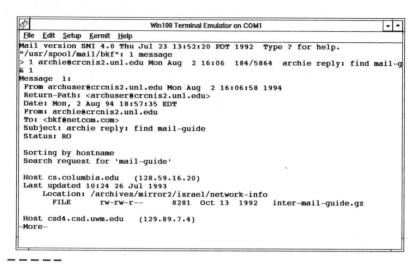

```
┌──────────────────────────────────────────────────────────────────┐
│ ◇│            Win100 Terminal Emulator on COM1              │▼│▲│ │
│ File  Edit  Setup  Kermit  Help                                    │
│ Mail version SMI 4.0 Thu Jul 23 13:52:20 PDT 1992  Type ? for help.│
│ "/usr/spool/mail/bkf": 1 message                                   │
│ > 1 archie@crcnis2.unl.edu Mon Aug  2 16:06   184/5864  archie reply: find mail-g│
│ & 1                                                                 │
│ Message 1:                                                          │
│  From archuser@crcnis2.unl.edu Mon Aug  2 16:06:58 1994            │
│  Return-Path: <archuser@crcnis2.unl.edu>                           │
│  Date: Mon, 2 Aug 94 18:57:35 EDT                                  │
│  From: archie@crcnis2.unl.edu                                      │
│  To: <bkf@net.com.com>                                             │
│  Subject: archie reply: find mail-guide                            │
│  Status: RO                                                         │
│                                                                    │
│  Sorting by hostname                                               │
│  Search request for 'mail-guide'                                   │
│                                                                    │
│  Host cs.columbia.edu   (128.59.16.20)                            │
│  Last updated 10:24 26 Jul 1993                                   │
│     Location: /archives/mirror2/israel/network-info                │
│         FILE     rw-rw-r--     8281  Oct 13  1992   inter-mail-guide.gz│
│                                                                    │
│  Host csd4.csd.uwm.edu   (129.89.7.4)                             │
│ -More-                                                             │
└──────────────────────────────────────────────────────────────────┘
```

Figure 5.8   E-Mail response to an archie query.

only compressed versions of the file. Still, there are several sites from
which we can copy this file. One of the sites is ftp.nau.edu, and we'll
work with that site in using ftpmail below.

Errors by E-Mail

Archie queries submitted by e-mail don't always go as planned. In a
separate session, the query for files matching the "mail-guide" pattern
was submitted via MCI-mail to the archie server at rutgers.edu.
(We'll discuss the mechanics of sending mail between Internet and
MCI-mail after we have retrieved a copy of the Internet Mail Guide.)
This command ended with an archie server time-out error, and a no-
tice of that error was sent back to the user who originated the query.
The error notification is shown in Listing 5.1.

Listing 5.1:

Error Returned via E-Mail from an Archie Query

```
Command: read 1

Date:     Tue Aug 02, 1994 7:15 pm EST
From:     archie errors
     EMS: INTERNET / MCI ID: 376-5414
     MBX: archie-errors@dorm.rutgers.edu

TO:     * Bennett Falk / MCI ID: 601-9949
Subject: archie [prog mail-guide] part 1 of 1

>> path Bennett Falk <0006019949@mcimail.com>
>> prog mail-guide
# Error from Prospero server - Timed out (dirsend)
>> quit
```

The command prompt for the MCI-mail mailer program is Command:. In the MCI system the read command is used to display messages. Structurally, the message is very similar to UNIX e-mail. There is a short header with fields identifying the time the message was sent, the sender, the receiver, and the subject. The body of the message includes the text of the original query (the lines set off with >>), and the archie server error (the line set off with #). The message that reports the error gives us a chance to check the query that was submitted. In this case, there is nothing wrong with the query; something out of our control kept the server from responding in a timely way.

Ftp via E-Mail: Ftpmail

With archie's help, we've located a file that is of interest (/internet/inter-net-mail-guide at ftp.nau.edu). To retrieve a copy of that file, we'll use the ftpmail server at decwrl.dec.com. Use this site for ftpmail if you're in North America. A separate site is available for

European users. (Ftpmail was developed by Paul Vixie at the Digital Equipment Corporation's Western Research Laboratory.) As with many other things on the Internet, the first step in using ftpmail is to get ftpmail to tell us how to use it. We do this by simply sending a message containing the word "help" to ftpmail@decwrl.dec.com. Note that ftpmail will ignore the Subject line of your message.

The help message that is sent in response to this query includes a command summary, several usage notes about different features, and a number of examples. Frequently used ftpmail commands are summarized below.

reply *mailaddr*

Set return address to which files should be mailed.

connect *host*

Connect to the named host ("anonymous" is the default login name).

ascii

Files to be transferred are printable ascii.

binary

Files to be transferred are binary.

chdir *directory*

Change directory (only once per session).

compress

Compress binary files.

uuencode

Uuencode binary files before mailing.

```
chunksize size
```

Split files into *size*-byte sections for e-mail (default is 64000).

```
ls directory
```

Short listing of the named *directory*.

```
dir directory
```

Long listing of the named *directory*.

```
index pattern
```

Search for *pattern* in `ftp` server's index.

```
get file
```

Get the named *file* and have it mailed to you (max of 10 *get* commands per session).

```
quit
```

Terminate script, ignore rest of message.

`Ftpmail` uses `chdir` in place of `ftp`'s `cd` command, and it has a number of commands that filter files (through `compress`, `uuencode`, and `split`) to make them suitable for e-mail. Apart from these differences, however, the commands for `ftpmail` are very similar to the standard `ftp` commands.

You can start an e-mail file transfer by sending `ftpmail` a message containing commands very much like those you would execute in an interactive `ftp` session. The following message instructs `ftpmail` to connect to `ftp.nau.edu`, move to the /internet directory, and retrieve the file named inter-net-mail-guide:

```
connect ftp.nau.edu
chdir internet
get inter-net-mail-guide
```

Shortly after this message is dispatched, `ftpmail` returns the first of several status reports. (See Figure 5.9.) This report confirms that the request has been queued, repeats the commands contained in the request, and lets us know how many requests are ahead of us in the queue. It is not uncommon for the queue to contain several hundred jobs. Ftpmail's initial response to a request also contains some supplemental documentation explaining in detail what you can expect.

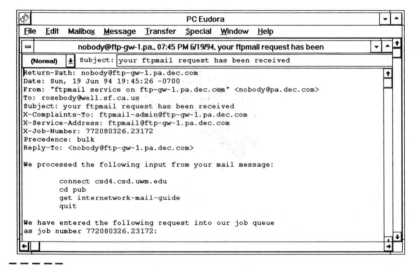

Figure 5.9 Response from ftpmail confirming a request.

Ftpmail will try five times to connect to the specified system. If it tries to connect and fails, you will receive a status message advising you of the failure and of the number of attempts still to be made.

When the transfer finally succeeds, you will receive the requested file as one or more mail messages (depending on the size of the file and the "chunksize" in effect for your transfer). You will also receive a status message describing the ftp session in which the file was transferred. Note that file transfers via ftpmail don't happen instantaneously. When John Chew's Internetworking Mail Guide was retrieved, roughly nine hours elapsed between request and completion.

Uuencode: Making Binary Files Mailable

Many of the files you'll find available through ftpmail are binary files. (The great divide between ASCII and binary files was introduced in Chapter 3.) "Binary" is an umbrella term for any file that contains data outside the ASCII character set, and it includes compiled programs, compressed files, and "archive" files produced with programs like PKZIP or the UNIX "tar" command. In their natural state, binary files don't mail well: mailers have a hard time transferring them intact. To remedy this problem there are two utilities (uuencode and uudecode) that are widely distributed on the Internet. These utilities were first developed in the UNIX environment, but there are now versions of them for other computers as well. Uudecode comes in particularly handy for PC users. (Uuencoding is also used for posting binary files to USENET newsgroups, and we'll discuss it again briefly in Chapter 8.)

Uuencode produces an all-ASCII copy of a binary file. Uudecode translates files produced by uuencode back into their natural format. The command line for uuencode on a UNIX system looks like this:

```
% uuencode destname < filename > filename.uue
```

In this command, *filename* is the binary file you want to convert to ASCII. *Destname* is the name you want the file to have when it is eventually decoded at its destination. Ordinarily you'd use the file's original name for the destination name. The `< filename` part of the

command line tells uuencode to use filename for its input. The >
filename.uue on the command line tells uuencode to create a file
named *filename*.uue and put the ASCII version of *filename* there. After
you've done this, *filename*.uue is perfectly safe to mail.

When you receive a piece of mail that has been uuencoded (as you
might using ftpmail), you can use uudecode to convert the file back
to its binary format. When you receive a uuencoded file in e-mail, it
will look something like this:

```
% mail
Mail version 5.2d (word-wrap) 9/22/91. Type ? for help.
"/usr/spool/mail/rosebody": 1 message 1 new
>N 1 rosebody Thu Sep 9 08:14 109/6271 "UNIX Tuna"
& 1
Message 1:
From bennett@optimism.wsqpd.com Fri Sep 9 08:14:32 1994
To:      rosebody
Subject: UNIX Tuna
Date:    Fri, 9 Sep 1994 08:13:49 -0700

begin 644 unix_tuna.Z
M'YV02-[<'>'D#1#1#1TO=----Z'$*%G*+]P$'&$*'@*['*+]P06=[4D=K
M#8$@A99=*@*3P*]L#OE%'NH[+/Qw$X(A)=RX*4/GH:]3::UB'4+]'CQNH+]Y+W=]4]"@](L(@@,QS6H]5].&.
MXI@I',DDH+9.G:1X2*3B.&3<0%BIX(@(.,K,:3Ib31J:6CL>Q%H&Q)HR><2\"2,G
MXQQLS'=WD'0&'+ITT8^JPH@ANb39@q66<>A:j':Lr1)=gl)9-f#m*j%+'*d7@&
```

The line that reads begin 644 unix_tuna.Z is the start of the uuencoded message. When you decode this message, it will produce a file
named unix_tuna.Z. This is the destination name that was provided
to uuencode.

When you receive an encoded file in mail, save the message in a file.
When you quit the mailer, you can use uudecode on this file to convert
the message to binary. For example, if the message above was saved in
a file named tuna, the uudecode command would be uudecode tuna.

168

Here is the uudecode command sandwiched between two ls commands that show what files are present before and after uudecode.

```
% ls -l
-rw-r--r-- 1 rosebody well       6281 Sep 9 08:17 tuna
% uudecode tuna
% ls -l
total 12
-rw-r--r-- 1 rosebody well       6281 Sep 9 08:17 tuna
-rw-r--r-- 1 rosebody well       4336 Sep 9 08:18 unix_tuna.Z
```

Notice that uudecode doesn't remove "tuna." If uudecode succeeds, you can remove this file. One other point of interest is that tuna contains the message we received complete with all the header information that mail supplied. Uudecode ignored everything in the file up to the "begin" line. It is possible (but not very likely) that a mail header could interfere with uudecode. If that happens, the file you're decoding can be edited (in an ASCII editor, of course) to remove everything above the begin line. Be careful not to change or delete the begin line itself.

By the way, unix_tuna.Z is a compressed file. After decoding, it still needs to be decompressed to be usable. Decompressing looks like this:

```
% compress -d unix_tuna
% ls -l
total 15
-rw-r--r-- 1 rosebody well       6281 Sep 9 08:17 tuna
-rw-r--r-- 1 rosebody well       8165 Sep 9 08:18 unix_tuna
```

Notice that decompressing replaced unix_tuna.Z with unix_tuna.

There are also versions of uudecode for DOS. Figure 5.10 shows a DOS uudecode session. In this example a uuencoded file named rtfm.uue is decoded to produce rtfm.gif, a binary graphic file. This example uses version 2.13 of uudecode for DOS by Richard Marks.

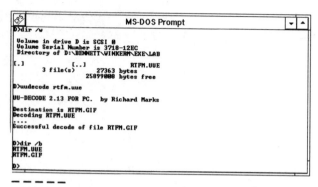

```
                          MS-DOS Prompt                  ▼  ▲
D>dir /w

 Volume in drive D is SCSI 0
 Volume Serial Number is 3718-12EC
 Directory of D:\BENNETT\WINKERM\EXE\LAB

[.]              [..]              RTFM.UUE
        3 file(s)        27363 bytes
                      25899008 bytes free

D>uudecode rtfm.uue

UU-DECODE 2.13 FOR PC.  by Richard Marks

Destination is RTFM.GIF
Decoding RTFM.UUE
....
Successful decode of file RTFM.GIF

D>dir /b
RTFM.UUE
RTFM.GIF

D>
```

Figure 5.10   Using a DOS Version of Uudecode.

Mail between Networks

Thus far, we've looked at e-mail primarily as an exchange of messages
between senders and receivers on the Internet. As large as it is, however, even the Internet has boundaries. Some of the Internet's points
of contact with other networks can only be crossed by e-mail, and
the familiar user@host.domain address format may not work for mail
delivery to a foreign network. We downloaded John Chew's Internetwork Mail Guide to have a reference work for e-mail to some of
the networks that make up the "outernet." Some of the networks discussed in the guide are private corporate networks, and some have
no point of contact with the Internet. The accompanying sidebar
summarizes e-mail addressing conventions between the Internet and
several of the networks with which Internet users commonly exchange mail.

What Are These Networks?

SprintMail and MCIMail are commercial e-mail services running on
networks operated by Sprint and MCI, respectively. Sprint and MCI

E-MAIL ADDRESSING BETWEEN NETWORKS - - - - - - - -

BITNET: To send mail from a BITNET site to an Internet user, use one of the following address forms:

```
user@host
```

or

```
gateway!domain!user
```

To send mail from an Internet site to a BITNET user, use the following address form:

```
user%site.bitnet@gateway
```

(Substitute for *gateway* the name of a host that serves both Internet and BITNET.)

CompuServe: To send mail from a CompuServe site to an Internet user, use the following address form:

```
>Internet:user@host
```

(Add the prefix `>Internet:` to the Internet address.)

To send mail from an Internet user to a CompuServe site, use the following address form:

```
71234.567@compuserve.com
```

(CompuServe user IDs are two numbers separated by a comma. Replace the comma with a period and add the domain name `compuserve.com`.)

MCIMail: To send mail from an MCIMail site to an Internet user, use the following address form:

```
create <CR>
TO:  User Name
EMS: Internet
MBX: user@host.domain
```

To send mail from an Internet user to an MCIMail site, use one of the following address forms:

acctname@mci_mail.com

or

acct_id@mci_mail.com

(Account names may not be unique; MCI *acct ID* is a 7-digit number.) SprintMail: To send mail from a SprintMail site to an Internet user, use the following address form:

C:USA, A:telemail, P:internet, ID:*user*(a)*host.domain*

To send mail from an Internet user to a SprintMail site, use the following address form:

/PN=Bennett.Falk/O=co.wsqpd/ADMD=SprintMail/C=US@sprint.com
UUCP: To send mail from a UUCP site to an Internet user, use one of the following address forms:

user@*host*

or

gateway!domain!user

To send mail from an Internet user to a UUCP site, use the following address form:

user%host.UUCP@uunet.uu.net

e-mail subscribers can send and receive mail with a local phone call anywhere in the United States. CompuServe is a commercial time-sharing and conferencing system that also offers e-mail subscription.

BITNET, which was introduced briefly above, is a world-wide network chiefly for educational and research institutions. It is home to discussion groups managed by the LISTSERV mailing-list manager.

The UUCP network is a loose association of computer sites that communicate via modems and phone lines using the UUCP (UNIX-to-UNIX Copy) protocol to transfer data. UUCP is essentially a store-and-forward network. (It is also the home of the USENET News, which many people mistakenly believe to have originated on the Internet.)

Interpreting Foreign Addresses on the Internet

Mail originating on the Internet retains the user@host.domain format wherever possible. This is not always easy. There are intuitively satisfying Internet domain-style names (compuserve.com, mci_mail.com, sprint.com, and so on) for the commercial networks outside the Internet, but there is no single domain name for either BITNET or UUCP addresses. To send mail to a user at one of these networks you need to know an Internet host that serves as a *gateway* between the destination network and the Internet. (A gateway is a machine, connected to two different networks, that is capable of passing information back and forth between them.) For BITNET, cunyvm.cuny.edu is one such gateway. A UUCP network gateway is uunet.uu.net.

The addresses that route mail through a gateway have an unusual structure. Everything to the right of the @ is the gateway's Internet domain name. To the left of the @, a percent sign (%) is used to separate the user's name from the host name in the destination network.

This *user%host* notation is interpreted when the message arrives at the gateway and is handed off to the destination network.

Each of the commercial services (CompuServe, MCIMail, and SprintMail) has a unique notation for identifying users. CompuServe uses two numbers separated by a comma. MCIMail uses both an account name and an account ID. Only the account ID is guaranteed to be unique. Finally, SprintMail identifies users with the notation proposed by the X.400 e-mail standard. This notation includes fields for personal name (PN), organization (O), and country (C). Once you know that SprintMail's user ID includes all these fields, it is a little easier to recognize that SprintMail addresses like

```
/PN=Rene.Descartes/O=COGITO_INC/ADMD=TELEMAIL/C=FR/@sprint.com
```

really do have a familiar structure:

```
a_very_long_user_name@sprint.com
```

Addressing Internet Users from Foreign Networks

Sending mail to the Internet from a foreign network is a little more straightforward, as you can see in the sidebar. Most foreign networks accept names in the user@host.domain format. UUCP and BITNET can deliver mail to Internet users with no further information. Users of the commercial networks should consult their documentation or on-line help to see how to indicate that Internet is the destination network. On CompuServe, you indicate that Internet is the destination network by adding the prefix >Internet: to the user@host name. SprintMail addresses include the destination network name in a field labeled P:. SprintMail also uses the format <user(a)host.domain>.

For MCIMail users, the destination network is specified in response to a prompt when creating mail. Listing 5.2 shows the procedure for MCIMail users to address mail to Internet users.

Listing 5.2:
Addressing mail to the Internet from MCIMail.

```
Command: create

TO:     Thalamus Backmatter
        Thalamus Backmatter not found in the MCI Mail Subscriber
Directory.
        You may enter an address for paper, telex, EMS or FAX
delivery.

        0 - DELETE
        1 - Enter a PAPER address
        2 - Enter a TELEX address
        3 - Enter an EMS address
        4 - Enter a FAX address

Please enter the number: 3
Enter name of mail system.

EMS:    internet
  EMS 376-5414 INTERNET     MCI Mail       Downers Grove,

Enter recipient's mailbox information.

MBX:    backmatter@wsqpd.com

If additional mailbox lines are not needed press RETURN.

Subject: Hi, this is a test...

Text: (Enter text or transmit file. Type / on a line by itself
➥ to end.)

This was sent from mci-mail to the Internet.
Please reply when you get this.

thanks,
bennett
```

```
  /
Handling:
Send? yes
One moment please; your message is being posted.

Your message was posted: Tue Aug 02, 1994 10:41 am EST.
There is a copy in your OUTBOX.

Command:
```

The Future of E-Mail

Mail is certainly here to stay. It is an extraordinarily useful tool for personal communication. It can be used as a networked application to bring resources within reach with relatively little overhead. It provides a medium for communications to be passed between networks, and it is rapidly adapting to the need to transmit binary as well as ASCII data.

With the addition of e-mail, your orientation to the Internet's basic tools is complete. For most of the Internet's history, users have gotten what they wanted from the Internet with these tools. It is unlikely that any of these tools will become obsolete, but the trend in Internet applications is to give these basic tools a more convenient interface. In Part III we'll look at some of these second-generation network applications.

HUNTING THROUGH THE INTERNET - - - - - - - -

Question   You've heard about wireless cable TV, but this is a new field and you're worried about doing business with people you don't know in a new industry. Where can you find out more?

Answer   A first step is to see what is available through `ftp`:

```
% archie -s wireless
<--output truncated-->
Host plaza.aarnet.edu.au
      Location: /usenet/FAQs/rec.video.cable-tv
            FILE -r--r--r--      24768  Sep  3 06:59
➨Wireless_Cable_TV_FAQ
<--output truncated-->
```

This looks promising. It's a list of Frequently Asked Questions about Wireless Cable. Unfortunately, it's in Australia. We could get a copy from there, but we can probably find it closer to home. Now that we know what to look for, another `archie` search to look for *Wireless* (a case-sensitive search, this time) might help:

```
% archie -c Wireless

Host plaza.aarnet.edu.au


      Location: /usenet/FAQs/rec.video.cable-tv
            FILE -r--r--r--      24768  Sep  3 06:59
➨Wireless_Cable_TV_FAQ


<--Output Edited-->
Host athene.uni-paderborn.de


      Location: /doc/FAQ/rec.video.cable-tv
            FILE -rw-r--r--      10126  Sep  3 06:59
➨Wireless_Cable_TV_FAQ.gz


Host charon.mit.edu


      Location: /pub/usenet-by-group/rec.video.cable-tv
            FILE -rw-rw-r--      24768  Sep  3 06:59
➨ Wireless_Cable_TV_FAQ
      Location: /pub/usenet-by-hierarchy/rec/video/cable-tv
```

```
        FILE -rw-rw-r--      24768  Sep  3 06:59
→Wireless_Cable_TV_FAQ
<--Output Truncated-->
```

The entry from MIT looks promising. We can confirm that by downloading it via `ftp`:

```
% ftp charon.mit.edu
Connected to charon.mit.edu.
220 charon FTP server (Version 6.6 Wed Apr 14 21:00:27 EDT
→ 1993) ready.
Name (charon.mit.edu:bkf): anonymous
331 Guest login ok, send e-mail address as password.
Password:
230 Guest login ok, access restrictions apply.
ftp> verbose
Verbose mode off.
ftp> cd pub/usenet-by-group/rec.video.cable-tv
ftp> get Wireless_Cable_TV_FAQ
ftp> quit
```

This file is compiled by Brian Carlin, and contains the answers to the following questions:

```
1.0  Abbreviations used
2.0  What is wireless cable?
2.1  What are the benefits of wireless cable to the customer?
2.2  How does it work?
2.3  What is the history of MMDS?
2.4  How does MMDS work commercially?
3.0  What frequencies are used?
3.1  How many channels can be transmitted?
3.2  What channels can be sent?
4.0  What is the range of wireless cable?
4.1  Does weather affect reception?
5.0  What equipment is in the subscriber's home?
5.1  Is wireless cable equipment reliable?
6.0  What about copyright issues?
```

7.0   What about security?
8.0   How are wireless cable systems regulated?
9.0   I saw one of those 'infomercials' about wireless cable. Are these companies legit?
9.1   How can I tell if a company is running a scam on me?
10.0   Is there an industry association?
10.1   Who do I contact for more information?

We answered this question using only the tools we know about so far. In fact, this FAQ is part of a USENET newsgroup, and we could have gotten to this file in several ways. Chapters 6, 7, and 8 will show you some alternate ways of retrieving this sort of information.

The

Internet

Community's

Applications:

Gopher,

WorldWideWeb,

and

Net News

- The growth of the Internet is changing the way people use it. The new generation of Internet applications (represented here by gopher and W^3) are designed to let you use resources without worrying about where they are on the network. These applications guide you to resources using menus or hypertext documents. In Chapter 6, you'll learn about gopher, the jughead and veronica databases, and the WSGopher client (for protocol dialup users). In Chapter 7, the World Wide Web is introduced along with a discussion of the Cello Browser for protocol dialup users.

- Finally, in Chapter 8, you'll encounter the USENET News, with more than 7000 discussion topics. Two news readers are introduced: tin for conventional dialup users and WinVN for protocol dialup users.

6

CHAPTER

Internet Access for the Armchair Explorer: gopher

Something woke Sarah up in the middle of the night. She got out of bed, poked her head out the door, and looked down the hall just to be sure nothing was wrong. Everything seemed okay, but there was a faint blue glow in the open door of her daughter's room. Selina must have fallen asleep and left the computer on, Sarah thought as she padded down the hall.

- She peeked in the doorway and was amazed to find that her daughter was not asleep but standing in front of the table that held the computer and its monitor. The desk chair had been rolled out of the way, and Selina stared intently at the screen. Her arms were stretched out like wings, and she stood on one leg, knee slightly bent. Her free leg extended just in front of her, toes pointed delicately ahead.

- Sarah looked at the monitor and saw that it was a patchwork of windows with pictures of brightly-colored birds. Selina, she realized, was mimicking one of the bird pictures. Sarah watched in silence as Selina moved slowly from one pose to another. She was piecing the bird postures together into a dance.

- "That's lovely, dear," Sarah said softly. "Do you have a dance project due at school?"

- Selina dropped out of her stance. "Yeah, I need something really good for the program we're doing next month, and I don't think they'll let me do the dance about frogs mating."

- "I liked your frog dance," Sarah said, but her attention had wandered to the screen. "Where on earth did you get all these pictures?"

- "I found this gopher server in Illinois with all this birding stuff on it. Great pictures, lots of other stuff. And would you believe it, the whole thing's on a computer run by *the Army!*"

- Sarah, unsure what a gopher server was, adopted an expression of great seriousness. "My dear, I certainly *would* believe it. I didn't march to Washington in 1967 and levitate the Pentagon for nothing!"

Just Do It

If you are fascinated with the Internet's information resources but have a low tolerance for FQDNs, IP addresses, directory names, user names, passwords, and file types, the Internet gopher is the tool you've been waiting for. If you connect to the Internet via a conventional dialup connection, log in to your access provider's computer and issue this command:

gopher

Your screen will display a menu similar to the one shown in Figure 6.1. (There's an outside chance that your gopher command won't result in a menu, and this means there's something wrong. See the sidebar "Getting Started with gopher" for tips on coping with this.)

The menu shown is the root menu of the Mother Gopher at the University of Minnesota. If you received a menu different from the one in Figure 6.1, your Internet access provider has set up gopher to

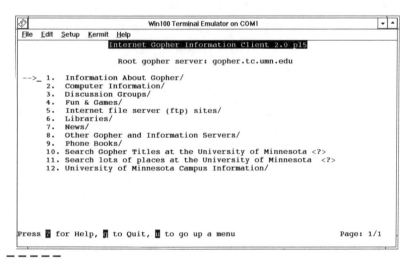

Figure 6.1 The root menu of the Mother Gopher

GETTING STARTED WITH GOPHER — — — — — — — — — —

If your gopher command did not start up a menu similar to the one shown in Figure 6.1, one of three things has gone wrong:

You received a message like "gopher: command not found": Try executing gopher by full pathname. This means spelling out in your command line exactly where the gopher program is. The following example will work for most Internet access providers. (The example is based on the UNIX operating system, which you'll find on many access providers' computers.) On UNIX computers, locally installed software is usually put in a special directory named /usr/local/bin. To run gopher by full pathname, type the following command:

```
/usr/local/bin/gopher/
```

If this fails and you get the same message, ask your Internet access provider if gopher is installed and what the appropriate command is to run a gopher client.

The gopher server isn't running and you received a message saying there was a network error and the connection was refused. In this case the problem is with the gopher server. You can still run gopher by connecting to a different server elsewhere. Try this command to connect to the Mother Gopher at the University of Minnesota:

```
gopher gopher.tc.umn.edu 70
```

This command includes the FQDN (gopher.tc.umn.edu) for the Internet host running the mother gopher and the port number at which that server listens for connections. Throughout this chapter there are examples of other gopher servers you can connect to in this way.

A menu appeared on your screen but it was scrambled and you couldn't make selections from it. Gopher is a "full-screen" application, and it needs to know some features of the terminal you're working on. On many Internet hosts, your terminal type will be set for you automatically when you first log in. If your terminal type can't be determined automatically, the system may ask you for a terminal type as part of the login procedure. In any case, if the display is scrambled when you run gopher, you'll still be able to quit the program by typing Ctrl-C. After gopher exits, you can change the terminal type. More information on logging in and setting terminal type can be found in Appendices C ("Logging In") and D ("Just Enough UNIX").

If all of these things fail (very unlikely, but possible), you can run gopher via telnet. Using gopher this way is not as versatile as running the client on the computer that gives you Internet access, but it will at least give you some exposure to gopher and its resources. Consult Table 6.1 or Yanoff's Internet Services List (Chapter 3 shows how to get a copy) for sites with public gopher logins. Telnet to one of the hosts in the gopher section of Yanoff's list. Use the login name gopher for most sites offering gopher access via telnet. (Exceptions to this practice are noted in the Internet Services List.) The list of sites that offer telnet access to gopher clients is subject to change.

connect to a different gopher server. Your actual starting point doesn't make much difference. To start cruising the Internet from a gopher server's root menu, select one of the numbered items and press Return. What you'll see next depends on what kind of item you selected. Most often your selections will lead to new menus (some of which will span more than one screen). Other selections will lead to files, to keyword searches on databases, to telnet sessions or to ftp archives. If you want to return from one menu to its parent, simply type u. If you want to see the on-line command summary for your gopher client, type ?. To quit, type q. You can do a fantastic amount of Internet exploration with just these commands.

Table 6.1: Internet Sites with Public Logins to Run Gopher

HOSTNAME	IP ADDRESS	LOGIN	AREA SERVED
consultant.micro.umn.edu	134.84.132.4	gopher	North America
ux1.cso.uiuc.edu	128.174.5.59	gopher	North America
gopher.msu.edu	35.8.2.61	gopher	North America
gopher.ebone.net	192.36.125.2	gopher	Europe
info.anu.edu.au	150.203.84.20	info	Australia
gopher.chalmers.se	129.16.221.40	gopher	Sweden
tolten.puc.cl	146.155.1.16	gopher	South America
ecnet.ec	157.100.45.2	gopher	Ecuador
gan.ncc.go.jp	160.190.10.1	gopher	Japan

GUI gophers

For protocol dialup users there are some very exciting alternatives to the ASCII gopher client pictured in Figure 6.1. A number of gopher clients for different graphical user interfaces (GUIs) are available at the University of Minnesota via anonymous ftp. The procedure for obtaining gopher clients is explained in the sidebar "Downloading and Installing gopher." Note that gopher clients do not include the basic network software for establishing a protocol connection to an Internet access provider.

DOWNLOADING AND INSTALLING WSGOPHER - - - - -

Gopher software (for both clients and servers) is available through anonymous `ftp` at `boombox.micro.umn.edu`. Underneath the directory /pub/gopher, you'll find subdirectories containing `gopher` software for various platforms (DOS, Windows, Macintosh, NeXT, UNIX, and others). Each subdirectory contains a README file that explains the directory's contents.

You will find several directories for `gopher` products for DOS and Windows. The contents of these directories are typically either "self-extracting" archives or archives in the ZIP format. (You'll need a utility, like PKUNZIP, to unpack the ZIP archives.) Both of these file types are binary, so remember to issue the `binary` command to `ftp` before you download from these directories.

The WSGopher software is in the directory /pub/gopher/Windows. Look for filenames that begin with wsg. WSGopher is distributed as a self-extracting archive, so the filename will have the .exe extension. The naming convention for wsg is to include the version number in the name of the archive, so WSGopher 1.01, for example, will be in the file named wsg-101.exe.

The GUI examples in this chapter will use the WSGopher client. WSGopher is the work of Dave Barry and is copyrighted by E.G.& G., Idaho, Inc. It was developed for the Idaho National Engineering Laboratory and is freely available for anyone to use. WSGopher is free, but it's also copyrighted and can't be sold. As a piece of freeware, it carries no warranty and no support. WSGopher is a "winsock-compliant" program; it will work with any networking software that supports the winsock interface. (Winsock is a standard interface for Windows programs that use the TCP/IP protocol. Your network software must comply with this standard for WSGopher to work.)

Download the archive for WSGopher and put the file in a directory by itself. Self-extracting archives are DOS programs. The safe way to unpack the WSGopher files is to execute wsg-101.exe from a DOS prompt. This will extract a few files, among which is wsgopher.exe, the gopher executable. You can run this program as you would any other Windows application.

Periodically, new versions of WSGopher are made available through boombox.micro.umn.edu. To upgrade your WSGopher, first be sure WSGopher is not active; then back up your WSGopher installation! Be especially careful to copy the wsgopher.ini file to another directory. Otherwise, it will be overwritten when you unpack the archive for the new version and you'll lose any bookmarks or configuration changes you had made. Go through the same steps as the installation procedure to install the new software. This will install a generic version of wsgopher.ini. Move that file out of your way (you may want to keep it for future reference), and then restore the wsgopher.ini that you copied before starting the upgrade.

WSGopher is configured by default to connect to the gopher server at the University of Illinois, Urbana-Champaign. Figure 6.2 shows a view of the root menu of this gopher from WSGopher. WSGopher puts each gopher menu in a separate window. You select a menu item by double-clicking its icon. Using the mouse, you can make any of the currently open windows active. The menu bar at the top of the WSGopher window provides commands to manage bookmarks and WSGopher's configuration.

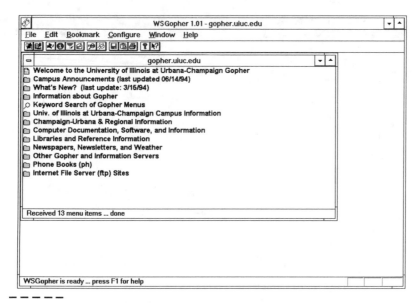

– – – – –
Figure 6.2   The UIUC gopher server as seen from WSGopher.

What gopher Is

Technically, gopher is a "distributed document delivery system." Fortunately, it's more appealing (and much more fun to use) than that description makes it sound. In practice, gopher is something like ftp and telnet all rolled into one and covered with menus. You can retrieve files via gopher without knowing which Internet host contains the file or what directory the file is stored in. You can connect to other systems just by selecting menu items. The aim of the gopher application is to bring you information from all over the Internet as seamlessly as possible. Unlike any other application we've discussed so far, gopher doesn't require you to memorize a domain name or login information. You won't even have to remember which gopher server manages the information you want to retrieve. Gopher is so successful at hiding the boundaries between machines and servers that the term "gopherspace" has been coined to refer to the complete pool of information resources managed by gopher servers throughout the Internet.

Because gopher is so easy to use, it has become an extremely popular vehicle for publishing information on the Internet. There are more than 1700 gopher servers spread throughout the Internet. In the last 12 months, the number of gopher servers has more than doubled. Many of these are devoted to specialized areas of interest. For example, there are at least five servers providing information on plant genome projects. Gopher has become a popular application among businesses trying to reach an Internet audience. There is, for example, a gopher server for *The New Republic*. There are also gopher servers for nonprofit organizations and advocacy groups such as the Electronic Frontier Foundation (EFF). Apart from its advocacy work, the EFF gopher is host to a number of electronic periodicals that challenge the conventions of mainstream journalism. Gopher provides a congenial medium for these and many more activities. And, of course, there are gopher servers for fun.

Gopher was developed in 1991 at the University of Minnesota. The gopher development team there continues to work on enhancements and extensions of the system, and the UM gopher server remains the Mother Gopher. Unlike ftp, telnet, and the UNIX mail command, gopher is an application designed for the current state of the Internet. It is built to accommodate lots of users, and it is designed to shield users from the details of managing client/server connections. Each connection from client to server should be as brief as possible. For this philosophy to work, the physical network must be fast enough to perform well even if the client program needs to open a connection for each query it sends to the server. If the Internet's physical network were slower or significantly more congested, gopher would not be as successful as it has been.

How gopher Works

What happens when you run gopher? First, your client program connects to a gopher server somewhere on the Internet. (The Mother Gopher at the University of Minnesota is the default, although your Internet access provider can change the default to a local server.) If you know the hostname and port number for a gopher server that manages information you're interested in, you can override the default and connect to any gopher server that you like. Starting your gopher session at the server you're interested in can cut down on the time you spend traversing gopher menus. As you use gopher, you'll also notice some differences in style between gopher servers, and you may choose a nondefault gopher as your starting point simply because you like the arrangement of its menus. Port 70 is usually reserved for gopher servers. If you're using an ASCII gopher client, supply the hostname and port number on the gopher command line. For example, to start a gopher session with the server with the Mother Gopher at the University of Minnesota, use this command:

```
gopher gopher.tc.umn.edu 70
```

Like the ASCII clients, WSGopher allows you to connect to any server for which you have a hostname and port number. First start WSGopher, then select the File menu button and the New Gopher item from the pull-down menu that appears. You can enter the connection information in the dialog box attached to this item. Figure 6.3 shows this dialog box filled out to connect to the Mother Gopher.

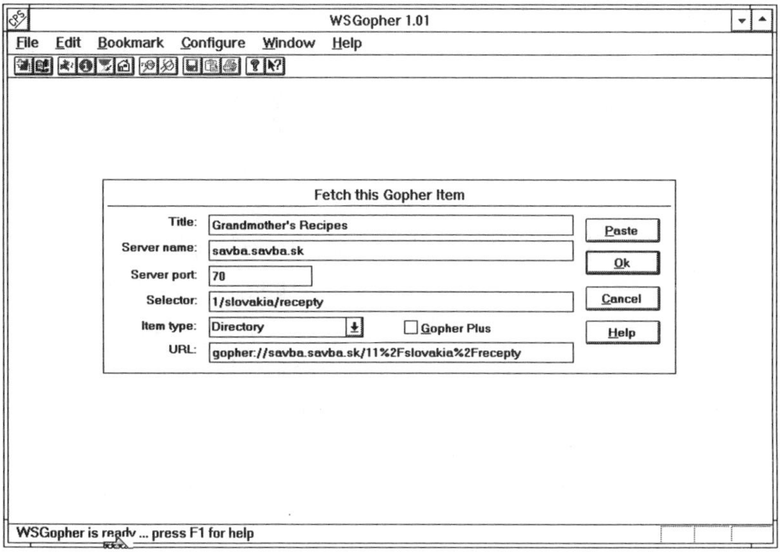

Figure 6.3 Entering connection information for a new gopher in WSGopher.

> **NOTE**
>
> The last item in this dialog box is URL, a style of identifying Internet resources that originated with the World Wide Web. URL stands for Uniform Resource Locator, and many gopher clients and servers have begun to use this kind of identifier in addition to the simpler format that originated with gopher. URLs will be discussed in more detail in Chapter 7 when we consider the World Wide Web.

After a connection is established, your client sends the server a request saying basically "Show me what you've got." A gopher server's resources are organized hierarchically, usually in a tree-like directory structure. The server will answer your first request with a listing of the root level of this directory hierarchy. Each item in this listing consists of a short description, an identifier that tells the client what kind of item it is, a hostname and a port number. After sending its list of items, the gopher server closes its connection with your client.

The client program turns the listing into a menu and displays it on your screen. When you select an item from this menu, the client figures out what kind of item you've selected, looks at the hostname and port number attached to that item, and connects to that host and port. The client uses this new connection to send a request for the item you selected. The server finds the item, sends it to the client, and closes the connection. If the item you selected is a directory, the server sends back a listing of that directory's contents, and the client presents that to you as a menu. If your selection is a file, the server will send the client the contents of the file.

When the client receives a file, it checks the file type and does whatever is sensible for a file of that type. If the file is text, the client displays it, and after you've looked at it, you'll have the option of printing, mailing, or saving the file locally. If the file is binary and you're working over a conventional dialup connection, the client will prompt you for a file name to use when saving the file locally.

Gopher Menus and the Objects Behind Them

The versatility of gopher depends a great deal on identifying the different kinds of items that can be encountered on the Internet. A gopher menu item can represent any of a dozen different things, and gopher menus include icons indicating what type of object each item represents. Internally, gopher uses single-character identifiers to name each object type. Most of the time the identifiers are safely out of view, but, as you'll see later, when you ask for information about an item, gopher displays the identifier without telling you what it stands for. The list of gopher objects, their identifiers, and icons appears in Table 6.2.

Table 6.2:   Gopher Objects, their Identifiers, and Icons

MENU ITEM TYPE	GOPHER IDENTIFIER	ICON
File	0	-none-
Directory	1	/
BinHexed Macintosh File	4	<HQX>
Uuencoded file	6	-none-
DOS Binary file	5	<PC Bin>
Binary file	9	<Bin>
Graphics File in GIF Format	g	<Picture>
Image File	i	<Picture>
Index Search	7	<?>
Telnet Session	8	<TEL>
Telnet 3270 Session	T	<3270>
CSO Phone-book Server	2	<CSO>
Error	3	-none-

A few of the objects gopher recognizes may be new to you. Telnet 3270 is a special implementation of the telnet program to connect to IBM computers that use the 3270 "block mode" terminal. A CSO Phone-book Server is a tool for maintaining a campus-wide phone directory. Index Searches are used to retrieve files containing keywords that you specify. Gopher provides an interface to index searching tools of various kinds. One popular indexing and retrieval tool on the Internet is the Wide-Area Information Server (WAIS). WAIS is a complicated application in its own right, but you don't need to know the details of using WAIS to query WAIS databases through gopher. (See Appendix E for information about WAIS.) Index searches are discussed in more detail later in this chapter.

Using an ASCII gopher Client

The basics of using an ASCII gopher client were introduced above. There are a few additional commands that will come in handy. When you run a gopher client and connect to the Mother Gopher at the University of Minnesota, you'll see the menu shown above in Figure 6.1. You can select a menu item by typing its number or you can move the cursor to the desired item with your terminal's arrow keys. Pressing Return will select the item, and the item type will determine what gopher does next. Typing a question mark will display a summary of the command that can be executed from a gopher menu. Figure 6.4 shows the gopher help message.

The commands you'll want to learn first are those that deal with menu navigation. With a terminal-based gopher client, there is usually room for 18 menu items on a single screen, and it is common for gopher to present directory listings that span several screens. In the lower-right corner of the display, gopher shows both the current page and the number of pages for the directory being listed. You can move your view of the listing forward and backward a page at a time with the > and < keys (that is, the shifted comma and period keys, not the arrow keys). If you want to jump to a particular menu item, you can do so by just typing its number. Notice that moving from page to page in one listing is different from going up to the parent menu (with the u command). If you want to end your gopher session at any time, you can type Q to quit unconditionally or q to quit only after you've confirmed that you really want to exit gopher.

Another tool for searching through long menus is the / command, which searches for a word or string in the names of the menu items in the current listing. Remember that the / command searches for the keyword only in the names of the menu items. Searching the contents of menu items requires an "Index Search" menu entry and a full-text index.

```
                     Quick Gopher Help
                     -----------------
Moving around Gopherspace
-------------------------
Press return to view a document

Use the Arrow Keys or vi/emacs equivalent to move around

Up ..................: Move to previous line.
Down ................: Move to next line.
Right Return ........: "Enter"/Display current item.
Left, u  ............: "Exit" current item/Go up a level.

>, +, Pgdwn, space ..: View next page.
<, -, Pgup, b .......: View previous page.

0-9 .................: Go to a specific line.
m   .................: Go back to the main menu.

Bookmarks
---------
a : Add current item to the bookmark list.
A : Add current directory/search to bookmark list.
v : View bookmark list.
d : Delete a bookmark/directory entry.

Other commands
--------------
s : Save current item to a file.
D : Download a file.
q : Quit with prompt.
Q : Quit unconditionally.
= : Display Technical information about current item.
O : change options
/ : Search for an item in the menu.
n : Find next search item.
o : Open a new gopher server
! : Shell Escape

The Gopher development team hopes that you find this software useful.
If you find what you think is a bug, please report it to us by sending
e-mail to "gopher@boombox.micro.umn.edu".


Press <RETURN> to continue,
   <m> to mail, <D> to download, <s> to save, or <p> to print:
```

Figure 6.4 Gopher Help

TIP –

To get a menu of all the gopher servers that are known to the Mother
Gopher, select Item 8 (Other Gopher and Information Servers) from
the root menu. This selection leads to a menu whose first item is "All
the Gopher Servers in the World." When you select this item, the server
will return a menu with more than 1700 items (about 100 menu
screens). The / command comes in handy when browsing this menu.

Most of the time, you will not need any additional information about
the items in a gopher menu. However, if you're curious about the access
information gopher has about an item, you can position the cursor on
that item and press the = key. Listing 6.1 shows what gopher reports
when you ask for information about an item. In this example, we asked
for information about the first item in the Mother Gopher's root menu.
Gopher tells us the item's name, its type (type 1 items are directories),
the path for getting to the object, and a host name and port number
that can be used to find the object.

Listing 6.1:

Getting Information about a Gopher Menu Item
– – – – –

```
Name=Information About Gopher
Type=1
Port=70
Path=1/Information About Gopher
Host=gopher.tc.umn.edu


Press <RETURN> to continue, <m> to mail, <s> to save, or <p> ➡
to print:
```

Using the WSGopher

WSGopher gives a Windows interface to gopher servers. We'll illustrate how to use it by connecting to the AVES gopher that contains information about birds. The AVES gopher can be reached at

```
vitruvius.cecer.army.mil 70
```

The root menu from this site is shown in Figure 6.5. To get information about any of the menu items, simply select File from the Menu bar and the Info on Item... entry from the pull-down menu that appears.

WSGopher allows you to specify which program to use as a viewer for files that you encounter. The AVES server, for example, offers a number of bird photographs in GIF format. If you have a program to display GIF files, you can tell WSGopher to start that

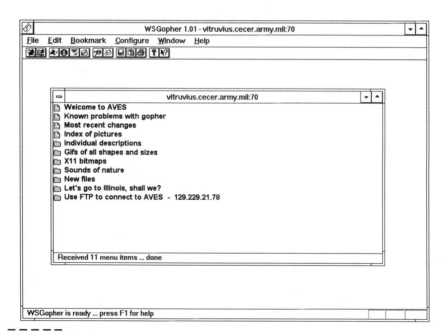

Figure 6.5 The root menu for the AVES gopher.

program whenever it downloads a file with the .gif extension. The pull-down menu attached to the Configure menu button has an entry for Viewers. Selecting this item will bring up the dialog box shown in Figure 6.6. Here, we are adding an entry to use Microsoft Word as the viewer for DOC files; the gopher is already configured to use WinGIF for GIF files and HiJaak for JPEG files.

When you select the GIF entry from the AVES root menu, you'll receive a menu of about 100 GIF files of various birds. When you select a an entry from this menu, WSGopher will bring up a dialog box prompting you for a local directory and file name. When you fill in this box and give the OK, WSGopher will download the file to your computer and, if you've requested immediate viewing of downloads, it will start the viewer installed for GIF files. Figure 6.7 shows the WSGopher screen after a download.

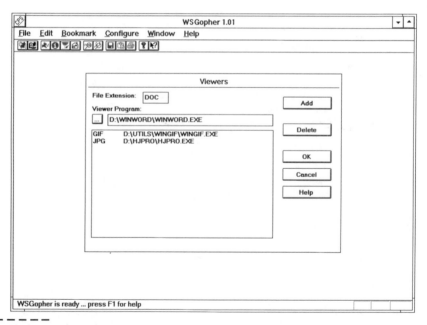

Figure 6.6 Configuring viewers for WSGopher.

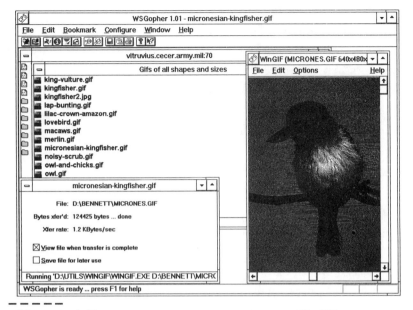

Figure 6.7 Viewing a GIF file with WSGopher and WinGIF.

A Menu of One's Own

One of the most powerful features of the gopher software is that you can generate custom menus tailored to your interests: you aren't stuck with navigating through someone else's preprogrammed menus, and you don't have to depend on trial and error to find interesting gopher resources. The more gopher servers there are, the easier it is to get lost in gopherspace. Tools that help you find things easily and record the location of interesting gopher items are invaluable.

There are four different tools to help you stay oriented in gopherspace: *bookmarks, index searches,* and the ever-popular jughead and veronica. Bookmarks are a feature of gopher client programs. Setting a bookmark allows you to keep a list of gopher menus and items that you visit frequently. This list resides on the computer where you run the gopher client. At any time during a gopher session, you can retrieve this list and use it as you would any other menu. Index searches are done outside of gopher by another application entirely (usually the Wide-Area Index Search system, WAIS). Fortunately, gopher provides a friendly interface to submit keyword searches to WAIS, and quite a few WAIS databases are accessible through gopher. To use WAIS from gopher, you'll have to depend on whoever maintains the WAIS database you're interested in to provide both an index and a gopher menu item that allows you to submit queries.

veronica and jughead are databases that contain information about what is available in gopherspace. They provide roughly the same service for gopher that archie provides for ftp. The veronica database stores the names of menu items in all the gopher servers that can be reached from the University of Minnesota gopher. When you query the veronica database you'll be prompted for keywords, and veronica will return a list of gopher items whose descriptions contain those keywords. jughead does the same sort of thing on a smaller scale, allowing you to query the menu items at a single site or at a small number of sites. jughead queries also require you to enter keywords for the subjects you're interested in. Menu items representing that subject area are returned to you as a menu. jughead gives a slightly different view of gopherspace, and it will allow you to combine keywords using AND, OR, and NOT as operators.

Bookmarks in gopher

Navigating through directories one level at a time using menus is easy but tedious. If there are gopher menus that you use frequently, bookmarks are a way to relieve the tedium and save some time. Bookmarks are shortcuts that take you directly to the desired menu or item without winding through all its parent menus.

If you're using an ASCII gopher client, and you've located a menu item that you know you'll want to visit again, simply position the cursor on that item and type **a** to add the item to your list of bookmarks. If you've found a directory that contains a number of interesting items, you can add a bookmark for the current directory by typing **A** at the gopher prompt. Doing this will add access information for the current item to a local file that stores the configuration of your gopher client. (If you're doing this on your Internet access provider's computer, your bookmarks will be kept in a gopher configuration file named .gopherrc.) You can view a list of your bookmarks by typing

ADDING BOOKMARKS BY HAND — — — — — — — — — — —

When you add a bookmark during a gopher session, you must first maneuver to the item or directory that you're interested in and then use the gopher client's command to add a bookmark. If you're using a conventional dialup session to reach an Internet access provider, you'll find your bookmarks in a gopher configuration file on your access provider's computer. On UNIX systems, for example, this file is called .gopherrc. If you use a protocol dialup connection from your home computer, there will be a gopher configuration file on your machine. On DOS systems look for a file named gopher.rc; Windows systems may store bookmarks in a file with the .ini suffix (WSGopher uses wsgopher.ini, for example); the bookmark file for the Macintosh TurboGopher is named BookMark. The TurboGopher's bookmark files are in a different format from those used by DOS and UNIX. The file Inside-TurboGopher that accompanies the TurboGopher release explains the format and procedures for handling bookmark files on the Macintosh.

On UNIX, DOS, and some Windows systems, you can add bookmarks manually by editing the gopher configuration files mentioned above. The changes you need to make are not complicated. The .gopherrc file will contain a section labeled "bookmarks," and each bookmark contains

the same five fields that are returned by a gopher client's "=" command.
In the .gopherrc file a bookmark will look something like this:

```
bookmarks:
Name=InterNIC Bibliography on the Internet
Host=gopher.internic.net
Type=0
Port=70
Path=0/infosource/getting-started/bibliography
```

The Name field provides the menu item name that you'll see when you
display bookmarks. The Host field contains a fully qualified domain
name for the host to which you wish to connect. The Type field describes what type of object this menu item represents. In the example
above, Type is set to 0 because the bookmark points to a file. (For the
names and identifiers for gopher item types, see Table 6.1.) The Port
field is the port number needed to connect to the resource the bookmark points to. The example bookmark indicates port 70, the port reserved for gopher servers. The file the bookmark points to can be
retrieved via the gopher server on gopher.internic.net. The Path
field repeats the item identifier (0) and gives the directory path that
leads to the file.

v at the gopher menu prompt. Gopher will display the bookmarks to
you as a menu, and you can move to any item by simply selecting it.
If you want to delete a bookmark from the list, first issue a v command to display the list. Position the cursor on the item to be deleted
and type d. Because bookmarks are stored in your local configuration
file, they are present whenever you start a gopher session. See the accompanying sidebar for information on adding bookmarks by editing your gopher configuration file.

GUI gopher clients also support the bookmark feature, and some, like WSGopher, have sophisticated features for managing bookmarks. WSGopher comes with a generous supply (more than 150) of predefined bookmarks. WSGopher divides bookmarks into categories to make them more manageable. Figure 6.8 shows the WSGopher Edit Bookmarks dialog box. One significant feature of WSGopher's bookmark handling is the ability to retrieve the root menu of the gopher server that a bookmark points to.

Veronica and Jughead: Indexes to Gopherspace

Veronica (besides being Archie's friend in the comic books) is also a tortured acronym that is usually interpreted as "Very Easy Rodent-Oriented Net-wide Index to Computer Archives." It performs for

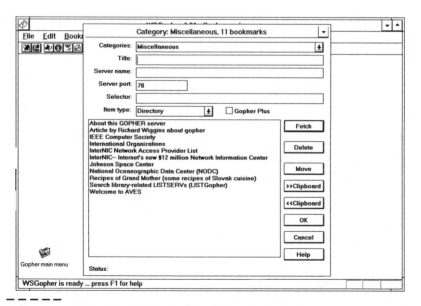

Figure 6.8 The WSGopher Edit Bookmarks dialog box.

LOCATING VERONICA SERVERS - - - - - - - - - - -

Veronica databases can be queried at any of the sites listed below in gopher bookmark format. You can add these entries to your .gopherrc file
as bookmarks so that you're never more than a menu away from being
able to query a veronica database. The availability of veronica servers
is one of the items discussed in the veronica FAQ.

University of Nevada at Reno:

```
Name=SCS Nevada
Host=comics.scs.unr.edu
Port=800
Path=
```

NYSERNET, New York:

```
Name=Search veronica database at NYSERNET
Host=nysernet.org
Type=7
Port=2347
Path=
```

Performance Systems International (PSINet), Virginia:

```
Name=PSINet
Host=gopher.psi.com
Type=7
Port=2347
Path=-
```

University of Pisa, Italy:

```
Name=U. Pisa
Host=serra.unipi.it
Type=7
Port=2347
Path=
```

University of Texas at Dallas:

```
Type=7
Name=U.Texas, Dallas
Path=-t1
Host=veronica.utdallas.edu
Port=2348
Type=7
```

SUNET, Sweden:

```
Name=SUNET
Path=-t1
Host=veronica.sunet.se
Port=2347
```

University of Manitoba, Canada:

```
Type=7
Name=U. of Manitoba
Path=-t1
Host=gopher.umanitoba.ca
Port=2347
```

UNINET/University of Bergen, Norway:

```
Type=7
Name=UNINET/U. of Bergen
Path=-t1
Host=veronica.uib.no
Port=2347
```

University of Koeln, Germany:

```
Type=7
Name=University of Koeln
Path=-t1
Host=veronica.uni-koeln.de
Port=2347
```

gopher the same service that archie provides for ftp archives: it is a searchable index of the titles of menu items on gopher servers throughout the Internet. gopher has become an immensely popular tool for publishing information in the Internet community. However, as more gopher servers have come on-line, the job of searching through gopher menus to find what you're looking for has become more complicated. veronica is an application that maintains a database of menu item titles from any gopher server that can be reached from the Mother Gopher at the University of Minnesota. There are veronica databases at a number of different sites, and their contents vary somewhat. You may need to query more than one of them to find the information you're looking for. (See the accompanying sidebar for the location of these databases.)

Veronica databases are queried from a gopher menu. The menu item you select to begin a veronica search has the same icon as other index searches (<?>). Figure 6.9 shows the screen that prompts for keywords in a veronica query. In this example, a dialup user working

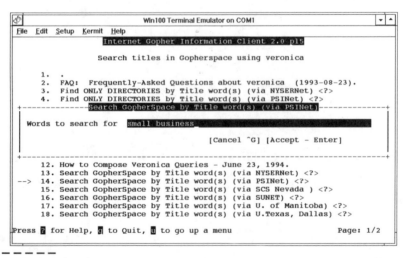

Figure 6.9 Entering keywords for a Veronica query.

with an ASCII gopher client queries the veronica database at PSI-NET. The menu from which we're querying provides access to several veronica servers and allows us to set the scope of the query. A query of gopherspace will return menu items of any type. You can choose a veronica search that only looks for a match in gopher menu items that point to directories. Directory queries generally return faster, but querying all of gopherspace will give you a more detailed picture of what is available. The prompt for keywords reminds you of which type of query you selected. To query for menu item titles containing the words *small* or *business*, you simply type those words and press Return. The results of this query will be displayed as a menu, and the first page of the result menu is shown in Figure 6.10. This query produced enough menu items to require 12 menu screens. Note that if you specify more than one keyword for your search, veronica will return menu items that contain either or both of your keywords.

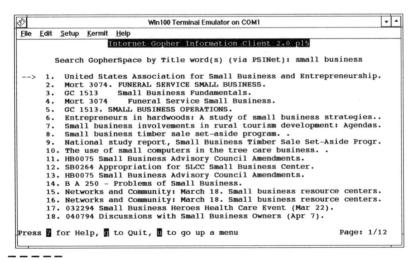

Figure 6.10 Veronica query results.

The interface for jughead queries is essentially the same. jughead, however, recognizes the operators AND, OR, and NOT in queries, so your queries can be phrased with much greater precision to retrieve just the directory items you want. (Just for the record, jughead is another tortured acronym, standing for "Jonzy's Universal Gopher Hierarchy Excavation And Display." Jughead is also, of course, another character from the Archie comics.)

TIP –

You can limit the scope of your veronica queries manually by including with your keywords a selector that restricts the query to items of a certain type. The format for this is -t<*itemtype*> where <*itemtype*> is the single-character identifier for one of gopher's menu item types. (See Table 6.2 for a list of item types and identifiers.)

Index Searches

Like any other menu-based system, gopher makes your access to information easier by giving you a clear view of your choices at every step of the way. Often, however, you will have only the names of the menu items to guide you in making selections from gopher menus, and you'll have to do a lot of browsing to find what you want. If the group of files you're interested in has been indexed, you can use the index to identify files that contain the keywords you specify. Usually you will be dependent on whoever publishes the files to provide an index.

One clear example of the power of index searches is The Electronic Newsstand, a service that carries excerpts from and subscription information for a number of current periodicals. *The New Republic*, for example, gets its Internet presence via the Electronic Newsstand gopher. The Electronic Newsstand is a prototype for one kind of commercial use of the Internet. It is a service that is free on the Internet, but carries information to facilitate doing business off-line. The root menu for this gopher server is shown in Figure 6.11.

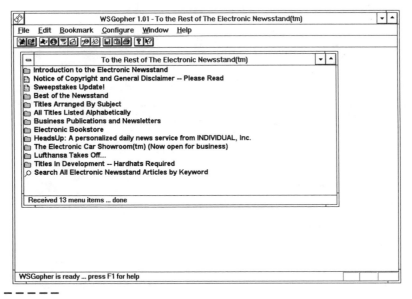

Figure 6.11 The root menu for the Electronic Newsstand seen from WSGopher.

The last item on the Electronic Newsstand's root menu is an index search of all the articles the Newsstand has on-line. The WSGopher icon for index searches is a magnifying glass. If you're using the terminal-based gopher client, index searches appear as menu items with the <?> icon. When you select an index search item, you'll be prompted for the keywords you want to look up in the index. Figure 6.12 shows this prompt from WSGopher. The keywords *biotech*

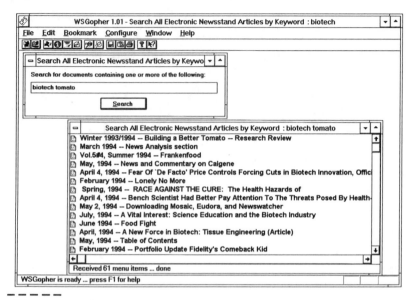

Figure 6.12 Index search prompt and results.

and *tomato* are already filled in. (If you specify several keywords, most indexes searchable through gopher will count a file containing any of the words as a successful match.) The query is executed by pressing the Search button, and the first screen of items found by the query is shown. If nothing in the index matches your keywords, the resulting menu will contain an item saying there were no matches and possibly offering suggestions for phrasing queries effectively or a description of the contents of the index. The important thing is that the responses come back in the form of a gopher menu. You can retrieve any article by selecting its menu entry, and you can create bookmarks for these entries if there are articles that you know you'd like to visit repeatedly.

Further into Gopherspace

A little gopher knowledge will go a long way. You've learned the basics of starting a gopher client and probing for information with menus, bookmarks, the veronica database, and index searches. Once you're comfortable using gopher to find Internet resources, you may find that gopher is the ideal tool for producing an information resource of your own and publishing it for the Internet community. Setting up a gopher server is only slightly more complicated than using a gopher client. To learn about creating gopher servers or to develop more advanced skills using gopher, you'll need some additional documentation.

Documentation on the Internet comes in many forms. There are FAQs (compilations of Frequently Asked Questions) about many topics. FYIs (For Your Information bulletins) and RFCs (Requests for Comment) are generated to inform the Internet community of (and invite commentary about) proposed standards. In the USENET Net News there are open forums about a wide range of topics (Net News is discussed in detail in Chapter 8). gopher documentation comes in all of these forms. There is a gopher FAQ that is updated periodically. Information about the design of gopher and the gopher protocol can be found in RFC 1436. And gopher is the subject of a USENET newsgroup named comp.infosystems.gopher. (For more information about the RFCs and FYIs, see Appendix B: Internet Documentation.)

The best way to get to all these pieces of documentation is, naturally, via gopher. The Mother Gopher's root menu contains an item titled "Information About Gopher" that will lead you to practically all the sources of information about gopher. (This is the first menu item on the Mother Gopher's root menu. The contents of the "Information About Gopher" menu are shown in Figure 6.13. A separate FAQ for veronica is maintained at the University of Nevada at Reno and is available via gopher. Finally, if you're working on a UNIX system

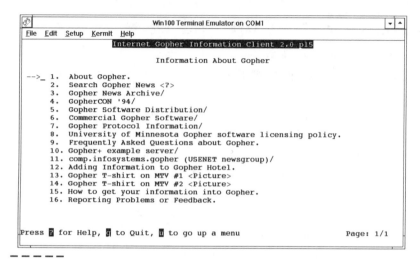

Figure 6.13 Information About Gopher Menu

HUNTING THROUGH THE INTERNET - - - - - - - -

Question   It's been a long time since 1967. Have there been any recent plans to levitate buildings?

Answer   An attempt was made to levitate the San Francisco Stock Exchange on October 29, 1993. We have no record of its outcome. Using gopher, navigate to a menu from which you can query veronica. Veronica offers two kinds of queries: one for directory names only and another for menu titles of all types. It's hard to believe there would be a whole directory about levitating public buildings. Querying for items of any type containing the word *levitate* produces two entries: one inquiring about magnetic levitation, and the other an invitation to join in the levitation of the S.F. Stock Exchange. This item once resided on the ecosystem.drdr.virginia.edu gopher. Attempts to retrieve it fail with the message that the item is no longer there. Its title, however, is still in the veronica database.

Question   Where does the nuthatch winter?

Answer   The white-breasted nuthatch is a small bird like a chickadee that resides in southern Canada, the US, and northern Mexico. It can be found in Alberta and Saskatchewan only in the Winter.
Another `veronica` query: From your favorite `gopher`, move to a menu from which you can issue a `veronica` query. Querying menu titles of all types for the word *nuthatch* will turn up two entries, both on the AVES `gopher`:

```
white-breasted-nuthatch.readme
white-breasted-nuthatch.gif
```

The readme entry includes a short paragraph about the bird's habitat, but it doesn't explain why the nuthatch would seek out Alberta and Saskatchewan in their coldest months.

---

that has the `gopher` client software installed, the first place to look for help is the on-line manual. Type `man gopher` to see the manual entry for the client program. If the `gopher` manual pages have not been installed, you'll get the message "No manual entry for gopher."

In the next chapter we'll learn about the World Wide Web, an application that uses hypertext to perform many of the same services as `gopher`.

Browsing the World Wide Web

It was lunch time, and the Completely Detached Observer walked down a sunny sidewalk, asking anyone who dared to make eye contact with him what the Internet was like.

- "It's a bulletin board for computer science graduate students," said a man in a suit.

- Someone nearby overheard this and took exception. "No, man, it's more like a sports bar," the stranger said between bites of roast turkey on rye. "I followed the Olympics on the Internet in February, the World Cup in June, and I can dabble in cricket and hockey if I feel like it. I haven't met any nerds yet."

- The first man was about to respond when a woman a few feet away suggested that the Internet was like a virtual reality game. A kid on a skateboard heard this and stopped to listen in:
- "Really," the man in a suit persisted, "I'm quite sure it's just for nerds."
- "Well, I got this great recipe for clam-parsley sauce from the Internet," someone else chimed in. "Whoever put that on the 'net cooks better than any computer science student I ever met."
- "Can we talk some more about sports?" the stranger with turkey on rye interjected.
- "No! I want to talk about music. A friend of mine got an actual recording off the Internet and played it on her computer at work. The speakers were awful, but the song was pretty good."
- "What about the Dead Sea Scrolls?" the virtual reality woman inquired. "I saw an on-line version of the Dead Sea Scroll exhibit, and it was very far out."
- Someone else walked up to the small crowd of people: "I've been reading Philosophy on the Internet, and I think it's the seedbed for a new humanism in the postmodern era."
- "Speaking of seedbeds, my tomatoes aren't doing too well. Has anybody found any gardening hints on the Internet?"
- "None of you knows beans about the Internet," the man in the suit shouted. There was an awkward silence.
- "I guess," the kid on the skateboard said at last, "we're all nerds, now."

From Trees to Webs

When you use a menu-driven application (such as gopher) to find information, you are guided through the complexities of the Internet in an orderly way. At every step, a menu provides a neat picture of your current location and your choices for further action. Many people find the "tree" metaphor useful for understanding menu-based systems: your search begins at the "root" menu and moves through various levels of branches until you finally arrive at the "leaf" level of the menu tree where you find the information you're after. If the information you retrieve through a menu-based system is incomplete, or if it raises new questions, you'll go back to the root menu and search through the menu tree again looking for something that addresses these new issues. In a conventional menu-based system, every search ends at the leaf level: the files to which the menus lead don't point to other resources that might be useful.

In the Internet community there are visionaries promoting a different way of organizing information, and this alternative view has become the fastest-growing application on the Internet and a mainstream phenomenon. In place of a tree-shaped menu structure, imagine a "web," in which there are as few "dead ends" as possible. In this vision of how to structure information, even the files and documents you retrieve should be capable of pointing beyond themselves to other useful or related resources. The application that implements this vision on the Internet is the World Wide Web (also known as W^3, WWW, or the Web).

The Origins of the Web

W^3 was developed at CERN (European Center for Nuclear Research), an institution for high-energy physics research in Geneva,

Switzerland. Its original purpose was to promote the sharing of research materials and collaboration between physicists at many different locations. W^3 quickly developed an eager following outside the High-Energy Physics (HEP) community, and there are now more than 3100 W^3 servers worldwide. This count and some other statistics about W^3's growth were done by Matthew Gray of MIT (`mkgray@mit.edu`). W^3 is very strongly represented in Europe, and has recently caught on in North America. The Web has also begun to attract an audience outside the academic world. You'll find Web Servers for the *Encyclopedia Britannica*, the city of Palo Alto, CA, and the 1998 Winter Olympics. CERN has very generously made W^3 available to this larger audience and continues to encourage the proliferation of servers.

W^3 is a client/server application that is similar to `gopher` in many respects. Like `gopher`, W^3 lets you retrieve information without having to know where on the Internet that information is stored. When you first use W^3, it will probably seem a lot like `gopher`. At every step of the way, you'll have clearly identified choices presented to you in menus. Like `gopher`, W^3 provides an interface to other Internet applications such as `gopher`, `ftp`, or WAIS (Wide Area Information Search). However, W^3 has included a subject catalog from the outset, and even though the catalog is incomplete, it is a tremendous help in guiding the curious to resources of interest. W^3 is also the only Internet application that is *hypertext-based*. Hypertext is what gives W^3 its web-like character.

The Web and Hypertext

Hypertext is a word first coined in the mid-sixties by Ted Nelson, the founder of the Xanadu Project, to describe texts that offer alternatives to sequential reading. Today hypertext has come to signify electronically annotated documents that are linked to other documents (and potentially to graphics or to recorded sounds) that may help interpret or clarify the parent document.

Imagine reading something and finding a word whose meaning you don't know. If you're reading plain text, you set it aside and look up the word in a dictionary. If you're reading hypertext, you select the unknown word to find any explanations that are linked to it. The explanation may in turn have links to other documents as well. Pursuing the links from document to document can lead to topics and ideas that might not have occurred to you just from reading the original document.

There is nothing about hypertext that forces it to be graphically sophisticated, and some of the hypertext resources you'll encounter on the Internet will be simple text files that happen to have links. You'll also encounter hypertext documents that are masterpieces of graphic design, and these give W^3 its reputation as an application that is best enjoyed from a graphical interface. The trail of hyperlinks isn't limited to documents alone. It can also lead to pictures or audio recordings. The word "hypermedia" has been coined to describe these annotated mixed-media presentations. If your computer has graphics and sound capabilities (and if you're using the right W^3 client), you'll get all the sights and sounds that have been programmed into W^3 resources. If your system doesn't support these media, the Web will deliver its resources to you as text only.

Creating hypertext is labor-intensive. Ideally every word in a document could have links to other sources of information, and links between documents don't just happen. They are made ("built") using a hypertext editor that encodes text in a language capable of expressing the text's links to other documents. Some of the resources you'll encounter on W^3 will be plain hypertext, and even the hypertext documents may not be as heavily linked as you would like. The influence of hypertext is apparent throughout W^3, however. The underlying protocol used by W^3 is the hypertext transfer protocol

(HTTP), and the Hypertext Markup Language (HTML) is used to produce and link documents. Working with W^3, you'll see that the distinction between menus and documents or files becomes fuzzy; W^3 menus tend to be wordy because they are actually documents. Documents, because they have links that lead to other resources, begin to take on a menu-like appearance.

How the Web Works

It's possible to build a collection of hypertext documents that don't use a network at all. In that case, all the linked documents must reside on the same computer. The Web successfully combines hypertext with client/server architecture. The startling thing about W^3 is that it is a hypertext system in which the links from a document can point anywhere on the Internet.

The interaction between W^3 clients and servers resembles the gopher client/server dialog: The client connects to a server long enough to submit one request and receive a reply. In W^3, client requests take the form of URLs, Uniform Resource Locators. At first glance, URLs may look like gibberish. However, with a little practice at identifying fully qualified domain names and e-mail addresses, you can learn to read URLs without much effort. URLs looks like this:

```
http://info.cern.ch/hypertext/WWW/TheProject.html
```

URLs consist of a resource type (`http` in this case), the name in FQDN format of the computer (`info.cern.ch`) that contains the resource, an optional port number for connecting to the computer just named, and a pathname for the resource itself (`hypertext/WWW/TheProject.html`). (The other characters are field separators.) Other information can be added to the URL as well, but file-type, machine-name, port number, and pathname are the essential fields.

When you browse through a W^3 document, the hyperlinks pointing to other documents all represent URLs. When you select a hyperlink, your W^3 client will read the attached URL and send a request to the appropriate server for the linked document. Most of the time this happens behind your back, and you don't need to be particularly conscious of URLs to use the Web. However, many browsers will also allow you to steer through the Web by entering URLs manually, and occasionally, this is just what you'll want to do.

Choosing a Browser

The client software you use to look at hypertext is called a browser. Browsers give you a clear view of where the links are in a hypertext document and a way of following links from one document to another. W^3 browsers are also client programs: they interact with a server to retrieve documents; and of course, the W^3 server must work with browsers in all sorts of display environments. Among W^3 clients, you'll find ASCII line-mode browsers, several full-screen browsers for use with ASCII terminals, and browsers for graphical user interfaces (GUIs) such as Xwindows, Microsoft Windows, and the Macintosh. If your Internet access is via a conventional dialup connection, you'll need either a full-screen browser like Lynx or the line-mode browser www.

If your computer has a graphical user interface and you access the Internet via a protocol dialup connection, there are a number of GUI browsers available. You can reach W^3 resources with any kind of browser, but GUI browsers can use your computer's audio and visual capabilities to make Web browsing more enjoyable. The examples in this chapter will use either the line-mode browser or Cello Browser for Windows. Cello is available from the Legal Information Institute at Cornell University. Another popular browser that is available for

Windows, X Windows, and Macintosh is the Mosaic browser from the National Center for Super-computing Activity (NCSA) at the University of Illinois, Urbana-Champaign. See the accompanying sidebar for instructions on locating W^3 browsers you can download from the Internet.

 LOCATING WORLD WIDE WEB BROWSERS – – – – – –

Browsers for W^3 are available via anonymous `ftp` from various sites. You can obtain the line-mode browser and a number of GUI browsers for different platforms from CERN. Connect to `info.cern.ch` and move to the directory /pub/www. The README file in this directory has up-to-date information concerning the software that is available. Already-compiled software can be found under the bin directory. This directory has subdirectories holding browsers for different computers and operating systems. Choose the computer platform you're interested in, and `cd` to that directory. The Cello browser for Windows is available at CERN. We'll discuss below how to obtain it from the Legal Information Institute at Cornell University.

The Lynx full-screen browser is available from the University of Kansas at `ukanaix.cc.ukans.edu`. The directory that contains the software is /pub/WWW/lynx. In this directory you'll find the Lynx browser compiled for several platforms and a compressed `tar` archive of the source code. Compiled versions of the www full-screen browser can be found at `www.njit.edu` in the /dist directory.

The National Center for Super-computing Activities at the University of Illinois, Urbana-Champaign publishes the Mosaic browser for Windows, Macintosh, and X Windows. You can obtain any of these browsers at `ftp.ncsa.uiuc.edu`. This is an extremely busy `ftp` site, and you may have difficulty connecting. The Mosaic distribution is also available at `sunsite.unc.edu`. Whichever site you choose will have a README file to direct you to the Mosaic releases.

The line-mode browser is the most primitive, but it has the great advantage that you can use it with almost any display terminal and with any kind of connection to the Internet. To start the line-mode browser, log into your Internet access provider's computer, type **www**, and press ↵. If all goes well, you'll see a "home page" similar to the one shown in Figure 7.1. If your **www** command results in a "www: Command not found" message, try again using the full path-name: **/usr/local/bin/www**. If this also returns a "Command not found" message, the line-mode browser is probably not installed on the machine you use for Internet access. If you don't have local access to the line-mode browser, you can still access W^3 by using `telnet` to connect to `info.cern.ch`. (CERN is the home of W^3.) The line-mode browser will start as soon as the `telnet` connection is made.

Full-screen browsers are a step up. They show you W^3 documents a screen at a time and use the display capability of your terminal (highlighting, reverse video, or underlining) and cursor-movement

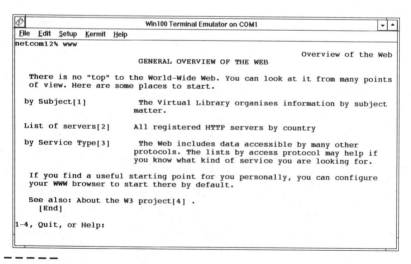

Figure 7.1 Reading the CERN home page with the line-mode browser.

keys. You can use a full-screen browser over any kind of Internet connection, but if you're working on a UNIX system, you'll have to tell it what kind of terminal you're using. There are several browsers available. The Lynx browser was developed at the University of Kansas, and offers a good selection of features. (Its home page display is shown in Figure 7.2.) It allows you to search through the current document for strings. This is particularly useful if the document contains more than a few links. It also supports bookmarks. If you'd like to test the Lynx browser, `telnet` to `ukanaix.cc.ukans.edu` and log in as www. Another full-screen browser is www. To use this browser, `telnet` to `www.njit.edu` and log in as www. Instructions for retrieving these browsers via `ftp` appear in the sidebar above.

Neither line-mode nor full-screen browsers will be able to display graphics or play sounds for you; for that, you'll need a GUI browser. For example, W^3 can lead you to the catalog for an exhibit of medieval art and historical documents from the Vatican. With a line-mode browser, you can read the modern commentary from the catalog, but

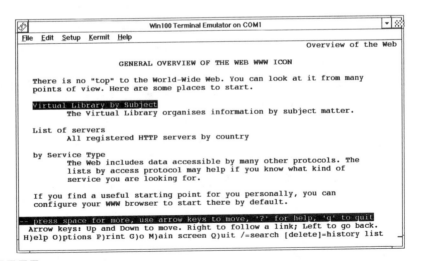

Figure 7.2 The W^3 overview from the Lynx browser.

INSTALLING CELLO - - - - - - - - - - - - - - -

The Cello Browser is a GUI browser for Windows. Cello is winsock-compliant. As with the other clients discussed in this book, you should already have your network software installed and working before installing Cello. (The Cello release consists of the browser only; no network protocol software is included.) It is available via anonymous **ftp** from **fatty.law.cornell.edu.** Here are the steps for copying the software and installing it:

1. Use anonymous **ftp** to connect to **fatty.law.cornell.edu.** When you connect, check for README files with up-to-date information on the location of the Cello distribution. Move to the appropriate directory, and read any instructions for downloading that are posted there.

2. Set **ftp's** file type to binary and download the Cello archive (cello.zip).

3. Put the archive in a directory by itself on your computer and unpack it. To do this, you'll need a utility (like PKUNZIP) that can extract files from ZIP archives.

4. Read the file readme.1st that accompanies each Cello release. This file contains detailed installation instructions. Cello should be ready to run immediately after you've unpacked, but it does need to be told which directories to use for downloads and temporary files. (By default, temporary files are stored in the directory that the DOS TEMP variable points to. See the Cello installation instructions for information about changing this.)

with a GUI browser, you'll be able to see the pictures and view facsimiles of the documents from the comfort of your own computer.

Some GUI browsers will allow you to look at several documents at once in different windows. Figure 7.3 shows the W^3 overview from the Cello browser. The drawback to GUI browsers is that they are very resource-intensive. Running a GUI browser on a slow modem, a slow computer, or a computer that has only a modest amount of memory installed can tax your patience. Running a GUI browser on a fast modem with a fast machine and lots of memory will remind you why you invested in the fancy hardware in the first place.

Using a Browser

When you first start any W^3 client, you'll see the browser's "home page," a page of information that contains links to other documents. The line-mode browser is set up to use a local copy of the home page

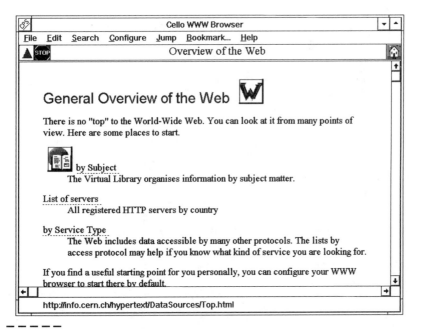

Figure 7.3 The W^3 Overview from the Cello Browser.

shown back in Figure 7.1, which was built at CERN. (The line-mode browser doesn't require a connection to a W^3 server until you select an entry from the local home page.) When you first start the Cello browser, it, too, loads its home page from a local file. (By default, this home page points to a W^3 server at Cornell. If you'd like a different starting point, an alternate home page could be installed in the Cello directory.)

In line-mode browsers, links to other documents are shown as bracketed numbers following the keyword or phrase to which the link is made. At the bottom of the screen there is a prompt that gives you the range of links from which you can choose (1–4 for the overview page shown in Figure 7.1) and a selection of the browser's built-in commands. To follow any link in the current document you type the number of the link. For help with the browser's commands, type **h** or **help**. The line-mode browser's command set is shown in Figure 7.4. All the browser's commands are triggered by pressing ↵. Pressing ↵ without first entering a command advances the display to

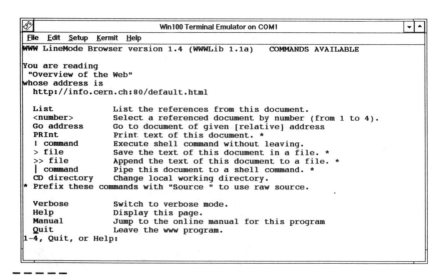

Figure 7.4 W^3 Line-mode browser commands.

the next screenful of the current document. A description of the most important line-mode browser commands appears in the following sidebar.

 BASIC WEB COMMANDS – – – – – – – – – – –

The W3 line-mode browser may not look fancy, but it has a generous set of commands to maneuver through hypertext documents and manage your Web session. GUI browsers also implement most of these commands. The basic commands are:

↵	Display the next page of the current document.
number	The line-mode browser identifies hypertext links with a number enclosed in square brackets. Typing the number of one of the hyperlinks by itself fetches the document that the link points to and displays it.
Back	Return to the parent of the current document.
Home	Return to the first document read in this session, usually a home page.
Recall	Display a numbered list of the documents you have visited. To return to one of these documents, type Recall followed by the number.
List	Display a numbered list of the links from the current document. To follow a link, type the number by itself as above.
Next, Previous	Fetch the document pointed to by the next or previous hypertext link in the parent of the current document.

Go *URL*	Fetch the document represented by the URL (hypertext address).
Up, Down	Scroll up or down one page in the current document.
Top, Bottom	Go to the top or bottom of the current document.
Help	List available commands.
Manual	Jump to the online manual.
Quit	End the current Web session and exit the browser.
> *filename* >> *filename*	On UNIX systems only, saves or appends the current document (without hyperlinks) to the named file.

GUI browsers mark the words or phrases that have hyperlinks attached in a way that doesn't disturb the document's on-screen format. Figure 7.5 shows the Cello browser's home page. This page is loaded from a file (default.htm) in the directory where the Cello browser is installed. Words that have links to other documents are underlined. To retrieve the contents of a hyperlink, you simply click on the link. This page contains hyperlinks for the top-level documents at CERN that we'll look at below. To get to these documents, scroll down in the home page (using the mouse or the PgDn key) to the hyperlink for CERN. Click on this and Cello will retrieve the Overview document from CERN.

GUI browsers typically provide a number of menu commands that can be used to manage your W^3 sessions. In addition to navigation from document to document, the Cello browser includes a Jump feature

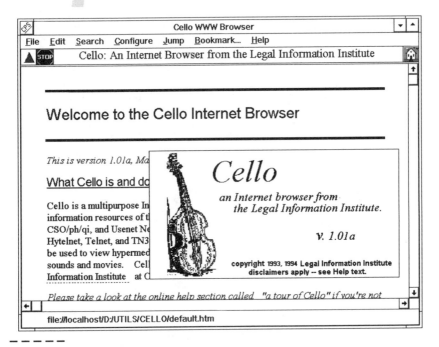

Figure 7.5 The Cello browser's home page.

for moving directly to different documents or even starting other Internet applications without going through intervening menus or documents. (Cello can also be used as a gopher client, for example.) Cello also maintains a history list of URLs visited in the current session and a bookmark list.

How Is Not What

As with gopher, the W^3 browser commands don't begin to describe what you can do with W^3. Fortunately the Web has been set up with a few key documents that serve as navigation tools to help you get and stay oriented. These tools are:

- the CUI W^3 Catalog
- the W^3 Virtual Library (a Subject Catalog of W^3 resources)
- the W^3 List of Servers
- the W^3 Classification of Resources by Type

The CUI Catalog deserves special mention: it is a searchable index of W^3 resources that provide for the Web the same kind of service that archie and veronica provide for other Internet applications.

The CUI W^3 Catalog

The CUI W^3 Catalog is a relatively new addition to the W^3 tool kit from the Centre Universitaire d'Informatique at the University of Geneva in Switzerland. The great advantage of this catalog is that you can submit keyword queries to find resources you're interested in. The response to your query will come back as a hypertext document with descriptive text for each resource and a hyperlink to take you to its full text. This catalog hasn't yet found its way to the CERN overview page. It is so important a resource, however, that it's worth learning the relatively simple URLs that lead to it and setting a bookmark that will get you to this catalog easily:

```
http://cui_www.unige.ch/w3catalog
http://cui_www.unige.ch/cgi-bin/htgrep/file=W3catalog/isindex.ht
ml
```

There are two URLs because the catalog has two interfaces. The main interface for the CUI catalog is set up for newer W^3 clients that support query by forms. (The NCSA Mosaic browsers for X Windows, Windows, and Macintosh have this feature.) The second URL is for clients (like the line-mode and Cello browsers) that don't yet support query by forms. If you're using the line-mode browser, you can use the URL above with the go command. From the Cello browser, choose the Jump menu button and the URL option from the pull-down menu that follows it. This will bring up a dialog box into which you can type the URL above.

The Cello browser's view of the CUI catalog is shown in Figure 7.6. In this figure, a query for entries containing the phrase *world cup* has returned several hits. Items that satisfy a query are returned in chronological order, with the most recent item first. The *world cup* query returned several items, among them a pointer to the W^3 server for Palo Alto, CA. That link led to the screen in Figure 7.7, describing World Cup events scheduled for Palo Alto.

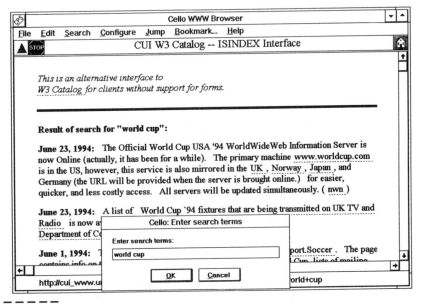

Figure 7.6 The CUI W^3 catalog.

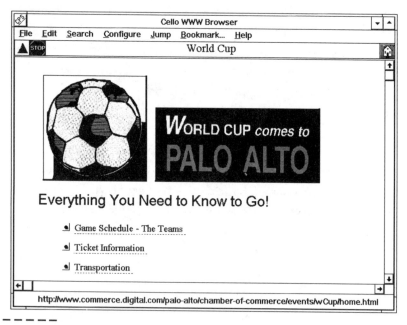

Figure 7.7 A page from the Palo Alto W³ server.

As this example shows, the CUI W³ Catalog is particularly adept at finding W³ resources that might slip through the cracks of a subject-oriented index. The Palo Alto Web server is just the sort of thing that might otherwise be missed.

The W³ Virtual Library

The W³ Virtual Library is a subject catalog of resources that can be reached from W³. The subject index covers everything from Aeronautics to Sports. Cataloging resources systematically by subject is not widely done on the Internet. (An effort is underway to classify gopher resources by subject, but it is far from complete.) It is a refreshing change to be able to think about the subject matter you want to investigate instead of guessing at likely names for files that might have something to do with the area of interest. The first screen of the Virtual Library (as seen from the Cello browser) is shown in Figure 7.8. Some of the subject categories are fairly brief ("Fortune Telling," for example); others have so many entries that they are listed separately in another document. Let's look at one of these in detail.

As you page down the list of subjects, you'll encounter the "Music" category. When you select this category, you'll be led to a list of W^3 resources devoted to various forms of music. Near the bottom of this document is an entry point for the Digital Tradition Database. Selecting that item, your browser will jump to the page shown in Figure 7.9, where you can search for lyrics in various folk songs. (If you're using the line-mode browser, you'll notice that the prompt has

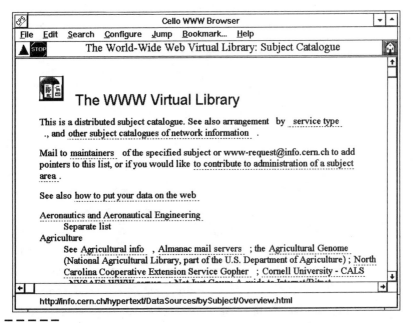

Figure 7.8 The W^3 Virtual Library from the Cello Browser.

changed to include the word FIND. In the Cello browser, a separate dialog box will prompt you for keywords.) To search for songs in this database that refer to the town of Carlow, you simply enter **Carlow** and press Return.

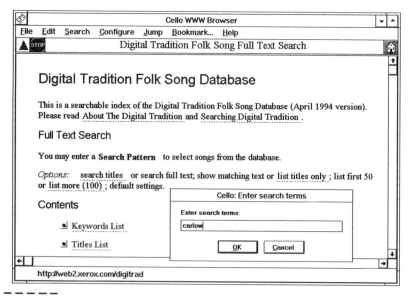

Figure 7.9 Searching the Digital Tradition database.

W³ Gateways to Internet Services

The CERN Overview document contains a hyperlink that leads to a classification of Internet resources by application type (that is, go-pher, ftp, WAIS, WWW). When you jump to this listing, your browser will bring up a W³ document that is a gateway to other Internet applications. (This page appears in Figure 7.10.) From this single page in W³ you can branch to approximately two dozen Internet applications or sources of information. Some of these services (ar-chie, ftp, gopher, and telnet) may already be familiar to you. You'll even find a hypertext version of Scott Yanoff's Internet Services List, containing links that take you directly to many of the resources it contains. Other services (Art St. George's list, WAIS, X.500, for example) may still be unfamiliar to you. You can get to them all from this menu. When you use W^3 as a gateway to other applications, the user interface will resemble W^{3}'s. Let's look at the W^3 gateways to Archie and ftp.

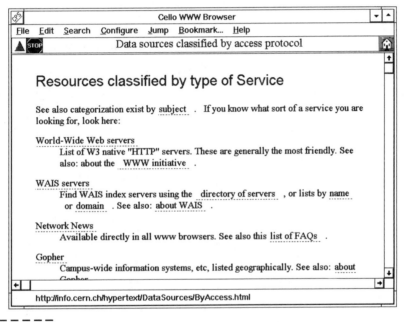

Figure 7.10 Internet services accessible from W^3.

The W³ Gateway to archie and ftp

In Chapter 3 we discussed the use of archie and ftp. You can also use W^3 to perform archie queries and retrieve files via ftp. From the

Web Overview document, follow the link to the "By Type" document. Then select "full hypertext archie gateway," and you'll see the menu shown in Figure 7.11. From this screen you can select any of several kinds of archie query and specify the keywords to be used in searching the archie database. As with the CUI W^3 Catalog, there are different selections for browsers that support form-based queries and browsers that do not. W^3 also provides a choice of archie hypertext servers for you to use. The databases at these sites vary somewhat, and a query that returns no results from one of these databases may find items on another.

In this example the keyword *tomato* is entered. The results of the query are displayed as a page of hypertext that provides hypertext links for the filename that matched the keyword, the directory that contains that file, and the site that maintains the ftp archive in which

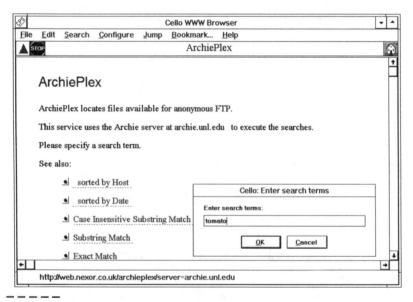

Figure 7.11 The hypertext interface to archie.

the file was found. Selecting any of these links will open an ftp session to the host selected. Selecting the file link retrieves the file and displays it on your screen. Selecting the directory link provides a menu of all the files in that directory. Selecting the host link opens an ftp session starting at the topmost ftp directory on that host.

The W^3 Index to FAQs of All Sorts

Another Internet institution is the FAQ, a compilation of Frequently Asked Questions about some topic. FAQ documents exist for hundreds of topics discussed on the Internet, and they're a very helpful form of documentation if you can find them. Many FAQs are posted to USENET newsgroups regularly, but finding the right newsgroup can sometimes be difficult.

W^3 simplifies this dramatically by collecting links to more than 300 FAQs (about all sorts of topics) in a single hypertext document. In the By Type document, move to the Network News item. In the short description that accompanies this item there is a hypertext link to a list of FAQs. Once you've jumped to this list, retrieving an FAQ requires only that you select a link from this list.

All the W^3 Servers in the World and Their Home Pages

Finally, if you want to get an overview of the world of W^3 servers, W^3 itself is one of the resources in the classification of services by type. When you select the WWW Servers item from the Services By Type document, a menu of available W^3 servers will be displayed. (A portion of this menu is shown in Figure 7.12.) You can connect to any of the servers listed by simply selecting its link from this document. From the list of W^3 servers there is a link to an automatically collected list of "home pages" for various servers. This is a particularly useful list if you are working with either a full-screen or a GUI browser that supports bookmarks. (The line-mode browser does not.)

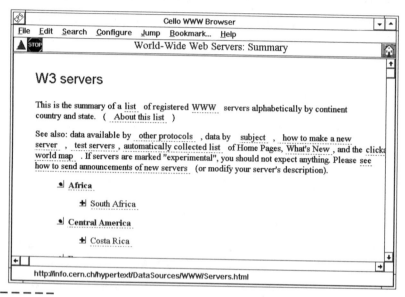

Figure 7.12 The list of World Wide Web servers.

The Appeal of the Web

W^3 is an application in transition. It is breaking out of its traditional role as a medium for academic communications, and being used for publishing all sorts of information in a visually exciting way to Internet audiences. For new users of the Internet, W^3 provides a uniform interface for network applications, effectively hiding the boundaries between those applications. The Web's phenomenal growth continues as it provides an easy way to take advantage of multimedia.

HUNTING THROUGH THE INTERNET – – – – – – – – –

Question 1 Where will the 1998 Winter Olympics be held and what is the official mascot for these games called?

Answer Using the CUI W3 Catalog, query for *olympics*. This will turn up a number of entries. As you scroll down the list, you'll encounter a link for the 1998 Winter Olympics in Nagano, Japan. Jump to this link and scroll down to the link for the official mascot. Jump to that link. If you're using a GUI browser, you'll see a representation of four owl-like figures called "snowlets," the official mascot of the 1998 Winter Olympics.

Question 2 What was the original form of Murphy's Law? Who first stated it and when?

Answer Connect to the Mother Gopher and select "Other Gopher and Information Servers" from the root menu. From this menu select "Search titles in Gopherspace using veronica." That selection will bring up a menu of sites with veronica databases. Pick one and query for *murphy law*. This will return a single menu page of titles that match. (Note that querying for the word "murphy" alone will return many more titles.) The resulting menu contains an entry titled "Murphy's Law," which provides the following information:

```
Murphy's Law: prov. The correct, *original* Murphy's Law reads:
"If there are two or more ways to do something, and one of those
ways can result in a catastrophe, then someone will do it."
<--Entry Truncated-->
Edward A. Murphy, Jr. was one of the engineers on the rocket-sled
experiments that were done by the U.S. Air Force in 1949 to test
human acceleration tolerances (USAF project MX981). One
experiment involved a set of 16 accelerometers mounted to
different parts of the subject's body. There were two ways each
sensor could be glued to its mount, and somebody methodically
installed all 16 the wrong way around. Murphy then made the
original form of his pronouncement, which the test subject
(Major John Paul Stapp) quoted at a news conference a few days
later.
```

CHAPTER 8

The USENET Bazaar

"In downtown Cleveland today, Elvis was sighted on a municipal bus. Stunned onlookers reported that the former king of rock and roll sat quietly at the back of the bus working on a crossword puzzle and whistling 'My Way.'

- "In other news, Silicon Valley chip makers announced plans to build a 64-unit multithreaded vector superprocessor with hardware support for asynchronous task generation. Prototype units, expected in early 1996, will also feature bidirectional optical waveguides and wormhole routing for virtual cut-through communications.

- "On the local front, `rosebody@well.sf.ca.us` pitched a hissy fit over the recent deluge of items in this broadcast regarding the changing of light bulbs. To quote rosebody: 'This is a fine kettle of fish. First, we had the anecdote, then, one respondent quoted the *entire original anecdote* simply to add a two-line comment, and now someone else has quoted that quote, included the original, *and* inadvertently failed to add anything new at all. I can't stand it.'
- "Thanks for sharing that, rosebody!
- "This just in: worms in hostage food! Details at 11:00.
- "New FAQs were posted to `news.answers` today from `soc.culture.hongkong`, `comp.lsi.cad`, and `comp.lang.modula2`.
- "From the weather desk in Chicago: tropical storm Emily now off the coast of Newfoundland is rapidly losing tropical characteristics.
- "And in news.groups, votes are being cast to decide the fates of `sci.chem.labware` and `soc.culture.berber`.
- "That's it for tonight's broadcast. In the words of Scoop Nisker, 'If you don't like the news, go out and make some of your own.' Good night and have a pleasant tomorrow."

The Biggest Bulletin Board in the World

In 1979 students at Duke University and the University of North Carolina constructed a system of UNIX shell scripts to move messages between two computers using the UUCP (UNIX-to-UNIX Copy) protocol over phone lines. (UUCP is a protocol used by UNIX systems to transfer files automatically. One system calls another at a prearranged time. The calling computer logs in to a special user account that runs the file-transfer program.) The messages that moved between Duke and UNC made up a floating bulletin board, a copy of which resided at each site. Discussions in this system were organized by topic, and when a reader of a topic at one site contributed something new to a discussion, that response would be distributed to all the copies of the bulletin board. The participating computers contacted each other regularly (with as little human intervention as necessary) to exchange new topics and responses to topics.

This system went on to become the USENET News, or simply Net News. Net News developed in the UNIX community, initially with no ties to the Internet. Until the mid-1980s, the USENET newsgroups were circulated primarily via UUCP. But more and more of the USENET sites were also Internet hosts, and in 1986, after two years of development, the Network News Transfer Protocol (NNTP) was introduced to the Internet community at large as a tool for distributing Net News. The already popular Network News was projected to an Internet-wide audience. NNTP dramatically increased the efficiency of transferring Net News articles from site to site, and it made the news available through client/server applications. Client/server access brought the Network News to people who did not have a local copy of the newsgroups. As the Internet has grown, so has USENET. Today there are more than 7000 newsgroups distributed via NNTP.

Net News is arguably the world's most comprehensive bulletin board. In spite of the symbiotic relationship between USENET and the Internet, they are not the same thing. There are, for example, sites that still depend on UUCP to exchange news with the USENET and Internet communities, and simply being on the Internet does not guarantee a News feed. Whether or not your local point of contact with the Internet has its own copy of the USENET newsgroups, however, you should be able to connect to a News server and read Net News from almost any Internet host.

Tools for Reading the News

To read the Network News, you need access to an Internet host that carries Net News and a news reader. Ordinarily, you'll get access to a News server from your Internet access provider. Scott Yanoff's Internet Services list contains a pointer to a list of publicly accessible News servers as well.

A news reader is a program that manages your subscriptions to newsgroups. It keeps track of what groups you're interested in and what articles you've already read in those groups. As new articles are posted to the newsgroups you follow, the news reader lets you read and respond to these postings. Before the development of NNTP, news readers were conventional, stand-alone programs, and could only be used on computers that had local access to the text of the newsgroups. NNTP fostered the development of news readers as client programs that could be used anywhere on a local network to read the news from a central location. You'll find news readers of both types in use throughout the Internet.

If you're using a conventional dialup connection to connect to an Internet access provider, you'll use either a line-mode reader or a full-screen reader. Line-mode readers present newsgroups and articles in groups one line at a time. Full-screen readers present a somewhat larger view of both the groups and articles, but to do this they need some information about what kind of terminal you're reading the news from. Readnews is a line-mode reader that is widely distributed, but not well-suited to reading a large number of newsgroups. Its main advantages are that it is in wide distribution, has a command set that is easy to learn, and can be run on almost any terminal available. Vnews, rn and nn are screen-oriented news readers that are also available at many sites. The ability to scroll through a list of newsgroups is a distinct advantage over line-mode readers, but the older screen-oriented readers like rn may be difficult for novices. Fancier still are the trn and tin readers. These, too, are screen oriented, but they offer the added benefit of organizing news articles into conversational *threads*. Each thread contains an original article and all responses to that article. Packaging articles and responses together makes for easier reading and cuts down on redundant and misinformed responses.

We'll use the tin reader for conventional dialup examples because it has an easy-to-read display and shows off threads nicely. Tin is a particularly good news reader for new users. It has a relatively simple command set, its help screens are uncluttered, and its documentation is succinct and written clearly. There are more popular news readers, but tin is widely distributed and easy to use.

If you use a protocol dialup connection to reach the Internet, you'll find news readers for various graphical interfaces (Windows, X Windows, and Macintosh) readily available via anonymous ftp. Trumpet and WinVN are popular news readers for Windows. The WinVN news reader will be discussed later in this chapter, where you'll find instructions for downloading and installing it.

You can get information about further developments in news reader software from USENET itself in the newsgroup news.software.readers. Here you'll find plenty of discussion about news reader features, and you're likely to find an article written by Gene Spafford (and now maintained by Mark Moraes) that gives a detailed view of the history of Net News software development. This article is also posted to other groups that help explain USENET news to newcomers: news.answers and news.announce.newusers. If you don't want to wait for the next posting of this article, it is also available via anonymous ftp in the pub/usenet/news.answers/usenet-software directory at pit-manager.mit.edu.

Reading the News with tin

Starting the tin news reader is just like executing any other program on your Internet access provider's computer: just type tin and press ↵. A first-time user starting tin on an Internet host will see a screen like the one shown in Figure 8.1. Some versions of tin may precede this Group Selection screen with a page of instructions and command help.

Tin has a structured approach to news reading. First, you select a newsgroup from a list of groups. Tin organizes any messages in that group that you haven't read yet into threads (groups of related messages). The threads are presented in a screen that you can scroll through. When you choose a thread to read, the articles in that thread will be displayed one at a time.

The first screen tin presents is the Group Selection screen shown in Figure 8.1. This screen gives an overview of the groups you've subscribed to and allows you to pick a group to read. When you run tin for the first time (and haven't yet subscribed to any newsgroups), you'll be

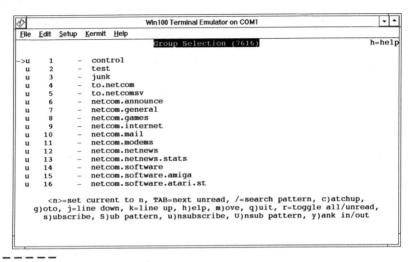

Figure 8.1 Starting the tin news reader for the first time.

given a list of *all* the newsgroups that are active at your site. This list can be quite long. Your Internet access provider does not have to accept all the newsgroups that are offered to it, but many access providers try to carry as many newsgroups as possible. The center portion of the Group Selection screen is a window showing 16 newsgroups. At the left edge of the screen is a single-letter status indicator. In this case, none of the groups has been read previously (u indicates unread). Following the status indicator is a selection number. After your first session of reading news, the selection number will be followed by the number of articles currently posted to the newsgroup. The number of articles is based on articles you've left unread plus any new postings since the last time news was read. If you're reading news for the very first time, a dash will be substituted for the number of articles (as in Figure 8.1). Following the numbers is the name of the group.

YOUR NEWSRC FILE – – – – – – – – – – – – – – –

When you first read Net News, you'll be presented with a list of *all* the active newsgroups as though they are all of equal interest. Even a broad-minded person with renaissance proclivities, however, will become more selective when faced with more than 7000 newsgroups. You can make your newsgroup reading more enjoyable by establishing a subscription list tailored to your interests.

Most news readers offer commands to subscribe to and unsubscribe from groups. Information about what you've subscribed to is kept in a local news configuration file. On UNIX systems, this file is named .newsrc, and most news readers are configured to keep subscription information in this file. (Conventions vary on DOS and Windows systems. Usually, however, subscription information will be kept in a file named NEWSRC.) The .newsrc file contains a complete list of the current newsgroups, some indication of which groups you've subscribed to, and a marker identifying what messages you've read in each group. Your news reader expects to manage .newsrc without any human intervention. Don't try to edit a .newsrc file manually.

When you first start a news reading session, your reader will ask the server for the names of any newsgroups that have been added since you last read news. These will be added to your newsrc file, and you'll be asked whether you want to subscribe to these groups and where they should be placed in the sequence of newsgroups you subscribe to. If you're not in the habit of reading news daily, there can be a lot of new groups to make decisions about. Some news readers allow you to start a news session without reviewing new groups. (Tin users can do this by using the command tin -q to start a session. The -q flag will suppress checking for new groups.)

Tin includes a command summary at the bottom of the screen, describing key commands that can be executed from the current screen. This on-screen help can be toggled on and off with the H command. In the Group Selection screen there are commands to manage your subscription to newsgroups and commands to move around in the list of available groups. Type h for a complete list of tin commands.

Subscribing, Unsubscribing, and Catching Up in tin

When you first start tin, take the time to subscribe to newsgroups that interest you. Tin has subscription management commands that can be applied to individual newsgroups or to collections of newsgroups. For individual newsgroups you simply position the current group pointer on a group in your list and issue the subscribe (s) command to subscribe to it. (If you later change your mind and decide to unsubscribe, position the pointer on the group name and issue the u command.) You can also apply a subscription command to any collection of newsgroups whose names share a common pattern; use S to subscribe and U to unsubscribe. After you've entered the command, you'll be prompted for a pattern or keyword that identifies the collection of groups.

In your first tin session, after you've marked the groups you wish to subscribe to, use the y command to yank all the unsubscribed groups out of the group selection screen. In future sessions, you will see only the names of the groups you've subscribed to. You can, in any session, unsubscribe from a newsgroup with the u command. The y command does double duty: in subsequent sessions, if you want to review all the newsgroups in your newsrc file, you can use y to yank them in, subscribe to any interesting groups, and then use y again to yank the unsubscribed groups back out of the list of subscribed groups that tin presents.

Even after you've created a subscription list that reflects your interests, you may not always want to read every posting in a group. If you leave too many things unread, finding new postings can be a chore. The "catch-up" command (c) helps you cope with this by marking everything in a newsgroup as read. After you use the catch-up command, you'll see only new postings for the newsgroup.

Newsgroup Navigation in tin

By default, tin uses reverse video to mark your current position in the newsgroup and article lists. Tin can be configured to use an arrow (->) instead, and we'll use this indicator for clarity's sake. (You can display all the configurable features of tin with the M command.) The highlighted group can be selected at any time by pressing ↵. There are three ways to move around in the list of newsgroups that the group selection screen presents:

- Use control characters to scroll forward (Ctrl-F) and backward (Ctrl-B) in the list of active newsgroups.

- Move to a specific group by typing its number. The group you jump to need not be on the current screen. The display will reposition to the group whose number you type.

- Search the newsgroup list for a word or pattern (the / command searches forward, ? searches backward.)

Searching the titles of the newsgroups is a particularly helpful feature. To find newsgroups about Elvis, for example, you would simply type /elvis and press ↵. (Tin will lead you to alt.elvis.sightings.)

One group that is particularly helpful in getting started with Net News is news.announce.newusers. To find this group with tin, type /newuser and hit ↵. The current group pointer will move to the first group whose name contains the word "newuser." In fact, there are two newsgroups that contain the word "newuser": news.announce.newusers and news.newusers.questions. You can repeat your most recent search by pressing / and then ↵. When the current group pointer is positioned by the group you're interested in, you can display the contents of this newsgroup by pressing ↵.

After you select a group, tin will give you an overview of the contents of the group as a series of threads. Each thread consists of an article and all the responses that have been posted to it. Like the group selection screen, the overview of threads in a newsgroup is organized into a menu. Figure 8.2 shows the overview of threads in the group news.announce.newusers. The name of the current group appears at the top of the screen, followed by the number of threads and the number of articles in the group. The threads are numbered sequentially and you can navigate through them with the same commands as in the Group Selection menu. A plus sign would indicate that the thread contains articles you have not yet read. The second number in each thread entry is the number of articles in that thread, and the last field contains the subject line for the thread.

When you're looking at the contents of a newsgroup, even in summary form, you have several options that were not available at the Group Selection Menu. A summary of these commands appears in the screen shown in Figure 8.2. You can list the contents of each thread by author and date posted with the l command.

When you select any of the threads from this menu, tin will bring up the text of the posted article. When you've finished reading the first

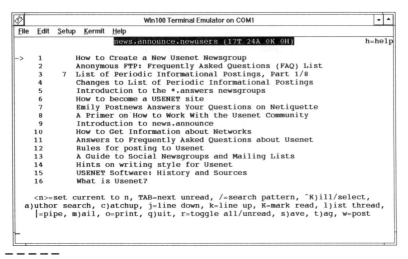

```
┌────────────────────────────────────────────────────────────────────────┐
│ ◊                    Win100 Terminal Emulator on COM1              ▼ │ ▲ │
├────────────────────────────────────────────────────────────────────────┤
│ File  Edit  Setup  Kermit  Help                                          │
│                    news.announce.newusers (17T 24A 0K 0H)      h=help    │
│ -> 1        How to Create a New Usenet Newsgroup                         │
│    2        Anonymous FTP: Frequently Asked Questions (FAQ) List         │
│    3     7  List of Periodic Informational Postings, Part 1/8            │
│    4        Changes to List of Periodic Informational Postings           │
│    5        Introduction to the *.answers newsgroups                     │
│    6        How to become a USENET site                                  │
│    7        Emily Postnews Answers Your Questions on Netiquette          │
│    8        A Primer on How to Work With the Usenet Community            │
│    9        Introduction to news.announce                                │
│   10        How to Get Information about Networks                        │
│   11        Answers to Frequently Asked Questions about Usenet           │
│   12        Rules for posting to Usenet                                  │
│   13        A Guide to Social Newsgroups and Mailing Lists               │
│   14        Hints on writing style for Usenet                            │
│   15        USENET Software: History and Sources                         │
│   16        What is Usenet?                                              │
│                                                                          │
│   <n>=set current to n, TAB=next unread, /=search pattern, ^K)ill/select,│
│ a)uthor search, c)atchup, j=line down, k=line up, K=mark read, l)ist thread,│
│   |=pipe, m)ail, o=print, q)uit, r=toggle all/unread, s)ave, t)ag, w=post│
└────────────────────────────────────────────────────────────────────────┘
```

Figure 8.2 Overview of articles posted to news.announce.newusers.

article, you'll have the option of reading to the next article in the thread, moving to the next thread, or returning to the overview of threads and articles.

Reading and Responding to Articles in tin

The text of a Net News article looks a lot like an e-mail message. Figure 8.3 shows the beginning of a posting to the news.announce.newusers newsgroup. (The posting shown is a portion of an article that describes "periodic" USENET postings: articles documenting some subject of public interest that are posted to newsgroups at regular intervals.) At the top of the screen tin provides information about the current newsgroup, which thread you're reading, and the number of responses.

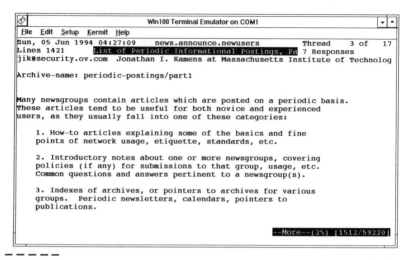

Figure 8.3 Reading a News Article with tin.

After you've read an article, you can save it in a file, send it to the printer, mail it to someone, send it as input to another program, or tag it as part of a collection of articles you'll work with later. Commands similar to those offered by `tin` are available in most other news readers as well.

Posting Articles with tin

If you're moved to respond to the article you've just read, you can either send a reply to the author via e-mail or post a follow-up response to the newsgroup, depending on the audience you want to reach. Replies sent to the author go directly to that person's mailbox and will probably come to his or her attention before follow-up postings in the newsgroup. E-mail replies don't become part of the newsgroup. If the point you want to make is of general interest to readers of the newsgroup, post it as a follow-up response.

When you respond via e-mail or with a follow-up article, your news reader will create a header for the response and start an editor for you to compose the message to be sent to the author or posted to the newsgroup. Tin uses the vi editor by default, but you can override this choice by setting the environment variable VISUAL to the full pathname (e.g., /usr/ucb/ex) for a different editor.

The procedure for posting an entirely new article to a newsgroup is very similar to that for follow-up postings. With the tin reader, you'll use the w command to start posting a new article to your current newsgroup. Tin will create a header template and start the editor for you. In the editor, you can write the body of your article. When it's complete, quit the editor. Tin will then prompt you with several choices: post the new article, return to the editor to change the article, or quit the posting procedure entirely. Only after you've chosen the "post" option from this prompt is your article submitted to the News server.

Using "test" Groups

Before you post your first real news item or follow-up response, practice posting with a "test" newsgroup. Test newsgroups are just that: newsgroups that you can use to practice reading and posting news articles without disturbing other readers of News. The original test newsgroup is test. There are other test groups as well, usually named "test" with a prefix that indicates a distribution area. For example, the test newsgroup for Chicago is named chi.test. You could also use the group misc.test. As a matter of courtesy, you should try to use the smallest locally distributed test newsgroup available: if you're in Los Angeles, use la.test unless there's some need for your test to be more widely distributed.

When you use a "test" newsgroup, *always put the word "ignore" in the subject header of your posting.* Test newsgroups are also used by news administrators to verify newsgroup distribution patterns. If you omit the word "ignore," your test posting will cause various USENET sites (as many as 30 or so) to send you mail saying that they've received your posting.

Note that there are newsgroups whose names contain the word "test" that are *not* for practice. A quick look at the subject lines of the messages in a group should give you a good idea of whether it's okay to use it for practice postings. (Subjects like "Testing, testing. Please ignore" probably mean it's okay to practice in this group. A group with subjects like "A Uniform Methodology for Software Testing" is *not* a group you should use for practice.)

Figure 8.4 shows the use of the UNIX vi editor to edit a new posting to the newsgroup misc.test. The lines beginning with the ~ character indicate that the message being edited is shorter than vi's screen. (For more information on vi and on path names and setting environment variables in UNIX, see Appendix D.)

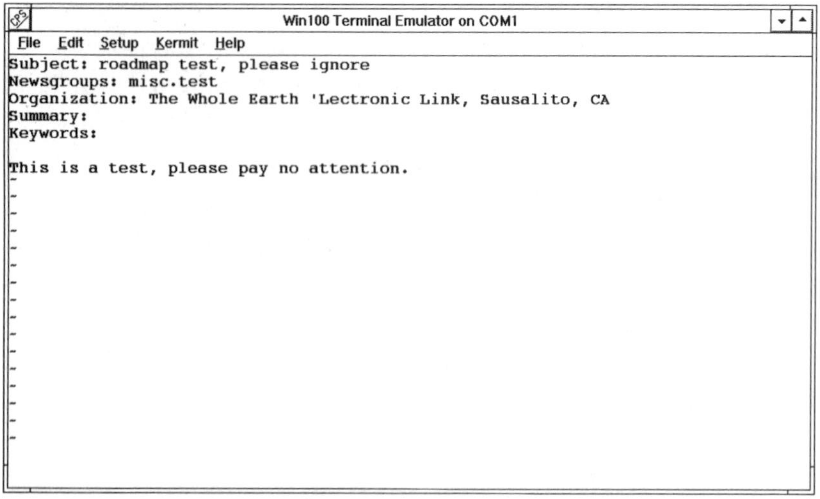

```
Win100 Terminal Emulator on COM1
File  Edit  Setup  Kermit  Help
Subject: roadmap test, please ignore
Newsgroups: misc.test
Organization: The Whole Earth 'Lectronic Link, Sausalito, CA
Summary:
Keywords:

This is a test, please pay no attention.
~
~
~
~
~
~
~
~
~
~
~
~
~
~
```

Figure 8.4   Editing a New Article

Picking an Audience

Depending on the news reader you use and the group you post to, you may have the opportunity to specify how widely distributed your article should be. The default distribution for new articles in the core USENET newsgroups is worldwide. (The core categories for USENET newsgroups will be discussed in detail shortly.) Your news reader may give you a choice of distributions that let you target your posting for the area to which it is relevant. The distribution choices will vary considerably from site to site, but common distributions are:

world	Worldwide Distribution (default)
can	Canada
eunet	European sites in EUNet
na	North America
usa	United States

You will probably have local or regional distribution categories available as well. Many states and local regions in North America have distribution categories (ca for California, ga for Georgia, and so on), and some newsgroups offer distribution by country.

Reading the News with WinVN

One of the most popular GUI news readers is WinVN, which was written by Mark Riordan at Michigan State University and is now maintained by a group of people under the leadership of Sam Rushing. WinVN is public domain software. The accompanying sidebar shows how to download and install it.

OBTAINING AND INSTALLING WINVN – – – – – – – – – –

Protocol dialup users interested in WinVN can get a copy of the latest version from `titan.ksc.nasa.gov`. (WinVN development is done at this site.) If you have trouble reaching this site, a reasonably current copy of WinVN can be found at `scss3.cl.msu.edu`. An `archie` search for *winvn* will turn up other sites that have WinVN as well. These may be older versions. When you connect to `titan.ksc.nasa.gov`, follow the instructions for finding WinVN. The directory pub/win3/winvn holds recent WinVN releases. WinVN is distributed as a ZIP archive with a name in this format:

```
winvn_91_6.zip
```

The name includes a version number (`91_6`). You will probably find several recent versions. Be sure to download the most recent version available. Note that the ZIP archive has a file name that is illegal under DOS. Most DOS or Windows FTP programs will convert the name to a legal DOS name automatically.

You'll need a utility that can unpack ZIP archives to use this release. Put the ZIP archive in a directory by itself and unpack it. One of the files extracted is named readme.txt. Read this file for information about the release and how to install it.

If you've already installed winsock-compliant networking software for your protocol dialup, you're ready to run WinVN. The first time you run the program, it will put up a dialog box to collect information about the NNTP server that gives you access to the News. (Your Internet access provider should give you this information when you open your protocol dialup account.) The dialog box for configuring WinVN is shown in Figure 8.5. When you're running WinVN, its main window contains a Config menu button that leads to dialog boxes in which you can change WinVN's configuration.

News Server Configuration

NNTP (News)	`nntp.netcom.com`
TCP port	`nntp`
SMTP (Mail) Server	`smtp.netcom.com`

Mail Transport
○ Disabled
○ Use MAPI
○ Use SMTP
◉ Auto Select

☒ Demand Logon

Optional news server authorization information:

Username	`bkf`
Password	`********`

[OK] [Cancel]

Figure 8.5 WinVN configuration dialog.

Reading the news with WinVN is like working with a GUI version of tin. Working with WinVN, you'll deal with three different windows: the Main Window, which lists newsgroups; the Group Window, which shows the subject lines for postings in a group; and the Article Window, which shows the text of an article.

When you first start WinVN, the main window shows information about the status of its connection to a News server. After a connection is made, WinVN asks if you want to check for any new groups that have become available since your last session. Downloading new groups can take several minutes. If there are new newsgroups, WinVN will list them in a separate window (as shown in Figure 8.6). You can subscribe to any groups you're interested in by double-clicking on the group name. When you've finished selecting groups, click the OK box and the window will disappear.

After this initial dialog, the main window will display a list of available newsgroups, like that shown in Figure 8.7. By default, WinVN displays the names of all the newsgroups in your newsrc file.

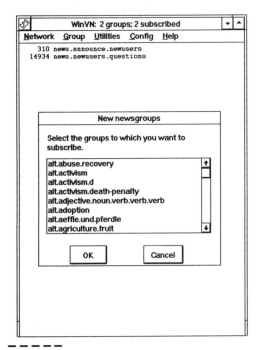

Figure 8.6 Selecting new newsgroups with WinVN.

Subscribed groups are shown first, followed by unsubscribed groups in alphabetical order. Subscribed and unsubscribed groups are shown in different colors. (WinVN can be configured to hide the unsubscribed groups entirely if you like.) To the left of each group name is a token that describes the group's status: a zero or a blank space in the status column indicates that there are no new articles in the group since your last session, or that WinVN was unable to get information about the group. Groups that have new articles are marked with an asterisk (*). Group names selected as a result of a Find command are marked with a "greater-than" sign (>).

As you scroll through the group names, you can read a group by double-clicking its name. If you want to manage your subscriptions, you can

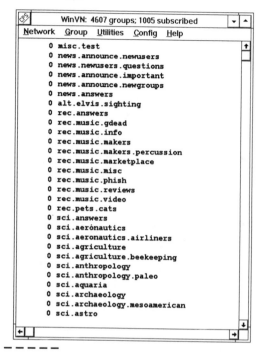

Figure 8.7 The WinVN Main Window.

click on a group name to select it. (You can also drag the mouse pointer across several consecutive group names to select them all.) The names of selected groups will be highlighted. When you have highlighted the groups you want to work with, pick the Utilities menu button at the top of the screen to see your subscription options.

After you double-click a group name, a group window will open and WinVN will get a list of current articles in the selected group from the News server. The subject lines from current articles will be displayed in the group window. With WinVN, you can open multiple group windows if you wish. Figure 8.8 shows the group window for news.answers, the newsgroup to which FAQ (Frequently Asked Question) compilations are posted. (The postings pictured in this figure provide some idea of the breadth of topics addressed in USENET newsgroups: discussions of Internet Talk Radio are side-by-side with notes on the cultures of Greece and India, a series of reports about ozone depletion, and information about Bob Dylan.)

Each group window allows you to scroll through the articles in a

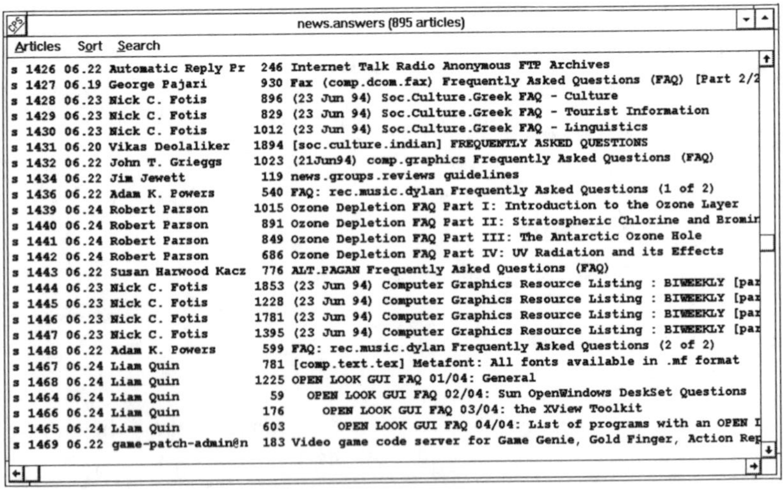

```
                        news.answers (895 articles)
Articles  Sort  Search
s 1426 06.22 Automatic Reply Pr  246 Internet Talk Radio Anonymous FTP Archives
s 1427 06.19 George Pajari       930 Fax (comp.dcom.fax) Frequently Asked Questions (FAQ) [Part 2/2
s 1428 06.23 Nick C. Fotis       896 (23 Jun 94) Soc.Culture.Greek FAQ - Culture
s 1429 06.23 Nick C. Fotis       829 (23 Jun 94) Soc.Culture.Greek FAQ - Tourist Information
s 1430 06.23 Nick C. Fotis      1012 (23 Jun 94) Soc.Culture.Greek FAQ - Linguistics
s 1431 06.20 Vikas Deolaliker   1894 [soc.culture.indian] FREQUENTLY ASKED QUESTIONS
s 1432 06.22 John T. Grieggs    1023 (21Jun94) comp.graphics Frequently Asked Questions (FAQ)
s 1434 06.22 Jim Jewett          119 news.groups.reviews guidelines
s 1436 06.22 Adam K. Powers      540 FAQ: rec.music.dylan Frequently Asked Questions (1 of 2)
s 1439 06.24 Robert Parson      1015 Ozone Depletion FAQ Part I: Introduction to the Ozone Layer
s 1440 06.24 Robert Parson       891 Ozone Depletion FAQ Part II: Stratospheric Chlorine and Bromin
s 1441 06.24 Robert Parson       849 Ozone Depletion FAQ Part III: The Antarctic Ozone Hole
s 1442 06.24 Robert Parson       686 Ozone Depletion FAQ Part IV: UV Radiation and its Effects
s 1443 06.22 Susan Harwood Kacz  776 ALT.PAGAN Frequently Asked Questions (FAQ)
s 1444 06.23 Nick C. Fotis      1853 (23 Jun 94) Computer Graphics Resource Listing : BIWEEKLY [par
s 1445 06.23 Nick C. Fotis      1228 (23 Jun 94) Computer Graphics Resource Listing : BIWEEKLY [par
s 1446 06.23 Nick C. Fotis      1781 (23 Jun 94) Computer Graphics Resource Listing : BIWEEKLY [par
s 1447 06.23 Nick C. Fotis      1395 (23 Jun 94) Computer Graphics Resource Listing : BIWEEKLY [par
s 1448 06.22 Adam K. Powers      599 FAQ: rec.music.dylan Frequently Asked Questions (2 of 2)
s 1467 06.24 Liam Quin           781 [comp.text.tex] Metafont: All fonts available in .mf format
s 1468 06.24 Liam Quin          1225 OPEN LOOK GUI FAQ 01/04: General
s 1464 06.24 Liam Quin            59    OPEN LOOK GUI FAQ 02/04: Sun OpenWindows DeskSet Questions
s 1466 06.24 Liam Quin           176    OPEN LOOK GUI FAQ 03/04: the XView Toolkit
s 1465 06.24 Liam Quin           603    OPEN LOOK GUI FAQ 04/04: List of programs with an OPEN L
s 1469 06.22 game-patch-admin@n  183 Video game code server for Game Genie, Gold Finger, Action Rep
```

Figure 8.8 News.answers seen from the WinVN group window.

newsgroup. Here, too, there is a status message: s indicates articles that you've already seen, n marks new articles, and > indicates articles selected with a Find command.

If you've configured WinVN to thread articles (as we've done in Figure 8.8), the group window will display related articles together.

If you've elected not to thread articles, the group window will list articles chronologically.

When you find an article you want to read, double-click on it, and WinVN will bring up an article window displaying the article's text. (With WinVN you can view more than one article at a time, each in its own window.) In Figure 8.9, WinVN is used to read the misc.test newsgroup, displaying a response to the test posting that was composed in Figure 8.5 above. Notice that WinVN sets off quotations from previous articles in italics.

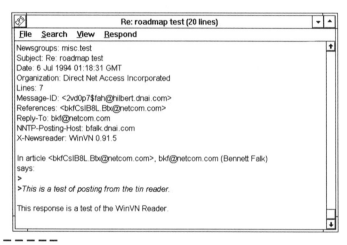

Figure 8.9   Viewing an article with WinVN.

The Article window allows you to respond to individual articles via either e-mail or a follow-up posting to the newsgroup. While you're getting used to WinVN, practice posting to "test" newsgroups. This will give you an opportunity to see what a posting looks like before it is dispatched to the live newsgroup.

The Taxonomy of Newsgroups

When you read Net News, you'll see scores of discussion groups, each consisting of articles posted by the people interested in the group's topic. As you've seen from the examples above, most USENET newsgroups have brief descriptive names that let the potential reader know what topic is under discussion. Not all the newsgroups are as whimsical as `alt.elvis.sighting`. With 7000-plus newsgroups in circulation, finding topics you're interested in can be difficult no matter how well-named they are.

One way of making the newsgroups more manageable is to classify them into very general areas of interest, and that classification produces names in the format shown above. In any newsgroup name the leftmost word (`comp`, `misc`, `rec`, `soc`, `alt`, etc.) indicates a general category for the discussion. The rest of the newsgroup name is not as orderly, but by convention, the words in a newsgroup name represent more specific spheres of interest as you read from left to right. For example, groups dealing with computer-related issues begin with `comp`. The `comp` groups that discuss artificial intelligence add `.ai`, and there are groups named `comp.ai`, `comp.ai.edu`, `comp.ai.philosophy`, `comp.ai.shells`, and `comp.ai.vision`.

Categories of USENET Newsgroups

At the most general level, there are seven categories for official USENET newsgroups. Groups in these categories are distributed worldwide to all USENET sites. A local administrator may elect not to carry groups in these core categories, but everything in these categories is offered to each USENET site. These global newsgroup categories don't change often, but they do change, and new newsgroups are added to each category nearly every day. Changes to these categories and a classification of the currently active newsgroups are posted periodically in news.groups. (See Table 8.1 for a brief description of the globally distributed groups.)

Table 8.1: Global USENET Newsgroups

CATEGORY	DESCRIPTION
comp	Newsgroups dealing with computer-related topics including hardware, software, commercial applications, and distribution of public domain and shareware programs.
misc	Newsgroups that cut across categories or that address themes not easily classified under any of the other groups.
news	Discussions related to Net News distribution and software.
rec	Groups discussing recreational activities, the arts, and other enjoyable things.
sci	Discussions related to topics in the sciences.
soc	Discussion groups for social issues.
talk	Groups providing an opportunity for open-ended debate.

Where New Newsgroups Come From

Starting a new topic in one of these core categories begins with submitting a proposal to the group news.announce.newgroups and to any newsgroups related to the proposed new topic. Submitting the proposal begins a period of discussion in which the charter and the name of the proposed new group are defined. At the end of the discussion period (usually 30 days), if the proposal is generally received favorably and if the name and charter have been agreed upon, a vote is taken via e-mail. Interested parties have 21 to 31 days to express an opinion about the formation of the new group. To be approved, the new group must be approved by at least two-thirds of the votes cast and must receive at least 100 more affirmative votes than negative votes. The approval process is the USENET community's way of guaranteeing two things: that new newsgroups have an initial constituency that will keep the new group active and that no newsgroup is added that the community feels to be a waste of resources.

The Alternative Newsgroup Hierarchy

In addition to the core USENET News categories there are a number of alternative newsgroup classifications. Groups in these categories are distributed locally by agreement between sites. The newsgroups in these alternative categories are technically not part of the USENET News, even though they are distributed via the same channels and read with the same news readers. The alternative groups are not governed by the same evaluation process as the USENET groups. Because the alternative groups are distributed by local agreement, they may not be as widely circulated as the core USENET groups. When you read the Network News, however, the USENET groups and the alternative groups will show up side by side. A list of the categories for alternative groups appears in Table 8.2.

Table 8.2: Categories for Alternative Newsgroups

CATEGORY	DESCRIPTION
alt	A collection of "alternative" newsgroups distributed voluntarily by a collection of sites. Many Usenet sites do not receive these groups.
bionet	Newsgroups for topics of interest to biologists, originating from net.bio.net.
bit	Newsgroups redistributing discussions from popular BitNet LISTSERV mailing lists.
biz	Newsgroups concerned with business products, particularly computer products and services. Postings include product reviews and announcements of product releases, bug fixes, and enhancements.
clarinet	Newsgroups publishing material from commercial news services and other sources. Sites carrying the ClariNet groups pay a licensing fee for the groups.
gnu	Newsgroups connected with Internet mailing lists of the GNU Project of the Free Software Foundation.
hepnet	Discussions dealing with High Energy Physics and Nuclear Physics. These groups, too, are connected to mailing lists and automatically archived.
ieee	Newsgroups related to the Institute of Electrical and Electronics Engineers (IEEE).
Inet/DDN	Discussions, many affiliated with Internet mailing lists. Groups in this category do not have a unique category name.
Info	A diverse collection of mailing lists (many technical, some cultural and social) connected into news at the University of Illinois.

Table 8.2: Categories for Alternative Newsgroups (continued)

CATEGORY	DESCRIPTION
k12	Conferences concerned with K-12 education: curriculum, language exchanges, and classroom-to-classroom projects.
relcom	A hierarchy of Russian-language newsgroups distributed mostly on the territory of the former Soviet Union (non-CIS countries included). These groups are available in Europe and Northern America; because of the 8-bit encoding (KOI-8) of Cyrillic letters, minor software modifications may be required.
u3b	Groups dealing with AT&T 3B series computers.
vmsnet	Topics for VAX/VMS users. Maintenance of these groups is a project of the VMSnet work group of the VAX SIG of the US Chapter of DECUS (the Digital Equipment Computer User's Society).

The Human Dimension

The Network News is a source of information unlike any other. Nowhere on the Internet is it more apparent that information is something made by human beings. When you read the news you'll encounter not just information, but the people who make it. You'll find emotion, opinion, sarcasm, humor and many other human qualities—good and bad—in ample supply throughout Net News postings.

You may encounter postings on the USENET that you find offensive. You may also discover that someone else has taken offense at something you've posted. There are a few precautions that anyone can take to avoid either giving or taking offense:

- Direct your postings to the most appropriate newsgroup. If you want to make a statement about abortion, for example, make it in the `talk.abortion` newsgroup.

- Avoid newsgroups and articles that you feel might be offensive. In addition to the "unsubscribe" feature, most news readers also support a "kill" facility that can be used to filter topics by keyword.

- If you must post something that is in questionable taste, state up front (in the Subject header or the first few lines of the posting) that the posting may not be suitable for everyone and take the additional precaution of encoding the offensive material. (See the accompanying sidebar for a description of rot13 encoding.)

 ROT13 ENCODING – – – – – – – – – – – – – – – –

Rot13 is a simple encryption formula that is used in some USENET groups (`rec.humor`, for example) to encode postings that some readers might find offensive. In rot13 coding, each letter is replaced by the letter 13 farther along in the alphabet. (A becomes N, B becomes O, and so on.) Here is a string of regular text and its rot13 equivalent:

```
Passwords are like underwear; both should be changed often.
Cnffjbeqf ner yvxr haqrejrne; obgu fubhyq or punatrq bsgra.
```

Many news readers (WinVN among them) can read and write rot13-encrypted text. If your Internet access provider's computer uses UNIX, you can use the UNIX `tr` command to translate rot13-encoded postings. This is the command to translate normal text into rot13 format:

```
tr A-Za-z N-ZA-Mn-za-m
```

Because Net News discussions take place between people who may never meet face to face, it is easy to forget that your on-line behavior has an effect on other users. A little common sense and a few rules of basic courtesy can do a lot to make the experience of using USENET more enjoyable. The following sidebar summarizes the basics of courtesy and common sense on USENET. This summary was taken from the USENET Primer, which discusses USENET etiquette more fully. The USENET Primer is regularly re-posted to the newsgroups news.answers and news.announce.newusers.

SUMMARY OF USENET ETIQUETTE

- Never forget that the person on the other side is human.
- Don't blame system administrators for their users' behavior.
- Be careful what you say about others.
- Be brief.
- Your postings reflect upon you; be proud of them.
- Use descriptive titles.
- Think about your audience.
- Be careful with humor and sarcasm.
- Only post a message once.
- Please rotate (rot13-encrypt) material with questionable content.
- Summarize what you are following up.
- Use mail; don't post a follow-up.
- Read all follow-ups and don't repeat what has already been said.
- Double-check follow-up newsgroups and distributions.
- Be careful about copyrights and licenses.

- Cite appropriate references.

- When summarizing, summarize.

- Spelling flames considered harmful. (English translation: Don't overreact to spelling errors.)

- Don't overdo signatures.

- Limit line length and avoid control characters.

Where to Go from Here

You can have a lot of fun and spend a lot of time rummaging through the recreational parts of the USENET. If you know where to look, you can also use it as a reference library for hundreds of topics. We've already alluded to a few key newsgroups that provide excellent points of departure for more serious excursions into Net News. To learn more about Net News itself, visit news.announce.newusers, news.misc, and news.software.readers. In these groups you will find periodic re-postings of and updates to the USENET Primer, the list of active newsgroups, and the Net News FAQ (Frequently Asked Questions).

The single most important newsgroup is news.answers. This group contains more than 800 FAQ compilations from various newsgroups. With the material in news.answers you can come up to speed on everything from object-oriented software design to historical costuming. When you've found an FAQ for the topic you're interested in, you'll also have a pointer to the newsgroup that produced it.

 **HUNTING THROUGH THE INTERNET** - - - - - - -

Question 1   Is this year's peanut crop larger or smaller than last year's?

Answer   On Yanoff's list, there are several sources for agricultural information. Use `telnet` to connect to one of these:

```
% telnet caticsuf.csufresno.edu
```

This connects you with the ATI-NET Bulletin Board at California State University in Fresno. The main menu for ATI-NET includes an item for Daily Agricultural Market Reports. When you select that item, a menu of Commodity Reports will appear, and one option on this menu is Statistical Reports. From this menu, select the Fruit and Vegetable Statistics, and you'll see a lengthy report that begins with a Crop Production Narrative. The narrative for peanuts is near the top of this file, and compares this year's production with last year's.

Question 2   Where can you get cricket scores?

Answer   Cricket has an avid following on the Internet. To get started, look at the `rec.cricket.scores` newsgroup. You'll get reports of scores, and pointers to other sources of cricket info, such as the CricInfo Gopher. Notice that a `veronica` search on the word *cricket* turns up five pages of menu items, many of which refer to a graphing program named Cricket. Looking for the newsgroup first is actually a more efficient way of finding the sources you want.

A P P E N D I X

Internet
Resources
Directory

Lists of Internet access providers are available on the Internet itself. Use ftp to connect to is.internic.net. Information about access providers can be found in the directory getting-started/getting-connected. The sites listed below are large-volume Internet access providers. When you connect to is.internic.net, you'll find many smaller providers in Peter Kaminski's Public Dial-up Internet Access List (PDIAL).

US Internet Access Providers

NAME (SERVICE AREA)	PHONE NUMBER	E-MAIL ADDRESS
Alternet (US and International)	(800) 4UUNET3	alternet-info@uunet.uu.net
ANS (US and International)	(313) 663-7610	info@ans.net
BARRNet (Northern/Central California)	(415) 723-7520	info@nic.barrnet.net

NAME (SERVICE AREA)	PHONE NUMBER	E-MAIL ADDRESS
CERFnet (Western US and International)	(800) 876-2373	help@cerf.net
CICnet (Midwest US)	(313) 998-6102	hankins@cic.net
CO Supernet (Colorado)	(303) 273-3471	kharmon@csn.org
CONCERT (North Carolina)	(919) 248-1404	jrr@concert.net
International Connections Manager (International)	(703) 904-2230	rcollet@icm1.icp.net
INet (Indiana)	(812) 855-4240	ellis@ucs.indiana.edu
JVNCnet (US and International)	(800) 35TIGER	market@jvnc.net
Los Nettos (Los Angeles, CA)	(310) 822-1511	los-nettos-request@isi.edu
MichNet/Merit (Michigan)	(313) 764-9430	jogden@merit.edu
MIDnet (NE, OK, AR, MO, IA, KS, SD)	(402) 472-5032	dmf@westie.unl.edu
MRnet (Minnesota)	(612) 342-2570	dfazio@mr.net

NAME (SERVICE AREA)	PHONE NUMBER	E-MAIL ADDRESS
MSEN (Michigan)	(313) 998-4562	info@msen.com
NEARnet (ME NH VT CT RI MA)	(617) 873-8730	nearnet-join@nic.near.net
NETCOM (California)	(408) 554-8649	info@netcom.com
netILLINOIS (Illinois)	(309) 677-3100	joel@bradley.bradley.edu
NevadaNet (Nevada)	(702) 784-6133	zitter@nevada.edu
NorthwestNet (WA, OR, ID, MT, ND, WY, AK)	(206) 562-3000	ehood@nwnet.net
NYSERnet (New York)	(315) 443-4120	info@nysernet.org
OARnet (Ohio)	(614) 292-8100	alison@oar.net
PACCOM (Hawaii and the Pacific)	(808) 956-3499	torben@hawaii.edu
PREPnet (Pennsylvania)	(412) 268-7870	twb+@andrew.cmu.edu
PSCNET (PA, OH, WV)	(412) 268-4960	pscnet-admin@psc.edu

NAME (SERVICE AREA)	PHONE NUMBER	E-MAIL ADDRESS
PSINet (US and International)	(800) 82PSI82	info@psi.com
SDSCnet (San Diego Area)	(619) 534-5043	loveep@sds.sdsc.edu
Sesquinet (Texas)	(713) 527-4988	farrell@rice.edu
SprintLink (US and International)	(703) 904-2230	bdoyle@icm1.icp.net
SURAnet (Southeastern US)	(301) 982-4600	marketing@sura.net
THEnet (Texas)	(512) 471-3241	green@utexas.edu
VERnet (Virginia)	(804) 924-0616	jaj@virginia.edu
Westnet (AZ, CO, ID, NM, UT, WY)	(303) 491-7260	pburns@yuma.acns.colostate.➥edu
WiscNet (Wisconsin)	(608) 262-8874	tad@cs.wisc.edu
World dot Net (OR, WA, ID)	(206) 576-7147	info@world.net
WVNET (West Virginia)	(304) 293-5192	cc011041@wvnvms.wvnet.edu

Canadian Internet Providers

NAME (SERVICE AREA)	PHONE NUMBER	E-MAIL ADDRESS
ARnet (Alberta)	(403) 450-5187	neilson@TITAN.arc.ab.ca
BCnet (British Columbia	(604) 822-3932	Mike_Patterson@mtsg.ubc.ca
MBnet (Manitoba)	(204) 474-8230	miller@ccm.UManitoba.ca
NB*net (New Brunswick)	(506) 453-4573	DGM@unb.ca
NLnet (New-foundland and Labrador)	(709) 737-8329	wilf@kean.ucs.mun.ca
NSTN (Nova Scotia)	(902) 468-NSTN	martinea@hawk.nstn.ns.ca
ONet (Ontario)	(519) 661-2151	bjerring@uwovax.uwo.ca
PEINet (Prince Edward Island)	(902) 566-0450	hancock@upei.ca
RISQ (Quebec)	(514) 340-5700	turcotte@crim.ca
SASK#net (Saskatchewan)	(306) 966-4860	jonesdc@admin.usask.ca

APPENDIX

B

**Internet
Documentation:
RFCs**

The Internet community has developed its own conventions for documentation. Topics that are of general interest to Internet users are documented in RFCs (Request for Comments). RFC authors submit their documents to an RFC editor, who reviews the document, assigns it a number, and makes the document available on-line. Once an RFC has been published and the requested comments start to arrive, if changes are required, a new RFC is generated that renders its predecessor obsolete. Both RFCs remain in circulation, however.

Many, but by no means all, RFCs address technical topics. Some RFCs are identified as For Your Information (FYI) documents discussing issues the entire Internet community needs to be aware of. Another subset of RFCs contribute to the definition of standards, and these are known as STDs.

The RFCs themselves (and an index listing RFCs by number and title) are available from many `ftp` sites, including `ftp.nisc.sri.com` (once connected, `cd` to the rfc directory) and `nis.nsf.net` (`cd` to internet/documents/rfc).

Following is a selection of introductory RFCs:

RFC 1118   Hitchhiker's guide to the Internet.

RFC 1175   FYI on where to start: A bibliography of internetworking information.

RFC 1206   FYI on Questions and Answers: Answers to commonly asked "new Internet user" questions.

RFC 1207   FYI on Questions and Answers: Answers to commonly asked "experienced Internet user" questions.

RFC 1150   FYI on FYI: Introduction to the FYI notes.

RFC 1208   Glossary of networking terms.

RFC 1087   Ethics and the Internet.

APPENDIX

C

Logging In

If your connection to the Internet is via a local UNIX network at your business or educational institution, you've probably already learned the login procedure, and you can skip this appendix. If not, read on...

When you connect to the Internet via phone you'll have to log in to your Internet access provider's computer. Internet access providers use all sorts of computers, but it's very likely that your Internet access will be via a computer running the UNIX operating system. Before you can log in to a UNIX system, you must have arranged with your Internet access provider for a login account. Your access provider will give you the login name and password for your account. Whether you have a conventional dialup connection or a protocol dialup connection, you'll have to log in to begin work. (The network software for most protocol dialup connections automates the login procedure.)

Logging in tells the computer who you are. Your login name (or user name) is your on-line identity. It determines what files, directories, and programs you can work with. Any files or directories you create will be stamped with this identity, so that you can control access to them. All login names should also be protected by a password known only to the authorized user of the login account.

Many UNIX systems have a bare-bones login prompt that looks like this:

```
login:
```

The prompt may be embellished with a brief message that identifies the computer or gives you any special login instructions for that system.

In response to the login prompt, enter your login name exactly as it was assigned by your Internet access provider. UNIX systems are case-sensitive, so be careful about capitalization. The characters you type in response to the login prompt are echoed on the screen as you type them. If you make a mistake, you can back over the letters you've already typed one at a time by pressing the Delete key. On some systems, you may find that the Delete key doesn't backspace over mistyped entries. If this happens, you can try using the Back-space key or simply press ↵ at both the login: and Password: prompts. Your login attempt will fail and return you to the login prompt where you can try again. When you've entered the login name correctly, press the ↵ key.

You should almost immediately be prompted for your password:

Password:

Enter your password. At this prompt, characters you type are not echoed on the screen. This is intentional: maintaining the privacy of your password protects your login account, the computer, and the network from unauthorized use. Even if you aren't concerned about your own account, carelessly publicizing your password could com-promise the security of other users or the network itself. When you choose a password, you should avoid words (your name, for ex-ample) that are easy to guess. You should also avoid words that might occur in common word lists (like the word list used by the UNIX spelling checker). It's a good practice to mix upper- and lowercase in your password and to include at least one number. Change your pass-word frequently. You can correct typing mistakes in your password entry by using the Delete key carefully to backspace over the mistyped letters. If you've entered your login name and password correctly, you'll be admitted to the system. What happens next depends on how the computer is configured.

After you've logged in successfully, the system may need some additional information to set up your session correctly. The most common piece of information asked for is your terminal type. Be prepared for something like this:

```
Term? (vt100)
```

This prompt asks you to enter the type of terminal you're using (for users connecting to the UNIX system from another computer, this means the type of terminal your communication software is emulating). The prompt above proposes vt100 as a default. Vt100 terminals were built by the Digital Equipment Company (DEC); but many terminals behave like vt100s, and vt100 is a common terminal emulation.

The selection of a terminal type affects the way things look on your screen. UNIX has a database of features for common terminal types, and some of the programs you run on the UNIX computer will check the terminal type you set and try to use features of that terminal. They do this by sending control codes the terminal recognizes. If the terminal type is set correctly, these control codes will do things like clear the screen, position the cursor, or turn special video attributes on or off. If the terminal type is not set correctly, your display may be difficult to read, and programs that try to control the screen may be difficult to work with.

If you know what sort of terminal you're emulating, enter an identifier for that terminal. Unfortunately, there is no universally appropriate response to the question about terminal type. On many systems the names "dumb" or "dialup" can be used to select a minimally featured terminal type that can be used safely.

Once you're past the login procedure and have specified a terminal type, you will receive a prompt from the UNIX command interpreter (or "shell"). Exactly what the shell prompt is depends on which UNIX shell you use and how it is configured. The shell prompt can be something simple like $ (the default prompt for the Bourne Shell) or a % (the default prompt for the C Shell). Some Internet access providers use programs other than the standard command-line interpreters for a shell program.

A Word about Terminal Servers

In some cases, the first piece of equipment you interact with may be a terminal server and not an Internet host. A terminal server is a special-purpose computer that does nothing but manage connections between terminals or modems and the computers on a local network. When you connect to a terminal server you should see a message identifying the terminal server and brief instructions. Typically the first prompt to which you must respond is a request for a user name. In the example below, the user name for the terminal server is the same as the UNIX login name. For some systems the name you use for the terminal server may be different from your UNIX login name.

```
CONNECT 9600

              Welcome to the Xyplex Terminal Server.


Enter username> bennett
XYRMT-7> c optimism
Xyplex -010- Session 1 to OPTIMISM established

SunOS UNIX (optimism)

login: bennett
Password:
```

```
Last login: Fri Sep 3 10:37:44 from yoda
%
```

Terminal servers are not usually protected with a password. After you've entered a username, the terminal server will start a session for you, and you can issue commands to the terminal server to start a login session with a host. You'll need to know the name of the host that you're authorized to log into. In the example above, the host was named "optimism," and the command c optimism made a connection to that computer so the user bennett could log in. Terminal servers recognize only a few commands. Most terminal servers include a help command that you can execute by typing help, h, or ?.

What Can Go Wrong?

There are only a few ways the login procedure can misfire. By far the most common is that the login name or password is entered incorrectly. When this happens, you'll see a "Login incorrect" message and be returned to the login prompt to begin again. Different systems respond to login failures in different ways, and you should read carefully any messages or instructions that are displayed after a login attempt fails. At any point you can interrupt the login procedure and start again by typing Ctrl-D.

Occasionally during the login procedure, the computer may decide that you're on a terminal that can't distinguish between uppercase and lowercase. When this happens, everything displayed by the computer will be uppercase, and letters that ought to be capitalized will be accompanied by a "\". Here's an example of this type of login sequence:

```
IBM AIX Version 3 for RISC System/6000
(C) Copyrights by IBM and by others 1982, 1991.
login: BENNETT
```

```
3004-030 YOU LOGGED IN USING ALL UPPERCASE CHARACTERS.
         IF YOUR WORKSTATION ALSO SUPPORTS LOWERCASE
         CHARACTERS, LOG OFF, THEN LOG IN AGAIN USING
         LOWERCASE CHARACTERS.
\B\E\N\N\E\T\T'S \PASSWORD:
3004-007 \YOU ENTERED AN INVALID LOGIN NAME OR PASSWORD.
```

In this situation, the system may have difficulty recognizing your login name or password. You can use Ctrl-D to recycle the login procedure and start again. On some systems you may be able to log in successfully even when the login program thinks you're on an uppercase-only terminal. When this happens, the system will continue to display everything in uppercase, using a "\" to introduce characters that really are capitalized. Once past the login procedure you can recover from this. In response to a shell prompt, type the command:

```
% STTY -LCASE
```

This lets the system know that your terminal can handle upper- and lowercase characters, and mixed case will be used from that point on.

APPENDIX

D

Just Enough
UNIX

So many of the computers on the Internet are UNIX systems that it is a real boon to be familiar with some of the basics of UNIX, even if the computer you work with directly is not a UNIX system (for example, if your Internet access is through a dial-up service that uses UNIX computers). UNIX is a multiuser, multitasking operating system developed twenty-five years ago at Bell Laboratories. Many of the design features of the original UNIX systems are still present in today's versions.

The elements of UNIX that most affect users are its file system (a collection of files and directories organized in a tree-like structure) and its operating environment.

The UNIX File System

The UNIX directory hierarchy is a tree-shaped structure that allows users to refer to any directory or file on any disk without having to know which disk contains the directory or file. (Many other operating systems, including DOS, organize their file systems into this sort of directory hierarchy.) The entire file system is a series of directory paths that branch off from a "root" directory. Directories can contain files or other directories, and the names of directories can be strung together to form *path names*. To refer to the root directory in a command, use a slash character (/) by itself. If the / occurs at the beginning of a path name, it is a reference to the root directory, and path names that begin with / are called *absolute* path names. The / character is also used in path names as a separator for directory or file names. Here are some sample absolute path names:

/	The root directory
/usr	A subdirectory of the root, named usr.
/usr/bin	A subdirectory of /usr, named bin.
/usr/bin/finger	The full pathname for the `finger` program in /usr/bin.

While you're logged in to a UNIX system, your login session has a current or working directory. By default, this is the home directory that the system administrator (whether for your local UNIX network or for your access provider) has allocated for your login name. During a login session you can change the working directory, but you'll always be in one directory or another throughout the session. Path names that don't begin with "/" are *relative* path names: they are interpreted in relation to your current working directory. When you're composing a relative pathname, you can use a period (.) to refer to the current directory and a double-period (..) to refer to the parent directory of the current directory.

UNIX provides many commands to manipulate files and directories. The commands you'll use most often are `ls` (list a directory's contents), `cd` (change directory), and `pwd` (print working directory). There are more detailed explanations of these commands at the end of this Appendix.

The UNIX Command Environment

When you log in to a UNIX system, you'll work with a command interpreter or shell program that accepts commands, executes programs for you, and manages the environment of your login session. There are three common shell programs in use on UNIX systems today: the Bourne Shell, the Korn Shell, and the C Shell. The Bourne and Korn shells are similar. The default prompt for them is $. The C Shell is different, particularly in its commands for managing the shell environment. The default C Shell prompt is %. Regardless of which shell you use, your login session's environment will consist of variables whose values control your access to commands and how the system behaves. By resetting these variables, you can customize your login session. Common items in the UNIX shell environment are

HOME	Full pathname for your home directory.
LOGNAME	Your login name.
MAIL	Full pathname to the file that is your system mailbox.
PATH	A list of directories that the system will search to find commands you execute.
SHELL	The default command interpreter for your login account.
TERM	The terminal type you're using.
TERMCAP	Either a description of your terminal's capabilities or a full pathname to the file containing the terminal capabilities database.

The environment variables that have the most dramatic effect on how your login session behaves are PATH and TERM. If the TERM variable is not set correctly, you may have difficulty using programs (such as terminal-based client programs for gopher or W3) that try to manipulate your screen. The PATH variable controls the list of directories that will be searched when the shell needs to look up a command for you. If you know what directory a program is stored in, you can always execute the program by typing its full pathname. For example, if the `finger` program is in /usr/bin, you can execute `finger` by typing:

```
% /usr/bin/finger rosebody@well.sf.ca.us
```

However, if the PATH variable in your environment includes the directory /usr/bin, you can execute `finger` by just typing its name:

```
% finger rosebody@well.sf.ca.us
```

On most UNIX systems, you can have access to everything you need with only a few directories in your path: `/bin`, `/usr/bin`, `/usr/local/bin`. You may also want to add `/usr/etc` and, if your system has it, `/usr/ucb`. If you're working with a commercial Internet access provider, you should not have to figure out for yourself what directories should be included in your PATH.

On some systems, your current directory won't be included in the PATH by default. This can be very frustrating when you try to execute a program in the current directory. The ls command shows that the program is there, but attempts to execute it by name fail with a "Command not found" message. You can execute the program by full path name, execute it by relative path name (./programname), or add the current directory to your PATH. (See the example below.)

Some application programs can be configured with environment variables as well. For example, if you want the World Wide Web line-mode browser to start up with a different home page, you can set the WWW_HOME environment variable to indicate which page should be used.

Setting and Displaying Environment Variables

How you set environment variables depends on which shell program you use. The Bourne and Korn shells use the same syntax to set variables. For example, this is how to set the PATH variable using either of these shells:

```
$ PATH=:/bin:/usr/bin:/usr/local/bin::
$ export PATH
```

The variable is set in the first command. The export command makes the variable available to any programs you start from the session in which the variable was set. To do the same thing in the C Shell, use the setenv command:

```
% setenv PATH :/bin/usr/bin/local/bin:
```

When you're entering directory names for the PATH variable, use a colon to separate the names. If the list of directories begins with this character, your working directory will be searched first. Directories are searched in the order they appear in the PATH variable. If you want to place your current directory elsewhere in the PATH variable, use :.: at the proper location. For example, Bourne shell users can put the current directory at the end of the PATH with this command:

```
$ PATH=:/bin:/usr/bin:/usr/local/bin:.:
$ export PATH
```

297

With the Bourne or Korn shells, the set command can be used to display all the variables in your environment. C shell users should use the command printenv. To examine the value of only one variable, use the echo command. For example, this command displays the current PATH setting:

```
$ echo $PATH
:/usr/local/bin:/usr/ucb:/bin:/usr/bin:
```

When a variable name is preceded by a "$", UNIX substitutes the current value of the variable. The same convention is used for all the shells.

The Shortest Possible Introduction to the vi Editor

UNIX systems offer a number of programs for editing files. (Among Internet tools, you'll need to edit files when sending mail or posting to USENET newsgroups.) One of the most convenient editors on UNIX systems is named vi.

From the UNIX command line, you can start the vi editor by typing its name and pressing ↵. If you want to edit a file that already exists, include the filename on the vi command line. Some mailers and news readers will start the vi editor automatically when you need to edit a mail message or news posting. When VI starts, the screen clears and the first screenful of the file you're editing is displayed. If you're editing a new file, vi will clear the screen and mark each line with a "~". Screen lines marked with "~" are *not* part of your file, and you can't move the cursor into this portion of the screen.

The vi editor has a rich command set, but you only need to know a couple of commands to use it for brief messages. Vi is a "modal" editor, and it is always in one of three modes: insert mode, cursor movement mode, or command mode. Vi starts in "cursor movement" mode. You can move the cursor around using four keys: h (left), j (down), k (up), and l (right). When the cursor is positioned where you want to enter text, you can enter "insert" mode by typing i. In insert mode anything you type will be inserted into the document. Vi does not break lines automatically. You'll have to press ↵ at the end of each line. While you're in insert mode, you can backspace over characters, but vi's cursor movement commands won't work. When you're finished entering text, press the Escape key. This turns off insert mode and returns you to "cursor movement" mode. To save your work and quit the editor, first enter command mode by typing a colon(:). The colon will be displayed on the bottom line of the screen. Next type **wq** and press ↵ to write your changes and quit the editor. (If you just want to exit the editor, type **q!** instead of **wq**.).

Sixteen UNIX Commands You Should Know

By design, UNIX systems use a large number of single-purpose commands. Here are brief summaries of sixteen of the most commonly used UNIX utilities. Some of the following commands require filenames or directory names on the command line. (Anything following the name of a UNIX command on the command line is called a command line "argument.") For many UNIX commands, arguments are optional. In the commands that follow, optional arguments appear in square brackets, with an indication of what sort of argument is expected. For example, an optional filename argument is shown as [*filename*].

`cat` *`filename`*

Display the named file on the screen. Similar to the DOS TYPE command.

`cd [`*`pathname`*`]`

Change the working directory to the named directory or to the user's home directory if *pathname* is omitted.

`compress` *`filename`*

or

`compress -d` *`filename`*

Compress (or, with the -d option, decompress) the named file. The compressed file is named *filename*.Z. `compress` appends a ".Z" suffix to the name of the input file, even if the input filename already had a suffix. Compressing `inet.services.txt`, for example, would produce a file named `inet.services.txt.z`. The compressed file will be one-third to one-half the size of the source file. Compressed files are binary and should be passed through uuencode before being sent via mail. The decompress option looks for *filename*.Z, decompresses it, and strips off the .Z suffix creating a destination file that has the same name and the same size as the source file.

`cp` *`filename newname`*

Make a copy of a file. If *newname* is a directory, a copy of the file will be placed in that directory.

`grep` *`pattern filename`*

Display any lines in the named file that contain the specified *pattern*.

```
head filename
```

Display the first few lines of a file.

```
ls [pathname]
```

List the contents of the named directory or the current directory if *pathname* is omitted.

```
mkdir dirname
```

Create a directory with the specified name.

```
mv oldname newname
```

Rename a file, or if *newname* is a directory, move the file to that directory.

```
passwd
```

Change your password.

```
pwd
```

Print the name of the current working directory.

```
rm filename
```

Remove the named file. Be careful; there is no way to "undo" the effects of rm.

```
rmdir dirname
```

Remove the named directory, which must be empty.

```
tail filename
```

Display the last few lines of a file.

```
uudecode filename.uue
```

Convert ASCII-encoded files to binary(see Chapter 5). Binary files can be converted to ASCII for e-mail or news posting with the command uuencode `filename < filename > filename`.uue

```
who
```

List currently logged-in users.

For a full explanation of these commands, use the UNIX on-line manual. For example, to see the on-line article about the ls command,s type man ls.

APPENDIX

E

WAIS and You

The Wide Area Information Server (WAIS) is a client/server application for performing full-text searches on databases containing indexed documents. (WAIS databases can also contain sound and pictures, but most of the databases are devoted to text.) There are more than 500 WAIS databases worldwide on a variety of topics. A large number of these are devoted to specialized academic subjects, but there are also general- interest WAIS databases containing USENET newsgroup archives, poetry, science fiction, government publications, and the like.

WAIS servers are scattered throughout the Internet. Each server can manage one or more databases, and finding the databases you're interested in can be a problem. Some sites maintain a directory of WAIS servers that can be queried to locate the WAIS sources you want. ("Source" is the WAIS term for a database.)

A listing of WAIS databases is also available via anonymous ftp. Connect to sunsite.unc.edu, move to the /pub/wais directory and download the file /pub/wais/waissources.tar.Z. This is a binary file that was created by the UNIX tar program and then compressed. You'll need access to a system with both tar and compress to unpack this file. (Most UNIX systems have both these utilities. If your Internet access provider uses a UNIX-based system, download the file to that computer, decompress it, and extract the tar archive's contents.) This archive contains the directory of WAIS servers. You'll find a file for each server with descriptions of the server's databases.

If you're just getting started with WAIS, `quake.think.com` (at Thinking Machines, where WAIS was first developed) serves as a home base from which you can maneuver through WAIS-based information. You can connect to `quake.think.com` via `telnet` to query its directory of servers. Use the login name `wais` with no password to start an ASCII terminal WAIS client. Instructions for using WAIS are presented as part of the login sequence, and the steps involved in querying a WAIS source will be described below.

Both `gopher` and W3 offer gateways to WAIS. You can reach the `gopher` gateway by connecting to the Mother Gopher at `tc.umn.edu`. From the main menu select Other Gopher and Information Servers. This will lead to a menu containing an entry for WAIS-Based Information. That menu entry leads to the WAIS gateway. The W3-WAIS gateway can be reached from CERN's list of Internet Services by type. If you prefer to jump directly to the WAIS information by URL, use either of the following:

```
http://server.wais.com/waisgate-announce.html
http://info.cern.ch/hypertext/Products/WAIS/Overview.html
```

In order to submit WAIS queries via the W3 gateway, you need a browser that supports form-based interaction. (The Mosaic 2.0 browser allows queries via forms.)

The `gopher` or W3 gateways depend on resources that are not always available, so you may not be able to get a connection reliably through these applications. If you want to do more than a smattering of work in WAIS, you'll probably want a client program of your own. For protocol dialup users, public domain WAIS client programs are available for Windows, Macintosh, and X Windows. Use anonymous `ftp` to connect to `sunsite.unc.edu` and browse through the /pub/wais directory for the client software you need.

Regardless of which client program you use, you'll go through the same procedure to query WAIS databases:

1. Connect to a WAIS server and select the "directory of servers." (To run a WAIS query, you must tell WAIS which databases to search. If you don't already know the name of a WAIS database that holds the information you want, you can look for one by querying the directory of servers, which is itself a WAIS database.)

2. Enter any keywords that describe the databases you're interested in. Remember that this query will scan only the short descriptions that the directory contains for each server. When querying the directory of servers, it's best to use general keywords that describe the subject you're interested in (poetry, for example, or home-brew). The names of any entries in the directory that match your keywords will be returned. (If a query produces no hits, you'll get a catalog of the documents in the database you're querying. For the directory of servers, this is just a list of all the servers. You can also repeat your query adding new keywords.)

3. From the list displayed as a result of your directory query, select the names of the databases you want to search. If you need more information about any of the databases, you can display the whole directory entry. Selecting a server adds it to the list of sites that will be searched for any keywords you specify.

4. After selecting databases that satisfied your subject query, you can enter keywords for the information you're after. This query will be run against the contents of all the databases you've selected. WAIS will get information about

documents containing these keywords from each of the databases you chose.

5. If there are documents that contain your keywords, WAIS will display the headlines of these documents. WAIS also assigns a "relevance score" to each of the documents that satisfies your query. (This can be especially useful if your query contained several keywords.)

6. You can retrieve the complete text of any document that satisfied your query by selecting its headline from the result set that WAIS returned.

Index

Note to the Reader: Throughout this index **boldfaced** page numbers indicate primary discussions of a topic. *Italicized* page numbers indicate illustrations.

G

Everything you need to start using the Internet today!

FREE SOFTWARE!

Windows, a modem and this comprehensive book/software package. That's everything you need to start using the Internet now. Includes economical, full-featured, direct Internet connection. Point and click interface. Gopher, World Wide Web, E-mail, Usenet Newsgroups, FTP, Telnet and much more.

Now available wherever computer books are sold.

250 pages.
ISBN 1529-2

SYBEX

Shortcuts to Understanding.

SYBEX, Inc.
2021 Challenger Drive
Alameda, CA 94501
1-800-227-2346
1-510-523-8233

Go from zero to 60 on the Information Superhighway— in a flash!

What's a good modem? Isn't there some *simple* explanation of the "Internet?" How is it different from Prodigy or CompuServe? What's the cost?

At last, here's *the* book on joining the online community, from SYBEX.

Now available wherever computer books are sold.

274 pages.
ISBN 1417-2

SYBEX

Shortcuts to Understanding.

SYBEX, Inc.
2021 Challenger Drive
Alameda, CA 94501
1-800-227-2346
1-510-523-8233

All the facts about WinFax.

Whether you got WinFax Lite free with your modem, or just went out and bought WinFax Pro 3.0 or 4.0, you'll appreciate the frank, troubleshooting approach of this companion for the popular Windows computer fax software.

Now available wherever computer books are sold.

376 pages.
ISBN 1462-8

SYBEX

Shortcuts to Understanding.

SYBEX, Inc.
2021 Challenger Drive
Alameda, CA 94501
1-800-227-2346
1-510-523-8233

Wacky games on a
FREE
high density disk!

Six categories of outstanding shareware and
freeware games for Windows, all on a single
disk. The accompanying book puts the rules of
the game right at your fingertips—even includes
strategies and secrets to help you win!

*Now available
wherever computer
books are sold.*

155 pages.
ISBN 1361-3

SYBEX

Shortcuts to Understanding.

SYBEX, Inc.
2021 Challenger Drive
Alameda, CA 94501
1-800-227-2346
1-510-523-8233

FOUR BOOKS IN ONE.

It's Microsoft Office made smooth and easy! This
step-by-step tutorial contains everything you'll need to
master Word 6, Excel 5, PowerPoint 4 and Microsoft
Mail–presented in a user-friendly, informative style.

Now available
wherever computer
books are sold.

779 pages.
ISBN 1483-0

SYBEX

Shortcuts to Understanding.

SYBEX, Inc.
2021 Challenger Drive
Alameda, CA 94501
1-800-227-2346
1-510-523-8233

GET A FREE CATALOG JUST FOR EXPRESSING YOUR OPINION.

Help us improve our books and get a *FREE* full-color catalog in the bargain. Please complete this form, pull out this page and send it in today. The address is on the reverse side.

Name _____

Address _____

Phone ( ) _____

Company _____

City _____ State ____ Zip _____

1. How would you rate the overall quality of this book?

❑ Excellent
❑ Very Good
❑ Good
❑ Fair
❑ Below Average
❑ Poor

2. What were the things you liked most about the book? (Check all that apply)

❑ Pace
❑ Format
❑ Writing Style
❑ Examples
❑ Table of Contents
❑ Index
❑ Price
❑ Illustrations
❑ Type Style
❑ Cover
❑ Depth of Coverage
❑ Fast Track Notes

3. What were the things you liked *least* about the book? (Check all that apply)

❑ Pace
❑ Format
❑ Writing Style
❑ Examples
❑ Table of Contents
❑ Index
❑ Price
❑ Illustrations
❑ Type Style
❑ Cover
❑ Depth of Coverage
❑ Fast Track Notes

4. Where did you buy this book?

❑ Bookstore chain
❑ Small independent bookstore
❑ Computer store
❑ Wholesale club
❑ College bookstore
❑ Technical bookstore
❑ Other _____

5. How did you decide to buy this particular book?

❑ Recommended by friend
❑ Recommended by store personnel
❑ Author's reputation
❑ Sybex's reputation
❑ Read book review in _____
❑ Other _____

6. How did you pay for this book?

❑ Used own funds
❑ Reimbursed by company
❑ Received book as a gift

7. What is your level of experience with the subject covered in this book?

❑ Beginner
❑ Intermediate
❑ Advanced

8. How long have you been using a computer?

years _____

months _____

9. Where do you most often use your computer?

❑ Home
❑ Work

❑ Both
❑ Other _____

10. What kind of computer equipment do you have? (Check all that apply)

❑ PC Compatible Desktop Computer
❑ PC Compatible Laptop Computer
❑ Apple/Mac Computer
❑ Apple/Mac Laptop Computer
❑ CD ROM
❑ Fax Modem
❑ Data Modem
❑ Scanner
❑ Sound Card
❑ Other _____

11. What other kinds of software packages do you ordinarily use?

❑ Accounting
❑ Databases
❑ Networks
❑ Apple/Mac
❑ Desktop Publishing
❑ Spreadsheets
❑ CAD
❑ Games
❑ Word Processing
❑ Communications
❑ Money Management
❑ Other _____

12. What operating systems do you ordinarily use?

❑ DOS
❑ OS/2
❑ Windows
❑ Apple/Mac
❑ Windows NT
❑ Other _____

13. On what computer-related subject(s) would you like to see more books?

_____

_____

_____

_____

14. Do you have any other comments about this book? (Please feel free to use a separate piece of paper if you need more room)

_____

_____

_____

_____

- - - - - - - - - PLEASE FOLD, SEAL, AND MAIL TO SYBEX - - - - - - - - - -

SYBEX INC.
Department M
2021 Challenger Drive
Alameda, CA
94501

E-mail Addressing between Networks

E-mail, discussed in Chapter 5, is one of the most popular uses of the Internet. Use the address forms summarized below to exchange mail between the Internet and other popular networks.

BITNET: To send mail from a BITNET site to an Internet user, use one of the following address forms:

    user@host

or

    gateway!domain!user

To send mail from an Internet site to a BITNET user, use the following address form:

    user%site.bitnet@gateway

(Substitute for *gateway* the name of a host that serves both Internet and BITNET.)

CompuServe: To send mail from a CompuServe site to an Internet user, use the following address form:

    >Internet:user@host

(Add the prefix `>Internet:` to the Internet address.)

To send mail from an Internet user to a CompuServe site, use the following address form:

    71234.567@compuserve.com

(CompuServe user IDs are two numbers separated by a comma. Replace the comma with a period and add the domain name **compuserve.com**.)

MCIMail: To send mail from an MCIMail site to an Internet user, use the following address form:

    create <CR>
    TO: User Name
    EMS: Internet
    MBX: user@host.domain

To send mail from an Internet user to an MCIMail site, use one of the following address forms:

    acctname@mci_mail.com

or

    acct_id@mci_mail.com

(Account names may not be unique; MCI *acct ID* is a 7-digit number.)

SprintMail: To send mail from a SprintMail site to an Internet user, use the following address form:

    C:USA, A:telemail, P:internet, ID:user(a)host.domain

To send mail from an Internet user to a SprintMail site, use the following address form:

    /PN=Bennett.Falk/O=co.wsqpd/ADMD=SprintMail/C=US@sprint.co